THE JESUS PUSHER

THE JESUS PUSHER

a 365 day exploration of Jesus

Stephen Manley

CROSS
STYLE
PRESS

The Jesus Pusher: a 365 day exploration of Jesus
Copyright © Stephen Manley 2014

Edited by Delphine Manley

ISBN-10: 0692327312
ISBN-13: 978-0692327319

CrossStyle.org

Introduction

I am a Jesus pusher!!! The root of the Greek word "doulos," translated "slave" or "servant," is used one hundred eight-two times in the New Testament. Some uses refer to an addiction. Peter wrote, "While they promise them liberty, they themselves are slaves of corruption; for by whom a person is overcome, by him also he is brought into bondage," (2 Peter 2:19). This is an emphasis of addiction and is highlighted many times with the word "doulos."

We must be addicted to Jesus. We were created by Him and for Him (Colossians 1:16). The absence of His presence creates a living hunger, which only Jesus can fill (Matthew 5:6). I am addicted to Jesus. One moment without Him and I have withdrawal pains. He is not a fix that wears off and I must seek Him again. His presence consistently fulfills my life. I must be aware of Him every moment. If He were removed from my life death would be immediate. Without Jesus I have no resource. Without Him I am a glove without a hand, an engine without fuel, a book without letters, supper without food, a car without a driver, or a job without a worker. Nothing happens without Him. I cannot get by without Him. He does not just make life better; He is life.

I am addicted to Jesus. I seek nothing but Him. I have no other desire in life. Join me in seeking Jesus. I am a Jesus pusher!!!

– Stephen Manley

Jesus PUSHER | 1

I am a Jesus pusher!!!! I am an undaunted, courageous, stouthearted, bold, adventuresome, brave, fearless, gallant, heroic, lionhearted, unafraid, unflinching, valiant Jesus pusher. I cannot help myself. He is startling and He has overwhelmed me. I do not speak of ideas about Jesus or historical information concerning Him. I speak about Him. I am a Jesus pusher!!!! I am a mastered, possessed, addicted and obsessed Jesus pusher. There seems to be no way to quit. But who would want to?

He is present in every situation of my life. There is no conversation in which I do not feel His presence. He participates in all my recreation. He is everywhere I go. Who would want to be without Him? He is the protection for my life. He is the fragrance I constantly smell. He is the flow of my spiritual blood giving me life. He is my constant nutrition making me healthy. I cannot survive without Him. I am a Jesus pusher!!!!

I want to push Him on you. I want you to join me in this obsession. You do not have to work at it; it is not a discipline. It is as natural as breathing. Please let Him pull you to His heart.

Jesus PUSHER | 2

I am a Jesus pusher!!!! I am not the first one. I have joined the heart of God, the first Jesus pusher. The moment man sinned (Genesis 3) God started pushing Jesus. He gave the first Messianic promise, declaring Jesus to be the solution to the curse on mankind. The focus of Noah and the ark was this one Man, Jesus. The significance of Abraham was Jesus. The only reason for Moses and the law was this one Man, Jesus. All the prophets spoke of nothing but this one Man, Jesus. Every sacrifice lamb offered in the temple was about this one Man, Jesus. The Old Testament pushed Jesus on us.

The New Testament is a Jesus pusher. Angels filling the sky with praise in the opening scene declares the focus. Shepherds captured by the news run everywhere pushing Jesus. A star pushes Jesus on the wise men. They go to Jerusalem to push Jesus on Herod the King. John the Baptist is a Jesus pusher. Everything is about Jesus. I am in line with a long heritage of Jesus pushers. I have not invented anything. I have only been captured by the same obsession. I am caught up in the stream of the rushing message of the histories, Jesus. There is nothing else about which to speak. I want to push Jesus on you. You must join me in this addiction. Let Him capture you. It is not a struggle, unnatural, or difficult. It is a flow; it fits my life. Let Him capture you anew.

Jesus PUSHER | 3

I am a Jesus pusher!!!! I have a choice. In all of the struggles and complications of life, I find Him the only solution. I can turn no other place. I cry out to God when I struggle with my temper. He gives me Jesus as the answer. I plead with God about my uncontrollable lust; He gives me Jesus. Hate fills my heart; God gives me Jesus. Each time I come to God in any searching, I only find Jesus. God is a Jesus pusher.

He does not push Jesus as a quick fix. Jesus is not an energy boost to get you through. He is not a rescuer of the moment. He is not a counselor to give advice to follow. He is not a cure for disease. He is not a bandage for the wounded. Jesus is life. He is the stage upon which I dance. He is the set of eyes through which I see. Everything is different in His presence. I am not inviting you to seek a solution, but to seek Jesus. He is not a way out, but a way in. He is not a theology; He is a living Friend. He is the Lover of my soul. I find everything in Him. He is my destiny. I am urging you to discover yourself (the real you) in Him. I am pushing Jesus on you.

———————————

Jesus PUSHER | 4

I am a Jesus pusher!!!! There is no other way. I have tried the latest psychology of my day. I am empty in its system. I have sought the distracting pleasures my society offers. That more than leaves me empty, it causes death. Where can I go? I do not need someone who knows the answer; I need someone who is the Answer. Jesus alone qualifies at every point. He does not give me solutions; He is the solution. He is not a supply of items I need for my life; He is what I need. He is my peace, joy, happiness, power, forgiveness, truth, strength, nutrition and life. He is everything to me. In Him I find all. God placed every spiritual blessing in Christ. All God dreams for me I find in Christ. Therefore, the place for me to be is in Christ.

The difficulty is I cannot get inside Christ. So Christ comes and gets in me. Christ in me is the hope of my glory. As Christ comes in me the intimacy of relationship takes place. I find myself in Christ. We fit together perfectly. Christ was made for me; I was made for Him. This is where I belong; I am at home. I want to go no other place. Why would I? I am pushing Jesus on you. Let Him find you in a new way.

Jesus PUSHER | 5

I am a Jesus pusher!!!! I have been captured by the One who is Light. I have discovered no darkness at all in Him. There is no shadow of turning in His ways. I am a deer caught in the head lights. I have been arrested by the glare of His presence. I cannot look to the right or to the left. His glow continually increases until I find myself, not unable, but unwilling to turn aside. What can I do? I am consumed by Jesus, the Light. I am a Jesus pusher!!!!

I am not attracted to the light bulb; I am mesmerized, spell bound, enthralled, entranced, charmed, enchanted, magnetized, allured, and transfixed by the Light. It is not what He does for me. It is not the beauty of His creation. It is He Himself. I am a Jesus pusher!!!! I am not caught in the organizational habit of an institution; I am possessed with the Light. It is not theology which thrills me; it is the Light.

I am a Jesus pusher!!!! I have been captured by the One who is Light. I cannot tolerate darkness. I am a person of the light. Even the shadows bother me. There is no shade of gray. The Light consumes me. There is nothing but the Light. I cannot dwell in the twilight; I have experienced the Light. I am a Jesus pusher!!!!

Would you walk with me in the Light?

———————

Jesus PUSHER | 6

I am a Jesus pusher!!!! It is not about being right or knowing more than others. It is about Truth. Jesus is the Truth. He is not the sum total of data, information, or facts. He is the Truth. In the embrace of His person I find perspective, the way things really are. He is not psychology, the manipulation of the mind. He is Truth.

He did not invent the truth or know truth no one else as grasp. He is Truth. If there is any truth anywhere in the universe, it is because of Him. To stray from Him is to walk in deception. In Him I see who I am and who I can be. Why should I settle for something less?

I am a Jesus pusher!!!! He is the single chance to see life without deception. Truth compels me. I will not settle for the lie. The lie is destructive. The comfort it offers only distracts me from the coming disaster. Distortion, exaggeration, misrepresentation, fabrication, falsification, misstatement, prevarication are not found in Him. Reality, accuracy, actuality, authenticity, certainty, correctness, genuineness bespeak His presence. I am a Truth pusher. I am a Jesus pusher!!!! Let Truth bath my heart and soul. May we dwell in Truth together?

Jesus PUSHER | 7

I am a Jesus pusher!!!! To push Him is to push happiness. He does not give me happiness; He is my happiness. I have lived too long in the allusion of happiness. Feelings of joy came and went determined by circumstances, financial stability, or material possessions. The gnawing ache of lacking soon returned if my possession were not bigger, better, and more elaborate. It was as if the entire universe fought against my happiness. I could not win.

Then Jesus came. In the intimacy of His person, all else shrunk to its proper size. The ebb and tide of circumstances ceased to control me. In the embrace of His person I found happiness. I am exuberant, cheerful, ecstatic, elated, glad, delighted, joyful, and jubilant. How could I not be? He has found me. I am a Jesus pusher!!!! I do not call people to happiness; I call people to Him. No longer is happiness a gimmick to allure people to join my religious program. This is beyond feeling or emotion. The One who is happiness can now be found. No wonder I push Jesus. To depart from Him is to leave my own sanity. Not to abide in Him is to dwell in depression. Not to be filled with Him is to be filled with the misery of myself. I must know Him.

Seek Him only. Do not be distracted. Allow nothing to get in your way. Fix your eyes on Him alone. Give Him all of your energy. He is seeking you. I am a Jesus pusher!!!!

Jesus PUSHER | 8

I am a Jesus pusher!!!! He is my prototype. In Him I have found who I am to be. God has placed in Jesus everything He wants me to have. In Christ I am complete. Outside of Jesus there is nothing. The New Covenant of the high level of intimacy with God began with Jesus of Nazareth, a Man. He is the first fruits of the new way. As He was filled with the Father, so I am now filled with Him. The same Spirit that enabled, empowered, and sourced Him now sources me.

Jesus is my standard, benchmark, criterion, gauge, measure, touchstone, yardstick, guideline, canon, and principle. The only way to go astray is to ignore Him. I am aligning my life with His person. I will compare myself to no one but Him. No man shall capture my vision; I am fixed on Him. I can push Him aside; but why would I want to? He pulls the best from me; because He supplies the best. He places me on a new level of living; because He is that level.

I am a Jesus pusher!!!! In discovering my prototype I have found my shape. Everything that is not essential to that shape is removed. I am stripped down to Him. The excess weight of duty, obligation, struggle, attempts, self-discipline, and I ought to is gone. I am free in Him. He is my source. Come! Jump into Him with me!

Jesus
PUSHER | 9

I am a Jesus pusher!!! "You are simply a slave," you reply. You are absolutely right. I have voluntarily given myself to Him. Love has constrained me to Him. I have placed my ear to the door post; an awl has pierced my ear. I am a love slave. It is not an emotional, sentimental love. It is not a love of convenience. The wonder of His Person has reached to the depth of my very system. Every cell of my being responds to Him. I believe I was made for Him.

I am a Jesus pusher!!! "You are simply a slave," you reply. You are absolutely right. I am a slave by addiction. One split second without Him and I am a devil again. Everything I have become in Him depends entirely upon Him. He has not given me supplies so I can maintain without Him; He is my supply. He has not saved me so I can now exist on my own; He is my salvation. His absence creates incredible withdrawal pains. I cannot tolerate one moment without Him. I am addicted to Him. It is a joyous addiction.

I am a Jesus pusher!!! "You are simply a slave," you reply. You are absolutely right. I am a slave by ownership. I have surrendered the right to live my own life. I have compared the chaos of exercising that right to the wonder of His life lived through me. Fulfillment, completion, security, development, accomplishment, purpose, meaning, direction are all inadequate words to describe the embrace and flow of His life. I choose to be His; I refuse to be my own. Join me in such slavery!

———————

Jesus PUSHER | 10

I am a Jesus pusher!!! I have experienced the growing awareness of despair. The inward relentless pressure has convinced me things are not right. Someone should do something; but it is so out of control. In every area of society things are in a downhill slide. It cannot be stopped. Even the church has joined the slide. All is lost; I slip into depression. But wait there is Jesus. He is my hope. He is the ray of light at the end of the tunnel. He is the large hand grabbing me from the slippery slide. Everything is all right; someone is in charge. He is adequate. Jesus is my hope.

Discouragement, dismay, defeat are words not found in my vocabulary. They do not exist in Him. He has lifted my eyesight to the view of His great purpose. He is working a plan; He is the plan. It is not positive thinking or wishful desires. It is the reality of all things working together for good as found in the midst of His person (Romans 8:28). He has repeatedly taken what was intended to be bad and gloriously made it good. He has come in the fullness of His Spirit to do this within; He is coming again in the physical to do this without. He is my hope. I rest comfortably in His arms. There is no worry there. We are safe in Him. I am a Jesus pusher!!!

Jesus PUSHER | 11

I am a Jesus pusher!!! I have a dream. My world views it as unrealistic and unattainable. But I still have this dream. In my dream I experience total victory over sin. No temptation can defeat me. No attitude of hatred dominates my life. Jealously disappears; envy is gone. My sexual body drives have been brought under control and my appetites balanced. I have a dream of living without sin. Perfect love is the constant attitude of every hour. There is no circumstance so great it controls my attitude; no wrong can take place that over powers my reactions. There is constant harmony within. Confusion is no longer present in the mind; my emotions are stabilized by an inward stability. Security has come to my life; fear has been removed. I have a dream. Life has become an adventure. It is like living on the edge. The adventure is found in investigation, learning, growing, and expanding. There seems to no end in sight. The discovery is so great it will stand an eternity of investigation. I have a dream of falling into an intimate relationship with someone who does not want to use me for his own ends. It would be an intimacy beyond sexual attraction, a spiritual embrace. Oneness experienced by a mutual surrender to each other that welds us together. A confidence would be present which would permeate every circumstance good or bad. I have a dream.

I want to tell you my dream has come true. It is not off in the future, nor is it partial. It is not heaven in the sense of going somewhere else after death; it is heaven in the sense that all I thought of heaven has come to me. My dream is Jesus. I am a Jesus pusher!!! Everything I described in my dream He has fulfilled in my life. Read about my dream again; embrace Him. I am a Jesus pusher!!!

Jesus PUSHER | 12

I am a Jesus pusher!!! I fear writing about Him lest all you see are facts, data, or information. I fear speaking about Him lest you only grasp ideas, concepts, or doctrine. How can I get you to embrace Jesus, the person? If I paint a picture of Him you may make it an idol. If I explain what He has done for you, you may simply honor His deeds. If I explain His crucifixion in your behalf, you may simply place a gold plated cross around your neck to celebrate. If I attempt to explain His thoughts for you, you may only comprehend theology. How can I introduce Him to you? How can I place you into His presence?

I am a Jesus pusher!!! I am afraid to preach about Him for fear you think it is my job, a career. Do I dare teach a Sunday school class? Will you think I am only fulfilling a role or working for the church? If I give my money to promote the spread of His name will you think I have simply given to get? How can I take your hand and place it in His? How can I get you face to face with Him?

I think I have found the answer! I am a Jesus pusher!!! I am going to love Him, get so tight with Him, and be so one with Him you will sense Him in my life. I am going to allow my life to be so filled with His presence you will be shaking hands with Him when you take my hand. I am going to expose you to Him because He is in me. I am going to allow my eyes to be His, my attitude to be His, my reactions to be His. You are going to meet Him through me. He is going to envelope you because I am going to envelope you. You will see Him! I am a Jesus pusher!!!

———

Jesus PUSHER | 13

I am a Jesus Pusher!!! Someone has described the Christian as simply one beggar telling another beggar where to find bread. Even if you do not agree with this statement, please acknowledge with me the deep internal hunger you and I have for Him. At the depth of my soul, there is an addictive craving which demands satisfaction. Have I tried other means of satisfaction? Indeed, I have, to no avail. Have I attempted to fill the void with a variety of worldly and religious activities? Indeed, I have, with no fulfillment. I have personally discovered the truth of the Preacher who cried, "Vanity of vanities, all is vanity," (Ecclesiastes 1:2).

Then I discovered Jesus. Oh, let me correct my statement! Then Jesus found me. To be discovered by Jesus is like walking into a great buffet. The buffet is great not because it offers multiple choices of food. It is not great because the food is in great abundance. There is only one item offered. Only one item covers the buffet. It is Jesus. He is the bread of life. He who comes to Me shall never hunger and he who believes in Me shall never thirst (John 6:35). Is there not total satisfaction found in the person of Jesus?

This is why I am a Jesus pusher!!! Regardless of your hunger need, Jesus will fulfill it. Regardless of what your spiritual taste buds require, Jesus will satisfy. It is amazing! Various people come with their various needs and Jesus is the complete answer! Whatever the need He easily fills it. Will you take my hand and let's rush to the banquet? Can we partake of Jesus together? I am a Jesus pusher!!!

Jesus
PUSHER | **14**

I am a Jesus pusher!!! He is the bread of life. He is not the baker of the bread. He has not gathered up the ingredients necessary and produced the bread. He is the bread! He does not offer you bread apart from Himself. He offers Himself alone. He does not simply offer you bread, but the bread of life. He said, "Whoever eats My flesh and drinks My blood has eternal life and I will raise him up at the last day. For My flesh is food indeed, and My blood is drink indeed. He who eats My flesh and drinks My blood abides in Me and I in Him," (John 7:54-56).

You partake of the physical food; your stomach digests it and your blood stream carries the nutrition to every part of your body. Every cell is served life. Thus is Jesus to my life. He does not visit me; He is digested into me. He becomes the nutrition of every area of my existence. My mind, emotions, nerves, attitude, and spirit, all derive life from Him. Jesus is the example of such a reality. He said, "As the living Father sent Me, and I live because of the Father, so he who feeds on Me will live because of Me," (John 6:57). Did you notice the interaction of the words "As" and "so?" Jesus was living because of the Father. This is the explanation of how I am going to live by Him. What the Father was to Him is what He is to me. As He was filled with the Father, so I am filled with Him.

I am a Jesus pusher!!! I will know no food except Him. I will have no resource for life except Him. I will allow no substitutes. I will not partake of junk foods. He is my bread. Will you eat of Him with me and live? I am a Jesus pusher!!!

Jesus PUSHER | 15

I am a Jesus pusher!!! I am focusing on Him. I want to concentrate on Him for so long He becomes my tradition. I want the routine of my life to be Him. The habit of my life will be the practicing of His presence. My inner spirit will be trained to immediately embrace Him in every troubled moment. I renounce the pattern of upset and anger. I must know Him in relaxation and surrender. I am a Jesus pusher!!!

We have many examples of established patterns in our past. The Pharisees and Sadducees had a consistent, automatic response. Whenever they were confronted with truth, they immediately reverted to their accepted tradition. They cried, "We have Abraham as our father," (Matthew 3:9). John the Baptist called them to repentance. He warned them not to allow this rut of tradition to be their defense. They were confronted with change. Their defense was their tradition. It was their consistent, spontaneous response. How often have I done this? Jesus calls me to embrace His attitude; I cry, "I am an elder in the church." He calls me to the appointment of His cross; I explain, "I must not miss the committee meeting; I am the chairman." He desires to pour His life through me to embrace a leper (or someone like him); I demand protection for my life. I must not be contaminated with the infection of my world for I am holy.

I am a Jesus pusher!!! I will surrender all of my defenses, patterns, responses, methods, systems, arrangements, schemes, plans, compositions, orderings, and groupings. He shall be the single response of my life. I will turn to Him alone. I am a Jesus pusher!!!

Jesus PUSHER | 16

I am a Jesus pusher!!! Everything else is a substitute, a replacement, a plastic misfit. I must not embrace my tradition instead of Him. If I do, I become like the Pharisees and Sadducees. Their automatic response to being confronted with truth was, "We have Abraham as our father," (Matthew 3:9). John the Baptist called them to embrace Christ, the Messiah, who was present among them. They reverted back to their heritage.

What a small, superficial, merger was their heritage in comparison to the presence of the King. John the Baptist quickly pointed out that their heritage was reduced to the level of a hard stone in light of Christ (Matthew 3:9). Jesus was able to turn stones into the children of Abraham. What they had held onto as precious was insignificant in the presence of Jesus. If they insisted on clinging to their heritage instead of Christ, it would become an ax which would cut them down (Matthew 3:10). What they thought would save them turned into their destruction in the presence of Christ. They would end up chaff instead of wheat (Matthew 3:12). At harvest time, no farmer boasts about the abundance of his chaff. He thrills only in the wheat. The chaff is simply burned and forgotten.

I am Jesus pusher!!! I will allow Christ to burn all the chaff of my life. This will include everything I have depended upon outside of Him. I want Him to remove every item which makes me feel secure. I have depended upon my education, financial gain, talent, contacts, experiences, traditions, knowledge, and possessions. I renounce all of these and declare Him as my sole security. I am a Jesus pusher!!!

Jesus PUSHER | 17

I am a Jesus pusher!!! I was not there. I did not embrace Him physically nor participate in His miracles. I did not help drive the physical nails in His hands nor stand in the crowd and jeer. I did not receive the free food as the miracle power of God wrought the multiplication of bread and fish. I did not see the empty tomb nor question His resurrection with the disciples. The historical Jesus of two thousand years ago was not then my acquaintance for I was not. But I have heard from those who did. That which was from the beginning, which we have heard, which we have seen with our eyes, which we have looked upon, and our hands have handled, concerning the Word of life – the life was manifested, and we have seen, and bear witness, and declare to you that eternal life which was with the Father and was manifested to us – that which we have seen and heard we declare to you, that you also may have fellowship with us; and truly our fellowship is with the Father and with His Son Jesus Christ (1 John 1:1-3).

I am a Jesus pusher!!! Therefore, do not think my experience is simply hearsay and invalid. I too have embraced Him. The historical Jesus of two thousand years ago has come to me as surely as He came to them. While the historical presence was absolutely necessary, it is not greater than the spiritual presence of the same Christ. I embrace Him, receive from Him, and hear from Him in a greater way than they ever dreamed in those three years of ministry. He is not different from then to now, but is the same Jesus. What He did for them, He is doing for me and greater. Would I trade places with them? Not on your life! I am a Jesus pusher for the eternal Christ has come to me!!!

Jesus PUSHER | 18

I am a Jesus pusher!!! I am His business partner. I do not work for Him. I do not serve Him as a slave would serve a master. He is not my foreman on the ministry job. He has not even appointed me foreman while He sits in the big office. I have not purchased a religious franchise from Him giving me the right to certain slogans and ceremonies. He and I have gone into business together.

I am a Jesus pusher!!! He and I are in "fellowship." The Greek word used often in the New Testament is "koinonia." It means far more than a potluck dinner after the Sunday morning worship service. It is used in reference to James and John who were partners with Simon (Luke 5:10). All three men had invested their money and time to join together in a fishing business. I am not on the assembly line, a mere employee. I do not punch a time clock to collect a wage. I am in the main office; I meet in the big conference room. Jesus and I are partners in the Kingdom of God. His heart has become mine; what He wants is what I want. What sources Him now sources me.

I am a Jesus pusher for He is my enterprise. All other activities are secondary; they only have meaning as they fit into Him. He does not provide vacation time apart from Him; who would want it? He is my relaxation, my rest, my sweat, and my hard work. We do not work side by side. We work inside and inside for I am in Him and He is in me. It is a dream job. The job security is certain; the benefits are outstanding. He and I have become one. I am a Jesus pusher!!!

Jesus PUSHER | 19

I am a Jesus pusher!!! I am message centered not organization centered. My concern is not the sharpness of the messenger, but the clarity of the message. Every aspect of the delivery which distracts from the message must be eliminated. When the music becomes so dominate I cannot see Him, the music must cease. When my stories become so vivid they are remembered instead of Him, I must shrink from telling them. You understand Jesus is my message. I am not referring to details about His life, or concepts He taught, or even commandments. I am only pointing to His person.

John strongly established himself as an eyewitness of Christ. He used words such as heard, seen with our eyes, looked upon, and hands have handled. Immediately he tells us the message he received from Jesus. He cries, "This is the message...." (1 John 1:5). The English language cannot properly translate his emphasis. John puts the stress on the verb "is" in order to convey the sense of "exists." In other words, "There exists this message." There is a timeless significance about the message. This message has not been subject to change or modification. It did not originate with John or you and me. In fact, it did not originate with the physical Jesus preaching the Sermon on the Mount. It comes from the heart of the Trinity.

What is the message? Jesus is the message. He is not a delivery system for the message or a bill board stating the message; He is the message of the heart of God. He is not one through whom God speaks; He is the speaking of God. Everything taking place in the heart of God is found in Jesus. I am a Jesus pusher; I want to push all that is found in God's heart. I want to engulf you and submerge you in His throbbing heart. This will be done by getting you into Jesus. I am a Jesus pusher!!!

Jesus PUSHER | 20

I am a Jesus pusher!!! What God desires for me to know is found in Jesus. Jesus said, "No longer do I call you servants, for a servant does not know what his master is doing, but I have called you friends, for all things that I heard from My Father I have made known to you," (John 15:15). He spoke this in the context of His coming to indwell us through the Spirit. Such intimate communication is taking place. It is far beyond words, gestures, or instructions. It is not on the academic level; it is not a result of education. It is Him. In being intimate with His person, He is able to communicate what cannot otherwise be revealed. I am discovering the heart of God.

I am a Jesus pusher!!! If Jesus is the message, not simply the messenger, then truth cannot be discovered outside of Him. Three times at the beginning of his epistle John relates we have heard (1 John 1:1, 3, 5). Is it simply sound waves coming from the lips of the physical Christ to the ears of John? The Greek word means "to hear," but more specifically means "to come to know." It goes far beyond the idea of physically hearing sounds to knowing and even obeying what is being revealed. Jesus ended many of the parables of the Kingdom with this statement: "He who has ears to hear, let him hear," (Matthew 13:9, 43).

I am a Jesus pusher for in intimacy with Him I am embraced by truth and am enabled to respond. He is the key element which makes everything else make sense. He is the glue which holds all the facts together. In the midst of chaotic situations, I find light, calmness in Him. He is proper perspective, ability to see things as they are, and truth instead of lies. There is great danger in life without His eyesight. I am a Jesus pusher!!!

———————

Jesus PUSHER | 21

I am a Jesus pusher!!!
I have been such a loser.
All my life I have pushed self;
The horror of guilt was not felt.
Battles raged in every circumstance.
They did not occur by chance;
They were a result of my own device.
I was attempting to save my own life.
I was so completely blind;
Light, in His presence, brightly shined.
It was the wonder of His countenance.
It penetrated the depth of my pretence.
I am complete in Him;
In every circumstance I now win.
I have ceased to be a God user.
I am now a Jesus pusher!!!

———————

I am a Jesus pusher!!! Therefore I am a pusher of light. Jesus is light! I am not referring to academic knowledge or information for this can be used to camouflage or hide (darkness). I am not pushing a perspective for it may be one among many. A perspective can be adjusted to cover certain aspects of one's life (darkness). This is not about a life style. The manner of my life may adjust what I believe in order to feel justified (darkness). This is not about doctrine; for an individual may embrace the doctrine that allows what they wish to do (darkness). I am not highlighting a set of circumstances; these may be used to excuse how I treat you (darkness). This is not about psychology. The opinions vary with the experiences and personalities of people.

I am a Jesus pusher!!! He is the light. He is the reality of the way things have been from the beginning. Go from the present to the beginning of all things and you will discover He has not changed. Circumstances, popular opinions of the present, nor personal agendas have not altered Him. Jesus Christ is the same yesterday, today, and forever (Hebrews 13:8). The light that He was is the light that He is. The light that He is the light He will be. I am secure in Him, the light.

What I know about Him today is not all I will know about Him tomorrow. I am growing in the light. This does not mean He has changed; it means I am discovering. What an adventure to investigate the light! It would be better stated, the light is investigating me. I am open, responding to the light going to the depth of my soul. I cry to be exposed. Let all darkness be consumed by the light. This light will not allow darkness to remain in my life. I and the light are becoming one. I am a light pusher, a Jesus pusher!!!

Jesus PUSHER | 23

I am a Jesus pusher!!! I am aligning my life with others who have been captured as I am. John declared God is light and in Him is no darkness at all (1 John 1:5). He is so emphatic about this truth. He reinforces the very idea of God is light by an additional negative statement of the very opposite thought. It highlights the fact that God is light is an absolute truth, without any exception or reservation. The absence of darkness is a quality of God. The Greek text uses two negative forms which reinforce each other. This expresses an emphatic negation.

I am a Jesus pusher!!! I am not attracted to the darkness; I am attracted to the light. I find no pleasure in confusion, dismay, depression, destruction, glumness, blindness, dimness, dejection, hatred, gloom, or sadness. I am not even interested in shade or shadow. My life cries for the brightness of His person. It is here I am exposed and changed. It is here I see clearly. I desire no deception. I do not want to live in the lie. Give me Jesus, the light. I will harbor no theology or concept which is not of the light. I want no style which is not of the light. No manner of living will be tolerated which is not of the light. No attitude will be allowed which is not produced by the light. Give me Jesus, the light.

I am a Jesus pusher!!! Flood my life with Him. May He brighten every dark corner. Let every hidden room be illuminated with His presence. May my countenance, my attitude, my eyes, the very tone of my life shine with the light. This is only possible when I am in Him and He is in me. Fill me the Jesus, the light. I am a light pusher, a Jesus pusher!!!

———————

Jesus PUSHER | 24

I am a Jesus pusher!!! It is such a positive way to be. To highlight Jesus is to present the best, the glorious, the answer, and the way out. It is not about what you cannot embrace but what you can embrace. He is not about what you give up but what you take on. Embracing Him is not about sacrifice but enhancing. Peter describes one who has known the wonder of Christ and turns from it as a dog returns to his own vomit, (2 Peter 2:22). Who would want to do such a thing? Every sacrifice I have made to know Christ can be clearly equated to "dog vomit." There is no sadness, sorrow, or regret connected to His fullness.

Having proclaimed this as true, I recognize the negative does exist. One cannot have a positive without the negative. There is light which verifies there is darkness. Darkness is simply the absence of light. It only exists where there is no light. If anyone wants to live in darkness, they must get rid of the light. One cannot live in darkness by accident. In a totally darkened room even the small flame cannot be ignored. It demands the attention of everyone. Why would anyone spend their life time extinguishing the light? It would be a constant battle one could never win. One must consistently fight to live in darkness. Embrace the light; it will grow in your life. I have become overwhelmed with it. It is not a struggle but a relaxed invading. Light is permeating the depth of every facet of my life.

I am a light pusher!!! Jesus is the light. In Him there is no darkness at all. But this is of no concern for all I want is light. I am not fighting against; I am fighting for. It is hard to call it a battle; the enemy is quickly dismantled as darkness disappears in the light. There is great victory in Jesus. I am a person of the light; I am a Jesus pusher!!!

Jesus PUSHER | 25

I'm a Jesus pusher!!! I have walked down the corridors of utter helplessness. I have regarded the iron doors clanging shut and knew there was no way out. I have experienced the strength of those in authority overpowering me. I was caught. I have gone up against the evil one and lost the battle. It was as if my very will had been conquered. I was so totally bound; I was helpless. No one came to visit; no one had a solution. Hundreds of voices cried out but each only provided an additional entrapment.

But in the darkest of my helpless estate, Jesus came! How can I describe His coming? Perhaps He did not come at all; perhaps He was already there. He did not come as a mighty conqueror able to overthrow all my defeats; although it was evident His power was adequate. He did not appear as the intellectual genius who could arrest all my confusions; although He impressed me as One who was the truth. He did not roar into my space as one who overpowered all other forces; although the foe trembled at His voice.

He came with the embrace of a passionate lover. He cared for me in my brokenness as a loving mother nursing me back to health. He found me like a father who had desperately searched for years. In that single moment of embrace I knew I was found. He was not one piece of my liberty; He was my freedom. Everything is complete in Him. No wonder I am a Jesus pusher!!!

———

Jesus PUSHER | 26

I am a Jesus pusher!!! I am completely embarrassed with the energy I have spent pushing other things. I speak not of drugs, pornography, or materialism as some have done. If those pushers have been misled, how much more have I.

I have pushed heaven with its streets of gold and great mansions. I have become emotional over a place where pain and suffering will cease to exist. I have promoted a location instead of Him. Do not be offended. All that is said about such a place is true; but why did that thrill me more than Him?

I have pushed theology with great vigor. I have become convinced of certain ideas which became so elevated in my spiritual life I could not tolerate those who did not agree. I found myself being intolerant, unloving, and judgmental. Perhaps my belief was correct, but did it create an attitude unlike Him?

I became so accustomed to certain religious activities; they became my traditions. I strongly pushed them upon everyone. I promoted them as the solution to the needs of mankind. If only they would follow my example and adhere to my patterns. Young people infuriated me with new patterns and customs. It brought division and argument. How could my patterns of seeking Him become so large in my life they overshadowed His presence?

I am a Jesus pusher!!! I renounce everything but Him. Everything must come under His presence; it must be subordinate to His presence. I will know Him only. Will you join me as a Jesus pusher?

———————

Jesus PUSHER | 27

I am a Jesus pusher!!! I have found Him as the total and only explanation of theology. Big words and philosophical concepts have often confused me. The arguments and debates of men have repulsed me. I have been repelled by the constant usage of certain theological jargon which did not relate to the pain of my life. If Christianity is only the complication of theological idea, I am damned. I have far too many unanswered questions plaguing my life.

I am a Jesus pusher!!! He is my theology. In intimacy with Him all the great questions of life find their answers. Is there life after death? Absolutely! I know the One who has conquered death. In Him the sting of death has been removed making it a simple transition to another plane of living. Did He not cry, "I am the life," (John 14:6)? Is there victory over sin? Can sin in its essence be cleansed and removed from my life? Who could claim such a condition? In Christ I have experienced the expanding righteousness of His person engulfing my life. Holiness had nothing to do with my doing but had everything to do with His embracing. He has become so united with me that His righteousness has become mine. I have become a partaker of the Divine nature (2 Peter 1:4). Is there purpose and meaning to life? All my plans and dreams have been temporary. Once a dream is accomplish what is left? In His indwelling presence I have moved from the temporal view to the eternal view. He has a plan. I was born out of the dreams and plans of God. I am important to Him forever.

I am a Jesus pusher!!! I will embrace Him as my theology. My doctrine will be a proclamation of Him. I will propose Him as the only answer, the total solution. We must know Him and be a Jesus pusher.

I am a Jesus pusher!!! When Peter was requested to explain Pentecost, he simply pointed them to Jesus. He must have been a Jesus pusher. Jesus of Nazareth, a Man was sourced by God in His living (Acts 2:22), His dying (Acts 2:23), and His resurrection (Acts 2:24). When the outside God came to indwell one hundred and twenty disciples at Pentecost, it was a duplication of what had already happened in Jesus of Nazareth, a Man. Jesus is the explanation of the theology of Pentecost. The fullness of the Spirit is no longer frightening; it reproduces the life of Jesus in you and me. How will I act if the Spirit of God comes to indwell me? I will act like Jesus. The same Spirit of God indwelling Him has now come to indwell me.

I am a Jesus pusher!!! His Spirit has become the source of my life. I refuse to live out of my best. Where has my best taken me? The pain and dissatisfaction of my own life is a product of my own efforts. I have ceased to blame others; I have lived out of my own resource. What is the potential of my future? How will anything be better? The common denominator of every crisis of my life is me. In every failure, I find myself? I have tried; but my attempts are insufficient. Could the Spirit of Jesus become my source? Could Pentecost happen to me? Jesus spoke of oneness with Him, "At that day you will know that I am in My Father, and you in Me, and I in you," (John 14:20). He is speaking of the Day of Pentecost. In the oneness of His Spirit I experience Him. He is my source. I am a Jesus pusher!!!

I am a Jesus pusher!!! It is not a job; it is an obsession. It is not a means to an end; it is a passion. I am not compelled by results; I am constrained by Him. I am not a con man attempting to manipulate situations for my benefit; I am captured by His love. I do not see people as individuals to entrap; I am compelled to embrace them because of Him. I do not have a self agenda; I have a Christ agenda. I am not performing before an audience; I am a lover. I am not an entertainer looking for applause; I am dancing with the God of the universe. He has come to indwell me. I am a Jesus pusher!!!

I am overwhelmed. I am standing on my tip toes stretching to grasp all that is found in Him. I am like a deer caught in the headlights of a car. I feel like a small child who has fallen into a swimming pool of chocolate; my only prayer is "please enlarge my capacity." I view the greatness of His person and know I have only begun in to discover who He is. As I am cradled in His arms, I realize the wonder of this love has only begun to penetrate my life. Every thought is captured by His presence. The very intent of my motive has become engulfed with His desires. My very body appetites are dominated by His presence. The craving of my heart is to know His mind. My desire is that He enlarges my heart with His wisdom. I want the mind of Christ.

I am a Jesus pusher!!! I am obsessed, possessed, mastered, dominated, addicted, caught up, thrilled, ecstatic, awestruck, and overwhelmed with Him. Would you please look at Him with me? Even a glance will capture you. Stop where you are and let Him draw you to Himself. I am a Jesus pusher!!!

I am a Jesus pusher!!! Is it true that you become like those you associate with the most? Do you remember the classic story of years gone by? There was a man's face which had been carved on the side of the mountain. It was created by nature. Over the years s legend developed that on occasion an actual man appeared who looked like the face on the mountain. A local boy heard the story and longed to see the man with such a face. Year after year he searched the face of every stranger who came to their town and compared it with the face on the mountain. By the time he reached his teen years he was dismayed. No one seemed to match the face on the mountain. Time quickly passed as he married and related the story to his own children. In old age, he wondered if he would ever see the man who resembled the face on the mountain. One day the people of the town looked at him and pointed to the mountain. They exclaimed, "You have the face of the man on the mountain!" Staring so long at the man of the mountain, he had become that man.

Oh, to be so absorbed into Jesus that I become like Him. Oh, for the cleft of His chin to become mine. Could I get so close to Him and become such a part of Him that I become like Him? Could who He is become who I am? I do not desire to be God; I am not speaking of power or fame. Could I have His attitude, reflect His glory, or display His beauty? Can all that He is be in all that I am; so that I can manifest all He is? If this is true my whole being can become a Jesus pusher!!!

Jesus PUSHER | 31

I am a Jesus pusher!!! From the lips of another Jesus pusher we hear, "He has delivered us from the power of darkness and conveyed us into the kingdom of the Son of His love," (Colossians 1:13). Are there not two kingdoms? We have all experienced the Kingdom of Darkness. The memories of guilt and defeat are still traps to draw us back into discouragement. The awareness of the multitude of people we have influenced for darkness instead of light could bring us to death. But God has not only taken us from the Kingdom of Darkness; He has conveyed us into the Kingdom of the Son of His love. "Conveyed" is a wonderful word to express what has happened to us. It means "to take or carry from one place to another." Jesus has taken His powerful redemptive hands and picked me up. He has nestled me in the strength of His arms as He has carried me into the place of safety. He did not call me to come on my own. He has not waited on me to come to Him; He has come to me. I was abandoned by all; yet He found me. I was blinded and knew no direction; He saw clearly and knew where to take me. I was confused and could not make right choices; He came with clarity and insight. I was dead but have awakened unto life.

The first thing I saw in the new kingdom was the wonder of His face. It is the Kingdom of the Son of His love. Everything in the Kingdom is like Him; because He is the Kingdom. It did not take long to go from the Kingdom of Darkness to the Kingdom of the Son of His life. The reason is the Kingdom came to be within me. The King is residing within me. What a wonder to sit next to the King at His table! What a delight to continually fellowship with this wonderful King! How relaxing it is to have this King at the heart of every problem confronting my life! I am not alone; I am in the Kingdom for the King is in me. I am a Jesus pusher!!!

Jesus PUSHER | 32

I am a Jesus pusher!!! I feel like Charles Wesley who wrote, "Oh, for a thousand tongues to sing my dear Redeemer's praise!" I have only one tongue and it shall be used exclusively to push Jesus. How could I ever speak of anything else as a solution to life except Him? I desire a thousand hands to raise in praise to His name. I have only two; they shall both be lifted constantly in His honor. I wish I had a thousand hands to do service for His glory. I have only two hands; they shall both be filled with His presence to be used for His glory. I crave a thousand feet to run throughout the world to speak His fame. I have only two feet; they shall be constantly available for His specific use. I will not be allured by size of crowd or the prestige of the group. I will not allow compensation to determine my location.

I am a Jesus pusher!!! He alone will be the inspiration of the message. A crowd of few will receive the same message with the same fervor as a crowd of thousands. The truth as sharp as a two-edged sword will come forth for those of power as well as for those of low status. The poor will see the same Jesus in my life as the rich. This is not about them; it is about Him. He is the same. May those who are repulsive know Jesus; let those who are attractive know Jesus. May the talented know Jesus; those who are without talent must know Him. The kings and the servants must both bow before Him. He is great enough to command the attention of everyman. If the demons leap at His voice, every individual must listen. If nature grows calm at His speaking, every heart must cease beating when He approaches. All the time, in every situation, with all available resource, with the entire fervor of my being I am a Jesus pusher!!!

———————

Jesus PUSHER | 33

I am a Jesus pusher!!! I see clearly in Him what I am to be. He is the shape, atmosphere, attitude, and image of all God intends for me. Peter leaves no room for doubt concerning this issue. After the Pentecost event, he is moved upon by the Holy Spirit to preach an explanation of the event for a large group of Jews. He boldly proclaims Jesus of Nazareth, a Man, sourced by God. What made Jesus the visible image of the invisible Father was the Spirit of the Father indwelling and sourcing Him. What would happen if I had the same resource living in me?

I am a Jesus pusher! This does not mean I simply talk about Him. This is not a banner I wave in the face of a crowd. Jesus pushing is not about correcting everyone who is wrong. I am not participating in a theological argument. It does not consist of a strong allegiance to an organization. I am sourced by the Spirit of Jesus. As Jesus was sourced by the Father so I am sourced by Him. This reproduces the life of Christ in my world. The life of Jesus is seen again. Christ likeness is far beyond my discipline. It is greater than bending my life style to achieve an ethical standard. It is not activity centered; it is person centered. It is the Spirit of Jesus indwelling and sourcing my life. This creates the possibility out of the impossible. An entire new level of living is now experienced. Being a Jesus pusher is His life generated through me. He pushes Himself! I am a Jesus pusher!!!

Jesus PUSHER | 34

I am a Jesus pusher!!! In the Book of Acts, Peter is moved upon by the Holy Spirit to explain Pentecost. His explanation is Jesus. He pushes Jesus! He explains that Jesus of Nazareth, a Man, was sourced by the Spirit of God as the one hundred and twenty disciples have just experienced. As Jesus was sourced by the Father, so we can now be sourced by Jesus. Sourcing has to do with what causes you. In fact, Peter boldly stated that God sourced the life of Jesus: "Jesus of Nazareth, a Man attested by God to you by miracles, wonders, and signs which God did through Him in your midst as you yourselves also know," (Acts 2:22). "Miracles, wonders, and signs" have to do with activities, attitudes, and manner of life. Everything about the life of Jesus is sourced by God. According to the dictionary "sourcing" has to do with what "causes, creates, or initiates." In the world of physics it means "the point or part of a system where energy or mass is added to the system." What is at the heart of your being which causes you to be as you are?

I am a Jesus pusher!!! I do not live out of myself. I have long since discovered my thinking is completely inadequate for the problems of life; I want to be sourced by the wisdom of the Spirit of Jesus. Self-control has brought nothing but collapse in my life. The temptations of my world have laughed at my feeble efforts to discipline myself. Is it possible to possess a different kind of control, the Spirit of Jesus? A fruit of His sourcing is "self-control." Oh, I want Jesus to spill forth from every aspect of my living. I want to be a Jesus pusher!!!

Jesus PUSHER | 35

I am a Jesus pusher!!! To speak of Jesus is to speak of the source of life. He does not give me life; He is life. Peter explained it to a crowd of Jews on the day of Pentecost. Jesus of Nazareth, a Man, is the explanation of what is taking place in one hundred and twenty disciples. Pentecost is all about the sourcing of God within the human being. Jesus was clearly the supreme example of such sourcing. God sourced the very life of Jesus (Acts 2:22). But Peter continues with a startling fact, an encouraging fact. God also sourced the death of Jesus: "Him, being delivered by the determined purpose and foreknowledge of God you have taken by lawless hands and put to death," (Acts 2:23).

Could I be so completely sourced by Jesus He not only causes my life, but He also plans and causes my death? This changes death from the scary, frightening unknown to the secure, confident embrace of His person. Death ceases to be the wasted life, a tragic end. It becomes the fulfillment, valuable, and held in high esteem. Death becomes ministry as we accomplish His will. Jesus' death has eternal significance because it is sourced by God. Can my death be used by God to fulfill His plan?

I am a Jesus pusher! I desire a life upon and through which He demonstrates Himself. I desire a death through which He can fulfill His plan. "Please Jesus, source me with Your life. May I not live, yet I am alive. May You live through me. Please push Your life and death through me. In my life and death I will be a Jesus pusher!!!"

Jesus PUSHER | 36

I am a Jesus pusher!!! Oh that I may know Him and the power of His resurrection, and the fellowship of His sufferings, being conformed to His death (Philippians 3:10). Was Peter correct in his explanation of Pentecost (Acts 2)? What God intended for you and me was taking place in Jesus. Jesus was sourced by the Spirit of God. If the Spirit which sourced Jesus lives in me, my life will exhibit everything of Jesus. My speech will be of Jesus. My actions will demonstrate Jesus. My attitude will be of Jesus. I will be a Jesus pusher!

Peter explained that Jesus was sourced by the Father in His life, death, and resurrection (Acts 2:22-24). If the resource of the Spirit of Jesus causes my life, can He also source my death? If He sources my death, can I depend upon Him to source my resurrection? He is the very internal cause of life which generates, quickens, and empowers life through me. This is true today; it is true in resurrection. Perhaps this is what is happening in my life today. Am I not living the resurrected life of Christ now? Has the eternal life of Christ so permeated my being that I have crossed the line?

I am a Jesus pusher! Pushing Jesus is not a hobby, a cause, or even a career. I cannot help myself. I do not have a choice (although I could quit, but why would I want to?). I have become saturated with His being. How could He not flow from me? My world must feel pressured by Him through me. They probably think I am a Jesus pusher, when really He is pushing me. Oh, what a relationship to be His! I am a Jesus pusher!!!

Jesus PUSHER | 37

I am a Jesus pusher!!! It is beyond my wildest dreams: He wants me! The Scriptures literally echo with this truth. It is not emphasized once or twice but continually. He wants me! Mark relates it in relationship to Jesus' disciples. And He went up on the mountain and called to Him those He Himself wanted (Mark 3:13). The subject of the sentence is He which refers to Jesus. There are three verbs in the sentence: went, called, and wanted. The first verb, went, is in the active voice. This means Jesus is responsible for the action of the verb. It is in the indicative mood; it is a simple statement of fact. The second verb is called. It is in the middle voice. This means the verb is focused on the personal desires and preferences of the subject. Jesus calls according to what He wants. This is strongly strengthened by the third verb, wanted. It is in the active voice which means the subject is responsible for this action. It is in the imperfect tense which indicates it occurred in the past and is continuing into the present. This is not just a fleeting moment, but is the enduring passion of His heart. While this was written about His disciples years ago, its truth relates to me now. I am His personal, desired, wanted, craved, loved, passionate choice. He has called me!

I am not one out of many. I am not the one who is left after everyone else has been chosen. He is not stuck with me. I am not the best choice He has because I am all that is available. I am His first choice. The driving motive of His heart is to have me. He has proven this by literally moving every obstacle to receive me. There is no distance He will not travel to come and get me. He has gone from heaven to earth to embrace me. There is nothing He will not suffer in order to possess me. He has gladly and willingly opened Himself to the crucifixion. He has experienced death and hell in all of it fury in order to have me. He is the lover of my soul; He is the entire fan club of my being. He is my great Supporter; He is my amazing Promoter. How can I not be His? I am a Jesus pusher!!!

———————

Jesus PUSHER | 38

I am a Jesus pusher!!! I never knew forgiveness outside of Him. I truly thought I had experienced forgiveness; however, after His embrace I know better. He did not try to appease me or make a compromise. He did not try to make things right or earn my respect. He did not simply set things aside and forget. He went to great expense in real forgiveness. When I realized His great expense I experienced the bathing of His forgiveness. I found myself in His embrace. He did not give me forgiveness and walk away. While He did not hate me, He could not have relationship with me. No! I was restored. It was as if I had never done anything against Him at all. He treats me as if I have always been His.

I am a Jesus pusher!!! I have discovered forgiveness is not a thing. It is an attitude expressed in an embrace. It is not something Jesus gave to me; but is the warmth of His affection expressed. I do not experience it apart from Him, but in Him. He has gathered me into His arms. In oneness with His heart I experience acceptance. It is a marvel! I have come to realize every sin has been against Him. I have wronged many people. Most people would not forgive even one offense against them. But all the offenses and hurts against everyone else have ultimately been against Him. He plunged through all the sins against Himself and forgave me. I am forgiven; I am forgiven; I am forgiven. I cannot say it enough. What a wonder! I am forgiven! No wonder, I am a Jesus pusher!!!

———————

Jesus PUSHER | 39

I am a Jesus pusher!!! He is the elimination of fear. He does not strain or whistle in the dark. He does not refuse or control emotions. When He is present confidence floods my soul. He is the very essence of assurance. I am not kept by my knowledge of Him or by the spiritual disciplines from His teaching. I am embraced by Him. I am not safe in academic information or data about Him, but in the warmth, oneness, and intimacy of His presence.

The disciples followed Jesus into a boat. If they had only known, it was totally safe to follow Him. They were experienced fishermen who had relied on their skills and training for years. But a seismic storm came their way. It was beyond their ability. They cried out, "Lord, save us! We are perishing!" (Matthew 8:25). This awakened Him from His sleep; for He was asleep in the storm. Why could they not be like He was? He arose and rebuked the sea which quickly became calm. They shook their heads in wonder and inquired, "Who can this be?" (Matthew 8:27). The answer is clear! He is a Man who is filled with the Spirit of God (Matthew 3:13-17). In the embrace of the Father He can sleep through any storm.

Could I be like Him? Oh, not because I imitate Him, or develop skills like His. I cannot create in through spiritual disciplines. Christ-likeness comes because as He is resting in the embrace of the Father, so I rest in His embrace. If I could know Him as He knew the Father. Isn't this the whole point? In knowing Him, I am embraced by His confidence. In being embraced by His confidence, I cease to fear. I think I will join Him and sleep during my seismic storms! I am a Jesus pusher!!!

Jesus PUSHER | 40

I am a Jesus pusher!!! After following Jesus for a few months, the disciples cried out, "Who can this be?" (Matthew 8:27). The answer is clearly stated in Matthew's Gospel account. Jesus is the beginning of the New Covenant. He is the first Man to walk over the threshold into the fullness of the Spirit. He is the first Man to experience Pentecost. God and man have become one in Him (Matthew 3:13-17). This is who He is! The disciples where astonished because He calmed the seismic storm. It was doubly amazing because He slept as the storm raged. The storm did not awaken Him. What immediately awaked Him was the cry for help from His disciples.

No wonder I am a Jesus pusher!!! He is not distressed by the circumstances around me, but is immediately touched with the pain of my heart. My cries deeply affect Him, while the chaos of the problem causes Him no worry. Where can you find such a solace as this? I want to live in His presence. I want His nature to so fill me that I am like Him. There are hundreds around me in upsetting circumstances. They do not need to see panic on my face, but feel love from my heart. The eyes of my soul must express the confidence of His presence not the fright of the situation. This is what I find in Him. There is no hopelessness or distress as the storm rages around me. He is focused on my need. I am His and this is enough. I am a Jesus pusher!!!

Jesus PUSHER | 41

I am a Jesus pusher!!!

I am joining with the centurion of old and those under his control. I want to share in their great revelation. This centurion was responsible for one hundred soldiers who were policing Jerusalem. A crucifixion always provided an opportunity for trouble. The crucifixion of Jesus was especially disturbing. The sky had turned dark at the noon hour. It was rumored the veil of the temple had been strangely torn from top to bottom. There were earthquakes taking place. Even resurrections of the dead had come to pass. It was as if the entire natural order was responding to this event. So when the centurion and those with him, who were guarding Jesus, saw the earthquake and the things that had happened, they feared greatly, saying, "Truly this was the Son of God!" (Matthew 27:54).

I want to join the centurion in proclaiming Jesus as the Son of God. This title is used twenty-six times in the Gospels. Jesus is called "Son of God" by Satan (Matthew 4:3, 6; Luke 4:3, 9), by demons (Matthew 8:29; Mark 3:ll; Luke 4:41), by John the Baptist (John 1:34), by His followers (Matthew 14:23, John 1:49; 11:27; 20:31), by angels (Luke 1:35), and by this Roman centurion. The content of this descriptive title is a focus on the Divinity of Jesus. I am overwhelmed that GOD would embrace me! Allow it to sink deep into your heart and mind. He who is above all has come to us. It is in His coming that our value is established. He has come for me! I have not been forced upon Him. How can anyone force God? I have not conned or manipulated God; does He not know everything? I did not earn His respect; He has simply loved me in the midst of my failures. I must have value for He cares for me. I will surrender to this love. I will allow my life to be shaped and molded by this love. Oh, Son of God, you shall have me! I am a Jesus pusher!!!

———————

I am a Jesus pusher!!! Who is it that I am pushing? He is the Son of God and the Son of Man. The content of the title, Son of God, is a focus on the Divinity of Jesus. The content of the title, Son of Man, is a focus on His humanity. No wonder, I am a Jesus pusher! God has become man, one of us. This title is used eighty-two times in the Gospel accounts. All of these occurrences, except for three, are spoken by Jesus. It is the preferred title Jesus gave to Himself. This title essentially means "The Man." Who can fully comprehend the reality of this truth? God has become Man. He set aside all that He had as God and limited Himself to the total resource available to man. It is too much to absorb. What a mystery!

If Jesus set aside all the advantages He had as God and became a total man, how did He live such an unordinary life? It is the proclamation of the resource you and I have available to us. Man filled with God! Jesus was Spirit-sourced. He did not do what He did because He was God (the Son of God); He lived as He lived because He was a Man filled with God (the Son of Man). No wonder, I am a Jesus pusher! This reveals an entire new level of potential and possibilities for you and me. I too can be sourced by God. As the Father indwelt and sourced Jesus, so Jesus wants to indwell and source me. The life He lived is realistic for me to live because what caused Him to live that life is now available to me. Who would not run to embrace such an opportunity?

There is no defeat here. Sin is conquered! But it is not just a defensive relationship with Him; it is offensive. We can change our world. When I say "we" I am speaking of Him and me. He is our only possibility! I am a Jesus pusher!!!

I am a Jesus pusher!!! He receives my total admiration. A great challenge to be like Him is contained within this admiration. I am awestruck with the complete humility and meekness I find in Him. Paul described this attitude as he pleaded for us to Let this mind be in you which was also in Christ Jesus. He gave us great details on the state of this mind. Jesus is God in the highest sense. He experienced no pressure or stress in maintaining who He is as God. But He emptied Himself of all the benefits of this position in order to become a man. He humbled Himself and became obedient to the point of death, even the death of the cross (Philippians 2:8). How can one describe this kind of surrender? He died to all He was in Himself and relied totally on the sourcing of the Father.

I am repulsed by every act of self-sourcing within me. Every tendency to hurt feelings, needing my own way, defending my position, or guarding and protecting, only remind me of how unlike Him I really am. Even my attempts to train myself to be like Him are self-sourced. I try to discipline my life to shape it in His image. Does He not want to shape me? Each time I use my energy to produce Christ-likeness, I have wasted energy which could have embraced Him tighter. Oh, for my total focus to be on Him. I cannot live with anything less. I will not reach this reality with more self-sourcing. He must bring me here. I will allow Him to do in me what the Father did in Him. Therefore, the life the Father lived through Him, He will live through me. Could I become the image of Jesus in my world? I am a Jesus pusher!!!

Jesus PUSHER | 44

I am a Jesus pusher!!! Temptations have been varied in my life. Each age had its additional temptations. I have often read how He was in all points tempted as we are, yet without sin (Hebrews 4:15). I always believed it because it was in the Bible. Yet, I have not been able to comprehend how this could be. Has He had every temptation just as I have had them? I have made a discovery of a life time. There is only one motive, center point, or heart of every temptation. This means all temptations have the same purpose and attempt the same thing. To experience one temptation is to experience them all; they are all alike. Jesus set aside all He had as God (Son of God) and became a total man (Son of Man). He was filled with the Spirit of God. He was constantly sourced by the Father. From this Pentecost experience, He was immediately led up by the Spirit into the wilderness to be tempted by the devil (Matthew 4:1). Every aspect in every circumstance of the temptation was about sourcing. The devil knew exactly who He was. He said, "If (Since) you are the Son of God, command that these stones become bread," (Matthew 4:3). This temptation was not about bread. It was about taking back His Divine powers. Since He is God, why should He not live from the powers that God has? He gave them up to become the Son of Man, but why should He not take them back? Why should He live a life of dependency on God when He Himself is God? The temptation was "source Yourself!"

This is the focus of every temptation you and I face. Don't rely on Him. Don't allow Him to source your life. Take charge of your own life. Do your own thing. You have your rights. Do it your own way; stand up for yourself. Have you discovered this attitude in your own heart? This attitude always produces death.

I must know nothing but Him sourcing my life. He alone can bring me to this life; He alone can keep me in this life. I must have Him and Him alone! I am a Jesus pusher!!!

———————

I am a Jesus pusher!!! He has clearly blazed the trail for me to follow. But not only has He made the way clear, He has become the way. The moment He was filled with the Spirit of His Father, He was led up by the Spirit into the wilderness to be tempted by the devil (Matthew 4:1). He will plainly demonstrate how to overcome Satan and all of his allurements. After experiencing spiritual warfare for forty days and forty nights, He realized that physical necessities had been forgotten. He was hungry (Matthew 4:2). The devil suggested a simple solution. Since being sourced by God had gotten Him into this situation, why should He not get Himself out of it? There was no solution for food in this barren wilderness. He could simply source Himself for a moment and solve the problem. Is it wrong to be hungry or to eat? Isn't this a God given desire?

Matthew is very distinct in describing Jesus' approach. But He answered and said is how Matthew phrases it (Matthew 4:4). He answered is a translation of a Greek word. It is a participle which means it is a verb used as a noun. It is in the nominative case which means it is the subject. While Jesus is directly involved in the action, He is not the focus of this sentence. The action of answering is the subject and focus. The actual Greek word means to evaluate, discern, or to separate. At the moment of temptation, Jesus lounges into the arms of His Father's embrace. He retreats into the sourcing of the Father. What is the Father's opinion? How does the Father feel? What is the Father's perspective? Jesus will not let any action come from His life which is not sourced by the Father! This was the pattern of Jesus' life!

Jesus has opened the door for me to know Him like this! In every situation I must lounge in the arms of Christ's embrace. In intimacy with Him I can know the mind and heart of God. I can see the situation through His eyes; the devil can no longer trick me. I can live sourced by Jesus. I am a Jesus pusher!!!

————————

Jesus PUSHER | 46

I am a Jesus pusher!!! I want to be sourced by Him in the exact same manner as He was sourced by the Father. I want Him to live through me as the Father lived through Him. When temptation arose, He immediately lounged into the arms of His Father. He wanted to see the situation exactly as the Father saw it. Jesus wanted the tone, attitude, and heart of the Father. It was not a matter of right or wrong. What was wrong with being hungry and needing bread (Matthew 4:3)? Upon discovering the perspective of the Father, Jesus responded to Satan, "It is written," (Matthew 4:4). He then proceeds to quote an Old Testament passage.

It is written is a phrase used sixty-one times in the New Testament. Each usage is referring to the Scriptures. Jesus uses it three times in this temptation scene (Matthews 4:4, 7, 10). The Scriptures were at the heart of the intimacy between Jesus and His Father. Jesus did not use the Scriptures as an academic study or a proof texting. He was not interested in bumper sticker slogans. He wanted to know the passion of the Father. He saturated in the Scriptures as He saturated in the fellowship of the person of His Father. It was through the intimacy of their oneness, He was able to understand and hear the voice of the Father through the Scriptures. The Scriptures were alive because the Father was alive in Him.

I am a Jesus pusher!!! I desperately want to know the mind of Christ as He knew the mind of His Father. At the heart of this intimacy will be the Scriptures. The Living Word wants to flow into and through my life through the Written Word. We do not worship the Bible; we worship Jesus, the Living Word. However, the Bible becomes alive because the author is speaking to me through His Word. In the sourcing of the Spirit, I see the lips of Jesus parting as He speaks to me through His Word. The Written Word becomes an extension of the Living Word. Oh, I know Him; I hear Him! I am a Jesus pusher!!!

———————————

Jesus PUSHER | 47

I am a Jesus pusher!!! I desperately want to be like Him. At one time that statement meant acting like Him, doing what He would do. It was WWJD (what would Jesus do?) I no longer want my life to be governed by that premise. I do not want to live for Him; I want Him to live through me! I want intimacy on the level of the sourcing of His person. I want Him to reproduce His life through me. At the moment of temptation, discovering "what Jesus would do" does not give me victory. I am not strong enough to accomplish it. I need Him to source me! This is how He had victory in temptation (Matthew 4:4). He lounged in the arms of the Father; He discovered the Father's voice through the Scriptures.

In the first of the three final temptations, Jesus quoted, "Man shall not live by bread alone, but by every word that proceeds from the mouth of God," (Matthew 4:4). He proceeds this quote by stating, "It is written," (Matthew 4:4). Evidently the content of "It is written" is "every word that proceeds from the mouth of God." Jesus considered the Scriptures as the actual speaking of God. God is speaking through His Word and God is speaking His Word. In fact, He based His entire life experience upon the Scriptures. After His resurrection at the Emmaus Road encounter, He stated, "O foolish ones, and slow of heart to believe in all that the prophets have spoken! Ought not the Christ to have suffered these things and to enter into His glory?" And beginning at Moses and all the Prophets, He expounded to them in all the Scriptures the things concerning Himself," (Luke 24:25-27). Following these moments, Jesus appeared to the disciples in the upper room in Jerusalem. He reminded them of what He taught them before His resurrection. He said, "These are the words which I spoke to you while I was still with you, that all things must be fulfilled which were written in the Law of Moses and the Prophets and the Psalms concerning Me," (Luke 24:44).

Jesus quoted the Scriptures in the moment of temptation not as a good luck charm or magical statement. He was intimate with the Father through the Scriptures. If I would know the Spirit of Christ as Jesus knew the Spirit of the Father, I must saturate in the Scriptures. As He is alive in me, so the Scriptures become alive to me. I want to hear His voice not as a command or order, but to know the tone and attitude of His life. Please source me, Jesus!!!

———————

Jesus PUSHER | 48

I am a Jesus pusher!!! In the crisis of temptation, Jesus proclaimed, "It is written." It clearly means "the Scriptures." He continued to give the content to the Scriptures as "every word that proceeds from the mouth of God," (Matthew 4:4). In other words, the content of the Scriptures is the words of God which are proceeding from His mouth! Therefore, the Scriptures are the actual speaking of God. How does this change our approach to the Scriptures? We come to the Scriptures to meet a requirement called "devotions." Preachers come to the Scriptures to select a Biblical text to validate what they have written in a sermon. Sunday school teachers grab the Bible to present a lesson to their students. Others jump from one verse to another as they flip the pages looking for guidance. Some search for proof texts to win an argument. Could all of these be completely discarded?

I must come to the Scriptures to know Him! I desperately want to be sourced by His heart and mind. If I could only think like He thinks, I could then respond as He responds. How can I know His heart and mind? I must listen to Him speak through His Word. To be sourced by God without knowing His mind and heart is a contradiction. Jesus did not receive the fullness of the Spirit and then go to the Scriptures for a list of activities to do. The Scriptures were not His instruction manual, rule book, or guidelines. The Scriptures were an intimate conversation between two individuals who love, live, and dream together. They not only received information from each other, but joined in attitude, heart, and opinion.

I want to lounge in the arms of Jesus through His Word. I want the sourcing of Jesus to take the shape of Jesus' mind gleaned from the saturation in the Scriptures. In every situation I want the clarity of Christ's thinking to produce my response. I want the throb of His heart to burst through my face. I want my life to radiate His atmosphere. How can I be sourced by Him without knowing His mind? Speak directly to me, dear Jesus!!

———————

Jesus PUSHER | 49

I am a Jesus pusher!!! I want to be captured by Him. I want the romance of His presence to be my constant delight. In the moment of strong temptation in the wilderness, Jesus said to the devil, "It is written," (Matthew 4:4). Immediately He quoted the Scriptures. In fact, in all three recorded temptations in this event, Jesus said this same thing. He consistently gained victory, saw through the tricks of the evil one, and avoided all demonic pitfalls through the Scriptures. Do not think we are making an idol of a Book. The Bible is simply black ink on white paper put together in a leather binding. It has no magical powers. I am not proposing the daily reading of the Scriptures will cause all things to be right. Even memorizing the Scriptures will not guarantee correct actions. The answer is not found in the Scripture, but in the connection between the Author and the Scriptures.

Jesus quoted the Scriptures in rebuke to the devil's temptations. However, the devil quoted Scripture right back to Him by saying, "For it is written," (Matthew 4:6). If Jesus desires to base His responses on the Scriptures, the devil can quote Scriptures as well. But Jesus would not act on what the devil stated from Scriptures. The devil interpreted Scripture from the perspective of his self-sourcing. Jesus knew the heart of the Father. He heard the Father's voice through the Scriptures. One can academically study the Scriptures and know its content. One can use and abuse the Scriptures for his own ends. It is not just the Scriptures as an historical writing which is so important. It is the interflow of the Spirit. He wrote the Scriptures; He must interact and source our lives as we hear His voice through the Scriptures.

I am a Jesus pusher!!! I must know Him intimately. But how can I know His heart, the tone of His life? How can I live in the flow of His attitude and have His perspective? I must hear His voice through the Scriptures. The answer is not just in the Scriptures; the answer is in knowing Him through the Scriptures. I will come to the Scriptures with only one purpose! I want to know Jesus! I am a Jesus pusher!!!

———————

Jesus PUSHER | 50

I am a Jesus pusher!!! Jesus was in all points tempted as we are, yet without sin (Hebrews 4:15). When tempted to self-source His own supply of bread, Jesus reverted back to the Scriptures. He said, "It is written." This is a direct reference to the Scriptures. Then He quoted, "Man shall not live by bread alone, but by every word that proceeds from the mouth of God," (Matthew 4:4). Jesus has just given us the content of the Scriptures. In other words, the Scriptures contain every word that proceeds from the mouth of God. The Greek word translated that proceeds is from the root word meaning "to go." However, it has a prefix which is translated "from." It specifically highlights motion from an original location. But the original location is always internal. This means the words coming from the mouth of the Father are proceeding from the very internal heart of God. He is not reading a document or quoting a secondary source. He is exposing His innermost thoughts. Jesus is stating that the Scriptures are the revelation of the heart and mind of the Father.

If I come to the Scriptures to know the Spirit of Christ, I will find the heart passion of God revealed to me. I cannot count on my visions to reveal Christ to me. They can be influenced by my personal experiences. I do not trust my wisdom to find the heart of God, for God has chosen the foolish things of the world to put to shame the wise (1 Corinthians 1:27). I dare not trust my emotions for they vary with circumstances. I must listen to the very heart of God spoken through the Scriptures to my heart which is anxious to receive. As I seek Jesus, the Living Word, the Scriptures, the Written Word, becomes alive to my soul. I begin to know the tone, attitude, and passion of God. I am a Jesus pusher! He is Jesus revealed through the Scriptures. The Scriptures are not a rule book or a set of guidelines. The Scriptures are not a road map to get me to heaven. They are the whispering of the Father revealing Jesus. To know Jesus is to understand the Scriptures and to truly understand the Scriptures is to know Jesus. When I saturate in the Scriptures, I am saturating in Him. Oh, I want Him in my life! I am a Jesus pusher!!!

———————

Jesus PUSHER | 51

I am a Jesus pusher!!! There was no chance to know God until Jesus came. All through the Old Testament God is revealing Himself; but it is a progressive revelation. The final and complete revelation of God is Jesus. Everything I can know about God is contained in Jesus. He is the bosom, the seat of affection, of the Father revealed to me (John 1:18).

Jesus is the declaration of what God is really like! Jesus told the devil, "Man shall not live by bread alone, but by every word that proceeds from the mouth of God," (Matthew 4:4). What is coming from the mouth of the Father, Jesus calls word. This is a translation of the Greek word "rhema." It means that which is spoken, a statement or word. I was amazed that Jesus did not use the Greek word "logos," (John 1:1). "Logos" is the expression of the thought, while "rhema" is the thought itself. "Logos" is the idea expressed and seen, while "rhema" is the subject matter of the expression or the thing about which we are speaking. Jesus is stating that the Father is making a bold declaration. It is coming from the very internal heart of His being. This bold statement is the Scriptures. Jesus, the "Logos," is the lived out expression of this statement. God is speaking; the statement or substance which comes from the very insides of God through His mouth is the word. When one looks closely at this substance, it is Jesus. He is the visible expression of this substance. In other words, Jesus is the Scriptures with flesh. If the Scriptures were to be taken off of the pages and put into flesh, they would look exactly like Jesus. Jesus is the Scriptures lived out!

If I am intimate with Him what new understanding would I have from the Scriptures? I can know the heart of God revealed through Jesus in the Scriptures. We no longer need to be ignorant of the heart of God. It is not dependent upon intellect, academic training, or personal ability. It is intimacy with Jesus. He wants to reveal the Father to us. The more I know Him the more I know the Father. In speaking of the fullness of the Holy Spirit to come Jesus said, "I am in My Father, and you in Me, and I in you," (John 14:20). I am a Jesus pusher!!!

———————

I am a Jesus pusher!!! There is no safe place outside of Him. I do not want to go anywhere unless He is sourcing me. There is no safety in circumstances, only in the resource of His person. Jesus was sourced by His Father. The moment this sourcing began, He was led up by the Spirit into the wilderness to be tempted by the devil (Matthew 4:1). The wilderness is a frightening place. Moses called it "that great and terrible wilderness, in which were fiery serpents and scorpions and thirsty land where there was no water," (Deuteronomy 8:15). At the mention of the wilderness I get an unsettled feeling. It is in the wilderness regions that many of the great battles between Israel and her enemies occurred (Joshua 8; Judges 20; 2 Chronicles 20). The wilderness conjures up feelings of dread, fear, and suspicion. I have no desire to go to the wilderness. But I am not a child; I understand sometimes one is led up by the Spirit into the wilderness to be tempted by the devil. If I am going, I want to be sourced by Him. I definitely do not want to wander into such a place on my own. Far too often I have manufactured my own wilderness. If He has been there, they would have been mere weeds in the back yard. I want to be sourced by Him!

I understand temptation in the wilderness. Forty days and nights of temptation occurred in such a place for Jesus. The first of three final temptation events occurred in the wilderness. Then the devil took Him up into the holy city, set Him on the pinnacle of the temple (Matthew 4:5). The entire surroundings changed. This was the beginning of the second of the three final temptations. What is the devil doing at the temple? He seemed to be familiar with this area. He had obviously been here before. I understand temptation in the market place, but not in the sacred place. Is there no place that is safe? Where can I let down my guard, relax, and escape the battle? Would we not assume that the temple where reading the Scriptures, praying on our knees, or worshiping in the sanctuary creates a place of safety? It appears there is no safe place. Safety is not found in circumstances. The devil can utilize any circumstance to his advantage in order to allure us from Jesus. From drugs to adultery, from church to preaching, he is comfortable in his trickery.

Circumstances are not the issue! I must not go to the wilderness without being sourced by Jesus! I must not go to the temple without being sourced by Jesus. He is the only safe place for me. I must be in Him and He must be in me. In the intimacy of His person I find my relaxation. I am a Jesus pusher!!!

Jesus PUSHER | 53

I am a Jesus pusher!!! John the Baptist knew his ministry was limited. He readily admitted his baptism of repentance was inferior to the baptism of the Spirit to come from Jesus (Matthew 3:11). I admire his perspective. He knew he must decrease and Jesus must increase (John 3:30). This certainly sounds like a man who is pushing Jesus! He encouraged his disciples to follow after Jesus. However, there was a group who did not make the transition. When John the Baptist was in prison, they identified with the Pharisees in asking Jesus a question. They asked, "Why do we and the Pharisees fast often, but Your disciples do not fast?" (Matthew 9:14).

There is only one place in the Old Testament which required fasting. It was on the Day of Atonement (Leviticus 23:17). The actual word "fasting" is not mentioned in this passage, but is linked to afflict your souls. People fasted often in the Old Testament when they were grieving, repenting, suffering or guilty. Fasting was a sign of mourning (1 Samuel 31:13; 2 Samuel 1:12; Psalms 35:13; Zechariah 7:5). There is some indication that the Pharisees developed an oral tradition of fasting twice a week. They would put on a sad face or even disfigure their countenance (Matthew 6:16).

Jesus answered the disciples of John with the illustration of a wedding feast. The bridegroom would choose his best friends as attendants to be responsible for the festivities which lasted for at least seven days. It was a party. Jesus, the bridegroom, was present with them so His disciples did not mourn or grieve. If this was true when Jesus was with them in the physical how much more must it be true because He indwells us? He is my celebration. He is the perpetual party of my soul. It is not the future events of

Christianity which excite me. His present embrace is my thrill. This is not the time of mourning or grieving, but of celebration and party. Jesus is my party! I guess I have a choice. I can grieve of my circumstances or I can party with Jesus. I am a Jesus pusher!!!

I am a Jesus pusher!!! He has definitely led the way as a Man sourced by God. After He was filled with the Spirit, He was ushered into a strong spiritual battle. The devil tempted Him on three levels. The second had to do with method of ministry. Jesus had been filled with the Spirit (Matthew 3:16); the Father had spoken of His love for His Son (Matthew 3:17). He is ready to bring redemptive ministry to His world as a Spirit-sourced Man. What will be the first step? How should He begin? While they stood on the pinnacle of the temple the devil had a suggestion. At first glance it appears to be a great suggestion. It was Scripturally based (Matthew 4:6). It was fitting for the cultural belief of His day; the Jews believed the coming Messiah would float down from heaven. The devil suggested Jesus leap off of the pinnacle and allow God to save Him in a great spectacular rescue. What could be wrong with it?

Jesus understood the very heart of relationship with the Father. It must never be forgotten. It is the standard for every action; the measuring rod for every deed. God initiates and we respond! This is what it means to be Spirit-sourced. The devil was suggesting the reverse of this principle. The devil was tempting Jesus to act and let God respond. The life of Jesus throughout the Gospels is one of response to the Father. Listen to His words, "Most assuredly, I say to you, the Son can do nothing of Himself, but what He sees the Father do; for whatever He does, the Son also does in like manner. For the Father loves the Son and shows Him all things that He Himself does;" (John 5:19, 20). "I can of Myself do nothing. As I hear, I judge; and My judgment is righteous, because I do not seek My own will but the will of the Father who sent Me," (John 5:30).

I want relationship with Jesus like Jesus had with His Father.

This is only possible if I grasp the heart of that relationship. I will live in a state of sensitivity to the slightest movement of the indwelt Spirit of Christ. All of my actions will be a response to Him. I will no longer respond to my circumstances, feeling, or rights. I want to live out of His mind. I want to beat with His heart. I am a Jesus pusher!!!

———————

Jesus PUSHER | 55

I am a Jesus pusher!!! But how often have I been a self pusher? There is always a fundamental principle which characterizes the sourcing of Christ. There is always a fundamental principle which characterizes self-sourcing. They are not the same. Self-sourcing is always characterized by sensationalism. It reeks of performance. It makes us a star. Regardless of how much I try to say that God helped me or I could not have done it without Him, the focus in on myself. I love to quote, "I can do all things through Christ who strengthens me," (Philippians 4:13). Isn't this verse true? It is in the Bible! But listen closely to how I quote it: "IIIIIIIIIIIIIII can do all things through Christ who strengthens MEEEEEEEEEEEEE." I readily acknowledge Jesus is a support; He helps me. But the emphasis of helping someone is that the one who is being helped is in charge. Jesus is a helper to what I want to do!

Jesus was tempted by the devil (Matthew 4:1-11). The second temptation took place on the pinnacle of the temple. The devil suggested Jesus' first act of ministry might be to leap off the pinnacle and let the Father respond to His leap of faith. After all, the Father had expressed great love for the Son. This great sensational feat would certainly win all of Israel and announce His coming. But it would not be sourced by the Father. He could give God credit later when He testified about it. But self-sourcing always focuses on the individual and is sensational.

Christ-sourcing always focuses on Jesus and is seldom sensational. The fundamental principle of Jesus-sourcing is cross style. It is not a sensational leap from the pinnacle of the temple, but a painful death on a cross. It will take three years to get there. There is little applause along the way. There will be betrayal and misunderstanding. The cross is not just an event, but it is a principle of Jesus pushers. The cross style demonstrates itself in washing the feet of the one who will betray as well as others. It is about pouring out your life, never living for self. It is not impulsive but is long range. It will eventually redeem a world. What a privilege! I am a Jesus pusher!!!

———————

I am a Jesus pusher!!! Jesus was tempted by the devil in the wilderness and then on the pinnacle of the temple (Matthew 4:1-11). Both temptations had the same principle. It was a sourcing issue. He had just been filled with the Spirit and was sourced by the Father. Look where it got Him! He ended up in a barren wilderness with nothing to eat for forty days. For the very sake of surviving He must take charge of the situation. He must source turning stone into bread (self-source). Jesus refused such a thought. He would rather die (cross) than self-source. The second temptation was a different location. In the comfort of Jerusalem, the big city, on the pinnacle of the temple the devil tempted Him to perform His first act of ministry. He refused to perform any action. The principle of a Spirit-sourced Man is to respond to the Spirit. God acts; we respond. The devil was suggesting that Jesus act and let God respond. Jesus was victorious (Spirit-sourced)!

However, this temptation never seems to disappear. It may lie dominate for a time, but it will strike again and again. Jesus will move into the Galilean ministry. The crowds will respond to the physical miracles and desire to make Him their King (John 6:15). But they wanted a king who would respond to their actions. They speak and He responds. The principle was wrong; it is self-sourced. Peter stated His great confession of Christ (Matthew 16:16). Only a few hours would pass and Peter would rebuke Him to His face for proposing His crucifixion. Self-sourcing will not tolerate a cross, the loss of one's life. Self-sourcing requires a life lived for self, out of self.

How ironic that I could be a self-sourced Jesus pusher. It could be my tradition, my religion, my theology, or my decision. I want to be a Jesus pusher who is captured by Jesus. I want His person to permeate my entire being until He sources mind, will, and emotion. Self can be religious; only Jesus can be Jesus. Oh, I want Jesus to be Jesus through me to my world. Jesus, source Me! I am a Jesus pusher!!!

––––––––––––

Jesus PUSHER | 57

I am a Jesus pusher!!! Jesus had such great victory in spiritual battle. In the midst of forty days of temptation Jesus would not weaken to the devil's suggestions. It was at the end of the second temptation, Jesus cried out, "It is written again, 'You shall not tempt the Lord your God,'" (Matthew 4:7). In all three of the temptations Jesus answered Satan with the words "It is written." It is a direct reference to the Scriptures. However, this time He adds the word again. The focus of this Greek word (palin) translated again is not just repeating. Although in relation to time, it can mean "one more time." But it also includes the idea of "back." It is the idea of simply returning back to a former place, state, or act. In other words, Jesus is taking Satan right back to His position from the start. Nothing new is presented; the defense is not altered. The core value of the Father's great love and the sourcing of the Spirit which provides intimacy in this love is still His position. In this second temptation, the devil may have taken Jesus to a new location, the temple, but Jesus refuses to move from His permanent location in the Father. The circumstances may change around Him, but His position will not.

As the Father was His position of safety and security, so Jesus is my haven. No amount of theology will add to it; no spiritual disciplines will increase it. He alone is my shelter. It is in the intimacy of His embrace I will dwell. If I must run into His arms, it indicates I have gone off on my own. I must not do so! One split second without Him and I am back in my failure and defeat. In every temptation or circumstance, I will simply state "again!" He is my permanent position. I am fixed in Him. Here I can rest. There is no worry or stress in His presence. I will dwell in His love. I am a Jesus pusher!!!

I am a Jesus pusher!!! In the temptations of Jesus, the devil has taken Jesus to the pinnacle of the temple. He is advising Him to leap off in a sensational act to launch His earthly ministry. Jesus replies, "It is written again, 'You shall not tempt the Lord your God,'" (Matthew 4:7). The key to His statement is the verb tempt. It is a translation of the Greek word "ekpeirazo." The normal Greek word for "tempt" is "peirazo" (see Matthew 4:1). One can easily see the prefix "ek" is the difference. This addition simply intensifies the action of the verb. It suggests that tempting man is one thing, but to tempt God is an entirely different matter. Satan has just crossed a line into a more serious suggestion.

The Greek word "peirazo" (tempt) is a morally neutral word. It simply means "to test." It is for good or for evil determined by the character or nature of the one who is testing. If a self-sourced person is tempting God, it would be for the purpose of evil. He is challenging God. He is attempting to prove God wrong. If a Spirit-sourced person is tempting God — but wait! If the tempting is Spirit-sourced, this would mean God is tempting Himself! Why would God tempt, test, or challenge Himself? He would not! Therefore, the only time God will be tempted or tested, is by a self-sourced person who wants His own way! Jesus would not tolerate this suggestion, nor will I. Regardless of how the circumstances appear, He trusts His Father; so I will trust Him. Satan would cast doubts about Jesus' motive. But I know Satan and I have embraced Jesus. As the Father loved Jesus, so Jesus has loved me. I will trust this love without question regardless of the appearances around me. I am a Jesus pusher!!!

I am a Jesus pusher!!! I am deeply aware that embracing Jesus will naturally result in testing. Jesus was tested; I am certainly not exempt. Jesus was led up by the Spirit into the wilderness to be tempted by the devil (Matthew 4:1). However, one must be very clear about the motive and purpose of this testing from God. There are several Greek words related to the area of testing, tempting, or proving. There is the Greek word "nouthesia." This word focuses on instruction by means of words. "Paideia" also focuses on instruction, but is mainly by deed. The author of the Book of Hebrews uses this Greek word in his discussion of the discipline of God. He asks, "If you endure chastening (paideia), God deals with you as with sons; for what son is there whom a father does not chasten?" (Hebrews 12:7) He emphasizes the lack of this discipline is a sign we are illegitimate. The purpose of this testing is not negative or evil; it is positive. God chastens (paideia) us for our profit, that we may be partakers of His holiness (Hebrews 12:10). Holiness is His nature. He wants us to be intimate with Him; He desires us to participate in the very core of His being. If this is true, I will welcome the discipline of Jesus in my life!

In light of this truth, I am willing to view every circumstance I face as an opportunity to receive the correction and instruction of Jesus. In this instruction, He will reveal Himself to me. I will be enabled to know Him better; we shall be intimate. I will face the difficult circumstances without complaints; I will embrace them as stepping stones to greater knowledge of His person. In the embrace of Jesus all things work together for good (Romans 8:28). My confidence is in Jesus! I am a Jesus pusher!!!

I am a Jesus pusher!!! If I am one with Jesus I will be tested as He was tested (Matthew 4:1-11). Through the inspiration of the Spirit, James offers clear teaching about this testing. He instructs us to count it all joy when you fall into various trials (James 1:2). The Greek word (peirazo) translated trials is the same Greek word translated tempted relating to Jesus (Matthew 4:1). When we are Spirit-sourced such trials take on the character and nature of the Spirit of Jesus. The ultimate purpose of this testing by the Spirit is that you may be perfect and complete, lacking nothing (James 1:4). If we are Spirit-sourced, even when the devil tempts us with the purpose of evil, we do not despair. For James states when we endure we will receive the crown of life which the Lord has promised to those who love Him (James 1:12). We are in a "win win" situation. Jesus bends everything to our benefit!

I am a Jesus pusher!!! I can totally trust Him regardless of the appearance of the situation in my life. Every circumstance completes my commitment to Him. Every trial only trims the excess from my relationship with Him. He is getting larger and larger in my eyesight. Every trap of the devil simply works for my benefit. It drives me to Jesus. The more pressure I experience in my circumstances, the more I am pressured to Him. I am convinced repeatedly I must cling to Him. The more the devil tempts, the more I am driven to Jesus. I am being "crowded" to Christ. I simply cannot survive without Him. I am a Jesus pusher!!!

Jesus PUSHER | 61

I am a Jesus pusher!!! He is my Hero, the King! In the New Testament, the Greek word (basileia) translated "kingdom" comes from the root Greek word (basileus) which is translated "king." The heart of the concept of the Biblical Kingdom of God is a focus on the King. This Kingdom does not emphasize territory, but royal reigning. Wherever Christ is reigning, the Kingdom of God is present. This is a mystical concept. Jesus said, "The Kingdom of God does not come with observation; nor will they say, 'See here!' or 'See there!' For indeed, the Kingdom of God is within you," (Luke 17:20, 21). However, while not the focus, there is a physical aspect to the Kingdom. The physical area where the King is reigning becomes dominated by the Kingdom. If Jesus is reigning as King in me, I become His territory. When He reigns He sources the activity of His territory.

Matthew began his Gospel account with the genealogy of Jesus. It traced His lineage through King David. This fulfilled the prophecy of the Old Testament. John the Baptist, the forerunner, proclaimed, "Repent, for the Kingdom of Heaven is at hand!" (Matthew 3:2). He was announcing the presence of Jesus, the King. At His baptism by John, He was filled and sourced by the Holy Spirit. It was His inauguration as the new King. Jesus was becoming the door to the Kingdom for us! His death, resurrection, and ascension were sourced by the Spirit and would enable the same Spirit to indwell us. Indeed, the Kingdom of God would be within us. The Spirit of Jesus, the King, would reign and source us. Jesus is my Hero, the King! I no longer need to do things on my own; I am enabled by my King. The trail of defeats in my life testifies to the disaster of my own reign as king. What a relief to belong to Him, my Hero, the King! I am a Jesus pusher!!!

I am a Jesus pusher!!! He is King of the Kingdom of God. He has included me as an avenue for the display of His reign! The devil attempts to defeat Jesus three times at the close of forty days of temptation. The third attempt deals with His reign as King (Matthew 4:8-10). The devil must win on this issue or experience constant war against his Kingdom of darkness. He lost this battle during the birth of the new King. All his efforts to eliminate the new King have failed. Now is his chance!

As they stand on an exceedingly high mountain, the devil offers Him a proposition. He displays, allows Him to see, all the kingdoms of the world and their glory (Matthew 4:8). The Greek word (doxan) translated glory comes from the idea "to think" or "to suppose." It is value or worth from your opinion or perspective. The devil shows Jesus everything which he considers valuable. He is sure Jesus will not be able to refuse it. Instead of Jesus being King over the Kingdom of God which is just being established, He could be King over the Kingdom of darkness already well populated. All the power, wealth, evil, perversion, self-centeredness, hatred, and jealousy could be His. He could be self-sourced and reign over it all. Jesus is repulsed by the very idea. There is no temptation at all; He has the perspective, opinion of the Kingdom of God, the sourcing of the Spirit. Jesus is my Hero, my King. I want to be so sourced by Him that I only have His opinion. Could all the allurements of this world repulse me because I am sourced by Him? Can I become His territory established by His reigning? Can I have the mind of Christ? I am a Jesus pusher!!!

I am a Jesus pusher!!! There is a significant contrast established by the use of the Greek word (doxan) translated glory in the New Testament. This word comes from the idea of "to think" or "to suppose." From the aspect of glory it has to do with thought or opinion, especially favorable human opinion. Thus it refers to reputation, praise, honor, splendor, and light. There is a strong contrast between man's opinion and God's opinion. During Jesus' ministry the leaders of Israel reject His message (opinion). Jesus calls upon the witnesses of the past to verify His message (John 5:31-35). He points out the testimony of the works of the Father through Him which validates His message (John 5:36). Even more convincing is the testimony of the Father who actually speaks of Him (John 5:37-40). Jesus quickly points out the problem they are having. He says, "How can you believe, who receive honor from one another, and do not seek the honor that comes from the only God?" (John 5:44). The Greek word (doxan) translated honor is the same as is often translated glory. Jesus was stating a basic condition within the leaders of Israel. They were not evil in the sense of deeds. They operated out of their own opinion (honor) and not the opinion (honor) of the Father.

The glory of man is human opinion; it is shifty, uncertain, and often based on error. This is contrasted with the glory (opinion) of Christ. It is absolutely true and changeless. God's opinion marks the true value of things as they appear in the eternal mind. Often I have been self-sourced; I did the best I knew. My consistent failures tell me I need another opinion. Jesus is my Hero, my King! I am not wishing Him to tell me what to do. I want Him to source me until His perspective is mine. The way He feels is the way I feel; His mind becomes my

mind. I want to be sourced by the King and live in His glory! I
am a Jesus pusher!!!

Jesus PUSHER | 64

I am a Jesus pusher!!! The devil tempts Jesus by showing Him all the kingdoms of the world and their glory (Matthew 4:8). The devil must have been grinning as he supposes the Kingdom of darkness would be alluring to Jesus. Self-sourcing, greed, hatred, bitterness, adultery, broken homes, and selfish power filled the lives of the entire Kingdom of darkness. Jesus could have it all. Do you picture Jesus as holding His breath, gritting His teeth as He is allured with great desire to be King over that Kingdom? I think not! This was not alluring to Him at all. He had the perspective, opinion of the Kingdom of God. He was Spirit-sourced.

Perhaps the "revealer" of the soul is found in what tempts or allures us. Could every temptation be brought under the authority of the perspective of the Spirit? Why are the kingdoms of the world and their glory alluring to me? As I find hate in my life, why do I justify it? What is present in my perspective which causes me to want to hate? Why does my opinion feel comfortable with using someone else for my own selfish ends? Perhaps victory over temptation is not found in resisting, but in a change of opinion! I must be sourced by Christ! His heart and passion must dominate my being. His eyes must become mine! Jesus is my Hero, my King! His thinking is true; His desires are clean; His actions redeem and restore. I must have the mind of Christ. I am a Jesus pusher!!!

———————

Jesus PUSHER | 65

I am a Jesus pusher!!! I love Jesus with my whole, entire heart. There is no "if" in Jesus. This is contrasted with the devil who is all about "if." In the great temptation event, the devil takes Jesus to an exceedingly high mountain and showed Him all the kingdoms of the world and their glory (Matthew 4:8). His proposition is simply, "All these things I will give You IF You will fall down and worship me," (Matthew 4:9). It is a conditional clause. If Jesus performs the necessary act of worship, then the devil will respond with the supposed gifts. The devil is not going to move, provide, or grant anything until Jesus responds; it is his leverage.

This is why I am a Jesus pusher!!! Jesus is the exact opposite. He is not waiting on us, but has graciously given us all things. He is not waiting to extend His full love; He has already surrounded us with complete grace. He has not withheld from us redemption; He has already died for us. He is not withholding any good thing from our lives; but has provided all things. His forgiveness is not dependent upon our repentance; He has already forgiven us. He wants to give us power over all sin; He has already given it to us. He loves me without "if!"

There is nothing that can keep me from experiencing all that He is. If this is not a reality in my life, it is not His fault. Don't I have to respond? Don't I have to accept what He has provided? YES! So there is an "if" in receiving all He is. But the "if" is not on His part, it is on my part. It is not in Him; it is in me. He has no "if." Such unconditional love consumes me. I am a Jesus pusher!!!

Jesus PUSHER | 66

I am a Jesus pusher!!! I am not going to be a Jesus pusher. I am not preparing to be a Jesus pusher. I AM a Jesus pusher. It is present tense! Everything with Jesus is present tense. This is strongly contrasted with the devil. It is seen in the great temptation event. After displaying before Jesus the kingdoms of the world, the devil said, "All these things I will give You if You will fall down and worship me," (Matthew 4:9). His statement is in the future tense. The devil is always alluring us with what might be. The promise of future fulfillment is always before us. How often I have fallen into this trap. His approach is like a great carrot dangling in front of me. It never seems to be mine in the present.

Jesus is not this way. His entire provision (Himself) is mine now! It is present tense! In the embrace of Christ I have everything He wants me to have. All is found in Him. We understand there is growth into maturity; there is heaven to come. However, He does not withhold from me, so I need to progress and grow in receiving more from Him. Progression is needed in my ability to grasp all He is in me. I am not waiting for Him to fulfill His promise and give me more; I need to enlarge my capacity for all He is in me. It is not an expanding of what He can give me. The expansion needed is in my comprehension of His provision for me. I am a little boy who has fallen into a swimming pool of chocolate. My prayer is not for more chocolate; my prayer is for an increase in my capacity. I must not live beneath my privileges, ignoring all He is in me. I am a Jesus pusher!!!

Jesus PUSHER | 67

I am a Jesus pusher!!! Let me remind you, I am not pushing doctrine, theology, or creed. My cry is about HIM! This is sharply contrasted with the devil. During the great temptation the devil promised Jesus, "All these things I will give You if You will fall down and worship me," (Matthew 4:8). "All these things" referred to all the kingdoms of the world. This phrase appears at the very beginning of the devil's statement. This means it is what he is emphasizing. I have found the devil is always about "things." He constantly attempts to distract me from one "thing" to another "thing." There is materialism, power, position, satisfaction of body drives, or stuff. It is always about "things."

I am a Jesus pusher; because He is about relationship not "things." Relationship is eternal; "things" are temporal. Intimacy with Him is not a passing issue, but will endure forever. This is His focus regarding you. He values you more than He values "things." Every "thing" was sacrificed for the sake of embracing you. Even His own life was not protected that He might embrace you. He held on to no position, even to the highest power as God in order to know you (Philippians 2:6, 7). To a scribe Jesus said, "Foxes have holes and birds of the air have nests, but the Son of Man has nowhere to lay His head," (Matthew 8:20). No "thing" has greater importance to Him than you and me. No wonder I am a Jesus pusher. He does not want what I can give Him; He wants me! His agenda is not service; I am not an errand boy. I am not a tool He uses. I am His beloved. He is my focus. I am a Jesus pusher!!!

Jesus PUSHER | 68

I am a Jesus pusher!!! Jesus captures my heart; He does something deep inside of me. In knowing Him, worship is spontaneous. I cannot help it. This becomes characteristic of my relationship with Jesus. It is never about rules and regulations; it is about passive and love. The Old Testament prophets looked forward to the day when intimacy with God would be the norm. God expressed it through them as, "I will put My law in their hearts; and I will be their God, and they shall be My people. No more shall every man teach his neighbor, and every man his brother, saying, 'Know the Lord,' for they all shall know Me, from the least of them to the greatest of them," (Jeremiah 31:33, 34). This is now a reality in my life. I am living in the day of which they dreamed!

This is contrasted with the devil's desires as seen in the great temptation. The devil promised great gifts to Jesus. "If You will fall down and worship me," was his appeal (Matthew 4:8). Notice there was to be the physical act followed by the worship. Perhaps the inner worship is not there, but the physical act is enough. Jesus is never satisfied with this in my life. He is not interested in a physical act which may be accompanied with worship; He wants the inner worship which will produce the physical act. No wonder I am a Jesus pusher. He wants my heart. Intimacy which comes from love binds me to Him. My relationship with Him is not about completing ceremonies or activities, but embracing and loving. My life flows from the inside out, from love to worship. I am a Jesus pusher!!!

Jesus PUSHER | 69

I am a Jesus pusher!!! I am not a Jesus pusher sometimes, once-in-a-while, or when I feel like it. I am a consistent Jesus pusher. Jesus is exclusive in my life. He is not one among several I am pushing. He is not just on my agenda; He is my agenda! He is not one of my priorities; He is my priority. Jesus is not my focus when it aids me or I have a need. I am mastered by Him. I am an exclusive Jesus pusher. I have no substitute for Him.

Do not consider this legalistic. Legalism has to do with law or rules. The Pharisees appeared to be very exclusive in their attitude concerning the law. Several times Jesus highlighted this difficulty (Matthew 23:3). Upon careful examination, the Pharisees were not exclusive about the law; they were exclusive about themselves (Matthew 23:5). They used the law for their own purposes. They would adjust, find loopholes, and highlight certain laws for their own personal convenience or benefit. If the Pharisees were exclusive, it was in their focus on themselves.

I am exclusive about Jesus who is not legalistic but relational. I am not concerned about meeting requirements, appearances, or traditions. My main goal is not to be right contrasted with wrong. There is only one focus; it is intimacy with Jesus. I do not want anything to distract or detour me from this obsession. He is so important to me; He is my life. Nothing can be allowed to interfere with His presence in my life. Everything is judged by how it affects this relationship. I do not have to elevate Him or defend Him in this position or priority. He is great enough to demand this focus in my life. Once I saw Him as He is, this focus became natural. I am abhorred at how long I focused on myself instead of Him. He has rescued me from myself. I am a Jesus pusher!!!

Jesus PUSHER | 70

I am a Jesus pusher!!! My focus is narrow and limited to Him. Do not consider this strange or a psychological problem. It is not an emotional reaction, something which has to be stimulated again and again. It is reasonable and quite logical. However, it is not a product of my reason, education, or wisdom. It comes from revelation. I have seen Him. Oh not in physical form, but in spiritual reality. This same reality was true between Jesus and His Father. During the great temptation, Jesus was confronted with a call. Satan wanted Him to set aside His relationship with His Father. The devil desired His worship and promised Him the kingdoms of the world (Matthew 4:8, 9). Matthew records His answer, Then Jesus said to him, "Away with you, Satan!" (Matthew 4:10).

The Greek word "lego" is translated said. It originally contained the idea of "to lay or let lie down for sleep, to lie together or to collect." The word evolved into the usage of "to lie before or to relate, recount." Thus the latter meaning "to say, speak, to utter definite words, connected and significant speech equal to discourse" became its usage. There is another Greek word (laleo) which means to utter sounds. This refers only to words spoken and not to their connected sense. What Jesus has to say to Satan is not an emotional response; it is not an immediate reaction with a light superficial meaning. This is a thought through, restated, a definite conclusion or discourse of Jesus' position on the matter. This is how focused He was on the Father. As the Spirit of His Father captured Jesus, so the Spirit of Jesus has captured me. I am saying (lego) this to you. It is not an emotional response; it will not change with maturity. It is a definite conclusion or discourse of my position on the matter. I am a Jesus pusher!!!

I am a Jesus pusher!!! The exclusive relationship Jesus has with His Father has been extended to us. I have been drawn into this intimacy. It was exclusive in nature. During the great temptation; Jesus turned to Satan and said, "Away with you, Satan!" (Matthew 4:10). This is statement emphasizes the exclusive nature of Jesus' position. Listen to the strength of His voice. Gaze at the stern look on His face. This is not a Man who will be swayed. He absolutely will not waver from the embrace and oneness with His Father. The Greek verb (translated away) is in the imperative mood. This means it is a command or order. There is no "maybe" involved. It is definite. This verb is also in the present tense which in the Greek language means "now with continual action." One can easily feel the exclusive intent of this statement. Jesus is distinctly drawing a line. He is excluding any and all suggestions of Satan. Jesus will not consider or even flirt with the idea of any relationship outside of the Father.

This relationship between Jesus and the Father has been opened up to us. Jesus died, was resurrected, and ascended to bring us into this same intimacy with His Spirit. Jesus has captured my life in the same way He was captured by the Father. There is no give or compromise to this intimacy, but why would I desire any? Jesus is not an addition to my life. He is not one of my many activities or interest. How can He be? All other interests fade in the presence of His greatness. He gives perspective to every other involvement; they are seen clearly as temporal. In the intimacy of His person, I hear His voice alone. His direction is my only command. He is the only One to be trusted with my life. I am a Jesus pusher!!!

Jesus PUSHER | 72

I am a Jesus pusher!!! It is marvelous to be captured by one emphasis. It settles all the issues of life; it determines every decision. It brings peace to every argument; it injects purpose to life. It is tragic when our focus is inferior. Everything in life is determined by this focus; life takes on the characteristics of the focus. Jesus is the only one great enough to demand the total attention of my life. Life becomes shaped by Him. Wow!! Jesus was confronted by the devil in the great temptation. In a final statement to the devil, Jesus quotes "You shall worship the Lord your God, and Him only you shall serve," (Matthew 4:10). He was actually quoting from a speech given by Moses (Deuteronomy 6:13). Notice the exclusiveness found in the statement. The Greek word (monoo) translated only is used in the sense of "being the only entity in a class, only, or alone." It expresses the uniqueness, isolation, or exclusiveness of persons, things, or actions. Is there any doubt of its usage as intended by Jesus in this passage?

The devil constantly attempts to get us sidetracked. He is not overly concerned about our relationship with Jesus as long as it is mixed with other loyalties. In China we visited a dark and cold temple. There was a constant stream of people offering sacrifices and making prayers to their gods. The difficulty was in deciding which god to honor. In one section, there was a statue of Buddha; but adjacent to him was a statue of Confucius; but immediately by him was a statue of Jesus. It was buffet religion. Take your pick; chose your god; cover all the bases. Adopting all three might be the best policy.

All other statues are gone; there is no one left but Jesus. He is in a category by Himself. He rises far above all other thoughts or suggestions. I will exclusively belong to Him. Even the gods of self-sufficiency, materialism, athletics, education, and position will be removed. My eyesight is on Jesus. I am a Jesus pusher!!!

———————

Jesus PUSHER | 73

I am a Jesus pusher!!! In the great temptation, Jesus' final statement to the devil was, "You shall worship the Lord your God, and Him only you shall serve," (Matthew 4:10). Out of all the Scriptures Jesus could have quoted, He states one that highlights worship. In studying this concept of worship, I have been extremely disappointed. I could not find any instructions in the Scriptures on HOW to worship. Jesus said to the woman of Samaria, "God is Spirit, and those who worship Him must worship in spirit and truth," (John 4:24). There is more emphasis in the Old Testament on worship. Music is highlighted and a full body worship experience is also described. However, where are the detailed instructions on how to worship? Should we conclude it does not matter?

Worship is not contained within the activities of an "event." Worship is found in the focus and attitude of the heart. Therefore, the physical activities or expression of the worship is not as important as the worship itself. Our tendency is to focus on the performance of the activities. At that moment the method of worship has become the object of our worship instead of Jesus. The central issue of worship is the inner action between the one who is worshipping and Jesus. Worship is stimulated by the intimacy between the worshipper and Jesus. It cannot be manufactured; true worship cannot be turned off and on. This means I have no right to criticize you for not worshipping. If you do not worship, it is because you have not been captured by Jesus. The issue is not how you perform but how intimate you are with Jesus. He has captured my heart and is the sole object of my worship. I have a single eye. He is the focus of my life. I am a Jesus pusher!!!

I am a Jesus pusher!!! I adore and worship Him, only Him. The Greek word (proskuneo) translated "worship" is used ninety times in the New Testament. It is only used in relationship to God. To do this to anyone else or anything else is considered idolatry. This Greek word (proskuneo) is a combination of two different words. The two words are "to" (pros) and "kissing" (kuneo). It literally means "to kiss toward someone." In the ancient oriental world, the mode of salutation between persons of equal ranks was to kiss each other on the lips. When the difference of rank was slight, they kissed each other on the cheek. However, when an individual was much inferior in rank, he fell upon his knees and touched his forehead to the ground or prostrated himself, throwing kisses at the same time toward the superior.

Often in the Greek lexicons to illustrate this word, the example is given of a dog licking his master's hand. This is a more accurate picture of worship coming from interaction and relationship. The master does not require such action from his dog. This flows from the inner nature of the dog. I am a lover of Jesus. My heart leaps at the very thought of Him. The last thing I desire to do is offend or hurt Him in any way. It is not about rules of duty; it is about love and passion. I want to spend every moment with Him; I want to yield and submit my entire life to Him. I desire no alone time. His approval is my only reward. I am privileged to know His thoughts and desires. His focus becomes mine. He is my one and only pleasure. I do not have to restrain myself from wandering. I am responding to His love. I am in love with Jesus. I am a Jesus pusher!!!

Jesus PUSHER | 75

I am a Jesus pusher!!! I have been reassured by other Jesus pushers. One of the great saints of years gone by is Saint Theresa. She was a young lady who died in her early twenties after prolonged illness from childhood. Her writings expressed an intimate relationship with Jesus through the attitude of worship. She cried out her desire to be a "rag doll" for Jesus. When I read this, I was not impressed. I want to be a soldier for the Kingdom. A great warrior fighting for my Master is my desired image. However, as I continued to read her writings, I was broken. She reported that a rag doll exists exclusively for the pleasure of the child. It serves no other purpose. The child will play with the rag doll and then discard it for hours, even days. Perhaps the rag doll is thrown under the bed and ignored. The child discovers the rag doll with great delight only to set it aside. The rag doll exists exclusively for the pleasure of the child.

Jesus is this great in my life. I have no agenda. My love for Him does not come from a beneficial relationship. I do not love Him because He meets my needs. If I never receive another blessing from Him, my passion is still for Him. If He throws me under the bed for long periods of darkness, I am content. I am at His disposal; I exclusively trust His plan. My worship is experienced in the depth of submission. I have relinquished all control or restrictions. There is only one thing which matters; it is Him. There is no mixture; it is exclusively Him. I worship Him alone. Every waking moment is about Him. The entire flow and direction of life is focused on Him. There is nothing happening in my life which is not under His control. He has won my heart. What can I say? How can I adequately express it? I am a Jesus pusher!!!

Jesus PUSHER | 76

I am a Jesus pusher!!! He has not only consumed by heart; Jesus dominates my energy, time, and activities. In the hour of great temptation, the devil offered Jesus, "All these things I will give You, if You will fall down and worship me," (Matthew 4:9). Jesus responded by quoting the Old Testament, "You shall worship the Lord your God, and Him only you shall serve," (Matthew 4:10). Notice that physical activity is involved in both statements The Greek word (proskuneo) translated worship is used ninety times in the New Testament. Every time a physical action is connected with its usage. Notice the difference between the devil's suggestion and Jesus' response. The devil suggests the physical action prior to the worship; Jesus refers to the physical action as a result of the worship.

This was the central conflict between Jesus and the Pharisees in the New Testament. They gave little attention to the inner core of their lives; they focused their lives on the outside discipline of their laws. Jesus was the exact opposite. Jesus understood that worship and service are intertwined. Service is not something an individual decides to do or disciplines his life to accomplish. Service is an automatic result of worship. It is not strained or attempted. It is not duty or obligation. It is spirited delight. Jesus has consumed my life; activities which others call service are expressions of love; I count them as privileges. Duty is what I have to do; delight is what I get to do. I am in love; I cannot help myself. I am a Jesus pusher!!!

I am a Jesus pusher!!! I love to speak of Him. The songs I sing are about Him. The answer to every question comes back to Jesus. My recreation is tied to Him. Even my hobbies are somehow connected to Jesus. I know there is a devil. In the great temptation, the Bible identifies him as a real being. Jesus was actually tempted by the devil (Matthew 4:1). At the close of this great spiritual battle, Matthew writes, Then the devil left Him (Matthew 4:11). We all understand the two fold nature of temptation. It is normally tied into the physical. However, this is only a beginning view of temptation. The spiritual battle rages in the heavenly unseen world. The mystical heavenly realm dips into the realistic physical world of our lives to bring about temptation. Paul reminds us, For we do not wrestle against flesh and blood, but against principalities, against powers, against the rulers of the darkness of this age, against spiritual hosts of wickedness in the heavenly places (Ephesians 6:12). This does not mean we are not tempted in the physical; it only means much more is taking place than appears in the physical.

We do not have a lot of information given to us in the Scriptures about the devil. But then why would we want to know details about him? We do not want to under estimate his ability and power; but he does not compare to Jesus. Instead of speaking about the devil, I want to highlight and focus on Jesus. I do not want to focus on the devil, when I can focus on the greatness of Jesus. Victory is found in Jesus. The answer to every trick of the devil is found in intimacy with Jesus. There is no darkness in Jesus. Nothing can hinder me when I am found in Jesus. Jesus is my total answer! No wonder I am a Jesus pusher!!!

———————

Jesus PUSHER | 78

I am a Jesus pusher!!! I have discovered a very significant verb in the New Testament Greek language. It is "aphiemi." It begins with the prefix "apo" which is "from." This has to do with motion from one location to another. The root word is "hiemi" which means "to send forth or away, or to let go from oneself." I found this word in the closing verse of the temptations of Jesus. Matthew concludes the entire event with Then the devil left Him (Matthew 4:11). In this case "aphiemi" is translated left. However, the flavor of the Greek word is not captured in the word left. It is absolutely true that the devil changed locations. But "aphiemi" tells you that he was repelled, forced, or sent away. The power of God operating in Jesus was so strong Satan was repelled from Him.

The Spirit of Christ repels all of Satan's attacks on my life. Victory is not found in resistance or self-control, but in intimacy with Jesus. Do not be misled! Satan is not equal with Jesus. Satan is not God; he is a fallen angel who was created. He is not all knowing or all powerful. He is no match for the indwelt Spirit of Jesus. There is no need to tremble in his presence unless you are alone. You and I are no match for him but with Jesus there is no contest. Jesus does not need weapons to defeat Satan; His very presence (nature) repels Satan. The safest place in the world is in Christ. No wonder the Apostle Paul speaks of us as being "in Christ" and also of "Christ in us." Jesus is so intimate in our lives; He is both outside and inside. We are covered with the wonder of His presence. It is in His embrace I see things as they are. In His presence the darkness of destruction is pushed back. Nothing can defeat me "in Christ." I am a Jesus pusher!!!

I am a Jesus pusher!!! Jesus is the answer in every area of my life. He is not strong in some situations and weak in others. He is not a pill that arrests some diseases but is inadequate in others. He absolutely conquers all. Whatever the need in my life, Jesus Himself is the solution. There is no need to look in any other direction. My eyes are upon Him. I am amazed at the Greek word "aphiemi." The prefix is "apo" (from) and the root word is "hiemi' (to send forth; repel). This Greek word is used sixteen times in Matthew's Gospel account for the act of forgiveness. Forgiveness is much more than simply forgetting the wrong deed. It is to actually remit, remove, or release someone from the actual sin. It is not to disregard the sins or do nothing about them; it is to liberate a person from their sins, from the guilt of sin, and the power of sin. Jesus has forgiven (aphiemi) our sins. He has removed the sin from us; we are no longer guilty of or under its power.

In a personal encounter with Jesus I received His forgiveness. But it was not an event; it was a relationship. Forgiveness is experienced within the warmth of this relationship. It is His personal presence which continually releases me from guilt. The moment He is not present, guilt overtakes me again. Jesus has pushed back the guilt and power of sin; He repels it. It has no hold on me because of His inward presence. I am living moment by moment in the releasing, removing, and repelling life of the Spirit of Jesus. He is holding at bay the forces of guilt and the entrapment of all my sin. In Him I am experiencing "aphiemi." How can I ever take that for granted or treat it lightly? I must shout His praises. I am a Jesus pusher!!!

Jesus PUSHER | 80

I am a Jesus pusher!!! There are many who are fascinated with angels. Angels definitely play a significant role in the Scriptures. However, in the four Gospel accounts they are only used by God during two periods of Jesus' life for revelation and instruction. They are strongly seen during His birth and resurrection. There are two other occasions in which they appear. Jesus includes them in the Parables of Judgment and Kingdom as aiding Him in the final hours. They also make an appearance at the close of the temptations of Jesus (Matthew 4:11). It appears a major shift has taken place. The role of revelation is not fulfilled by angels but by Jesus. Jesus has become the image of the invisible God (Colossians 1:15). Jesus is the preeminent disclosure of God.

It is through Jesus I have a complete revelation of God. I now know how God feels about children (Matthew 19:13-15). God has revealed His true feeling about His enemies (Luke 23:34). There is no question as to whether God will forgive me or not. Jesus has settled that issue! God has walked into every area of life through Jesus. I see the holy nature of God living before me in Jesus. The revelation is complete. In addition to seeing the life of Jesus, I experience the person of Jesus. He comes to be within me (Colossians 1:27). His mind becomes mine; He gives me His heart. He is now living His life through me (Galatians 2:20). My world is seeing Jesus again through me. As Jesus was filled with the Father and was the visible image of the invisible God, so I have been filled with the Spirit of Jesus and have become the visible image of Jesus. My whole existence has become a Jesus pusher!!!

Jesus PUSHER | 81

I am a Jesus pusher!!! Everything God has desired for mankind is inherited in Jesus, not in angels. We are joint heirs with Christ not angels (Romans 8:17). He has opened the door for us to join Him in the inheritance which is intimacy of the Father through the sourcing of the Spirit! Angels never experience anything like this. It is Jesus who became the Man who is Spirit-sourced who the Father calls Son. God promises to be to Him a Father (Hebrews 1:5). At the birth of Christ the angels of God worshiped Him (Hebrews 1:6). The angels are made ministers, but the Son is given a throne; He is King of the Kingdom (Hebrews 1:7-9). It is through Jesus that God is creative not an angel (Hebrews 1:10-12). It is Jesus, the Son, who is invited to sit at the right hand of the Father not an angel (Hebrews 1:13). What is the position of angels? Are they not all ministering spirits sent forth to minister for those who will inherit salvation? (Hebrews 1:14). Angels are destined to minister to those who are sourced by the Spirit!

I have no criticism for angels; I would not belittle their position or ministry. But I am not an angel pusher; I am a Jesus pusher! I would proclaim as the Hebrew writer did "Jesus has become so much better than the angels, as He has by inheritance obtained a more excellent name than they," (Hebrews 1:4). Jesus is the brightness of His (God's) glory and the express image of His person, and upholding all things by the word of His power, when He had by Himself purged our sins, sat down at the right hand of the Majesty on high," (Hebrews 1:3). Pardon my shouting! You must know Him, embrace Him, and let Him source you. Angels are not your answer; Jesus is. I am a Jesus pusher!!!

I am a Jesus pusher!!! David, the psalmist, was contemplating the value of man. In view of the vastness of the stars, man is insignificant. Why would God be mindful or take care of man (Hebrews 2:6)? The position of man is one who is lower than the angels. But even in this lower position God has crowned man with glory and honor (Hebrews 2:7). Man is like the victor in the public games; he is crowned as the winner. The glory and honor given to man is "You have put all things in subjection under his feet," (Hebrews 2:8). In creation man was given dominion over all the Garden of Eden (Genesis 1:26). Man was responsible for tending the garden (Genesis 2:15). Man was responsible for naming the animals (Genesis 2:19). Note carefully that man is in this position because he is relationship with God. He is Spirit-sourced.

The Hebrew author must have wept as he stated but we do not yet see all things put under him (Hebrews 2:8). Man in the Fall gave this authority and domain over to Satan, a fallen angel. But the Hebrew author wiped his eyes of those tears as he relayed the news, "But we see Jesus!" (Hebrews 2:9). He became one of us for the suffering of death crowned with glory and honor, that He, by the grace of God, might taste death for everyone (Hebrews 2:9). God became one of us. Jesus was a man who still had the authority originally given to man in the Garden. He came to restore us to this same authority. God accomplished this not through angels but through Jesus, a Man. Man got us into this mess and man would have to get us out. But he would have to be a man who was not in the mess. Jesus is the Man! He is your way out. I am a Jesus pusher!!!

Jesus PUSHER | 83

I am a Jesus pusher!!! God became man, not an angel. He came to restore us to the place of authority which comes through being Spirit-sourced. The Hebrew author calls Him "the Captain of their salvation," (Hebrews 2:10). It was through suffering Jesus would be completed (Hebrews 2:10). The Greek word (archegos) translated Captain means "trail blazer, scout, author, beginner, captain, and starter of a whole new breed of people." Jesus is the beginning of a new humanity. In describing our relationship with this Captain, we are all of one (Hebrews 2:11). The Greek word (pantes) translated "all" encompasses the Captain of our salvation and us. The Greek word (ek) translated "of" points to what was originally inside another object and has now come forth. The Greek word (henos) translated "one" refers to God, the Father (see Luke 18:19). Jesus, the Captain, you and I have come from the same Father. As He is sourced by the Spirit, so you and I are now sourced by the same Spirit. The life source which produces Him is also producing you and me. What is the title for two individuals produced by the same life source? They are called brothers; for which reason He is not ashamed to call them brethren (Hebrews 2:11).

A new species of humanity was born from a cross. The life of the Spirit is now yours. All residing in and sourcing Jesus can now be yours. We are His brothers; we are joint-heirs with Christ; we are sons of God. No wonder, I am a Jesus pusher!!! He is my brother.

———————————

I am a Jesus pusher!!! We often hear the statement, "I am no angel." It is an excuse to cover all those things of which we are not proud. Perhaps you should be grateful you are not an angel. It is amazing to contemplate the sin of one angel who had a following of one third of all the angels (Revelation 12:9; Isaiah 14:12; Luke 10:18). He sinned; God brought immediate judgment upon him. No plan of redemption was launched. Yet when man sinned God at great risk planned a restoration. But we are made a little lower than the angels (Hebrews 2:7). Why would God redeem us and not the fallen angels?

It has to do with the original purpose of God for mankind. Then God said, "Let us make man in Our image, according to Our likeness," (Genesis 1:26). His image must be understood in a relational context. It has to do with the source of our life. Mankind, not angels, is capable of being filled with and sourced by God. The image of the invisible God is Jesus, a Spirit-sourced Man, not an angel (Colossians 1:15). Mankind has been destined by God for this role. God's original purpose for our creation was to demonstrate His heart and character. Angels are destined to aid mankind in this demonstration, but they are not the demonstration. To be the sourced by God is to be like Christ; to be like Christ is to be in the image of God. As Jesus demonstrated His Father so we demonstrate Jesus. Thus, I am a Jesus pusher!!!

Jesus PUSHER | 85

I am a Jesus pusher!!! Peter was preaching to the Jews of the Dispersion (Acts 2:14-39). He was explaining Pentecost which the disciples had just experienced. The outside God has come inside man. Jesus of Nazareth, a Man is the explanation. Everything God is doing in Pentecost, He is doing in and through Jesus. The concluding statement of Peter's explanation is, "Therefore let all the house of Israel know assuredly that God has made this Jesus, whom you crucified, both Lord and Christ," (Acts 2:36). In the Greek text the first word in this sentence is "assuredly." The Greek word "asphalos" means safe, secure, or unshakable. What is placed at the beginning of the sentence is often the most important emphasis of the sentence. Here is a statement which is absolutely true. It is totally safe to rest your life upon it. Let this one sure truth shape your entire theology. There is no give or take, no compromise or adjustment in this reality. This is the fundamental which establishes the foundation of everything God desires for your life. If you grasp this all is well; if you miss this you are damned. This is the big, huge issue!

Notice it is about Jesus! He is the certainty of God's action in your behalf. There may be questions about creation, baptism, organizational structure and rules of the church. There is no question about Jesus. He is God's final statement to you and me. I am secure, safe in Him. There is no need for further argument. He is mine and I am His. I am a Jesus pusher!!!

———————

Jesus
PUSHER | **86**

I am a Jesus pusher!!! As Peter explains the experience of Pentecost, he highlights Jesus of Nazareth, a Man (Acts 2:22). The concluding statement of his presentation is "Therefore let all the house of Israel know assuredly that God has made this Jesus, whom you crucified, both Lord and Christ," (Acts 2:36). The sentence begins with the Greek word (asphalos) translated assuredly. It means safe, secure, or unshakable. This certainty rests upon the fact that God has made. This puts it beyond question or suspicion. The position of Jesus as both Lord and Christ is as secure as God.

The verb "has made" comes from the Greek root word "poieo." It is the Greek word used to describe the action of trees as they bring forth fruit (Matthew 3:10; 7:17; 13:23, 26). It is the picture of an artist whose creative, artistic nature is flowing through his brush to produce a masterpiece on the canvas. Jesus is the result of the creative flow of the inner heart of God. Jesus is an expression of His nature. Paul shared the mystery of the ages was hidden and revealed according to the eternal purpose which He accomplished (poieo) in Christ Jesus our Lord (Ephesians 3:11). The Greek word translated accomplished is the same word and grammar form as "has made." Paul said that we have become ambassadors for Christ. It is as if He is pleading through us. The foundation of this is for He made (poieo) Him who knew no sin to be sin for us, that we might become the righteousness of God in Him (2 Corinthians 5:21). Again Paul used the exact same word and grammar form as before. Everything occurring in Christ is a result of the certainty of the nature of God. Jesus is the sure expression of God's nature. Jesus is God speaking, embracing, and caring for you. I am a Jesus pusher!!!

Jesus PUSHER | 87

I am a Jesus pusher!!! Peter is addressing the Jews of the Dispersion concerning the event of Pentecost. His explanation is clear and concise. The outside God coming to live inside must be seen in the context of Jesus. Pentecost is explained and understood in and through Jesus. The creative flow which caused Jesus is now available to us. It comes from the very center of God's heart. Peter expresses this in the final statement of his sermon, "Therefore let all the house of Israel know assuredly that God has made this Jesus, whom you crucified, both Lord and Christ," (Acts 2:36). The strong emphasis of the statement is on what the creative heart of God is accomplishing in Christ (poieo). However, the undercurrent of the statement is the response of Jesus to God's heart. The creative "causing" came from the very center of God's heart; but there was also the consenting of Jesus' heart!

Listen to the words of Jesus: "Most assuredly, I say to you, the Son can do (poieo) nothing of Himself, but what He sees the Father do (poieo); for whatever He does (poieo), the Son also does (poieo) in like manner. For the Father loves the Son, and shows Him all thing that He Himself does (poieo); and He will show Him greater works than these, that you may marvel," (John 5:19, 20). All the Father is doing (poieo) is from His creative, artistic heart; the entire "doing (poieo)" of the Son is a result of the same heart. The Son is sourced by the throbbing heart of His Father. This is Peter's explanation of Pentecost. This same heart is available to us. I want the heart of Christ! I am a Jesus pusher!!!

I am a Jesus pusher!!! What Jesus are you pushing? Peter clarified it in his concluding sentence of his explanation of Pentecost. He said, "Therefore let all the house of Israel know assuredly that God has made this Jesus, whom you crucified, both Lord and Christ," (Acts 2:36). He leaves absolutely no room for a wrongful identification of Jesus. Peter strongly emphasizes this identity in his language. God caused this (touton) Jesus. The Greek word (touton) is often translated "this same." It is an adjective which modifies Jesus. Inserted between "this" and "Jesus" is the Greek word (ton) which is not translated in our verse. It is the definite article translated "the." A literal translation of this Greek statement would be "this same (touton) the (ton) Jesus." Peter is displaying the particular and specific Jesus, the Father has "caused." The action of God's causing is focused on this same "the" Jesus.

The next part of Peter's statement gives content to Jesus. He is the One whom you crucified. God did something marvelous in Jesus; how did we respond? We embraced our traditions instead of Jesus. We listened to our self-sourcing rather than Jesus. We believed our own wisdom instead of His. It was not a misunderstanding or misjudgment. God revealed; we crucified. But wait! He has given us another chance to embrace Jesus. He has not set us aside, but has brought new revelation concerning Jesus. What will we do about Jesus today? I am a Jesus pusher!!!

I am a Jesus pusher!!! Everyone is religious; it is a universal fact. Sociologists discover worship of a higher power in every tribe or group of people however isolated. There may be some atheists in our time. However, they are the result of several generations of religious men experiencing comfort and stability. These religious men eliminated God because they had no need of Him. There are no atheists in the pagan world. Religion is man's search for God. How can I get His attention, manipulate Him, and secure what I need?

But Christianity has an entirely different focus! It is God's search for man. God has initiated contact with us. We did not manipulate, perform, or merit His attention. He has searched and found us. His nature has demanded His involvement. Redemption is not a "pet project." He is not attempting an experiment. Redemption is driven by His nature. He is expressing Himself. The final and complete expression of Himself is Jesus. Jesus is God searching for us! He is the good Shepherd who is risking Himself for one lost sheep (Luke 15)1-7). He is the woman searching for the lost coin (Luke 15:8-10). He is the Father who is longing for His prodigal son to return (Luke 15:11-32). If He desired revenge He would have already eliminated us. If He delighted in punishment, we would already be in hell. His nature drove Him to the cross, the ultimate sacrifice of redemption. His nature is selfless love. Jesus is the full expression of this love for you. Everything you are looking for is contained in an intimate relationship with Him. I am a Jesus pusher!!!

I am a Jesus pusher!!! God's desperate search for man demanded that He become one of us! He did not dress up in human flesh as a fake man; He was not play acting. He really did become one of us. In order to do this, He had to eliminate all of His God-abilities (omnipresence, omniscience, omnipotence). He became all Adam was in the original creation. God gave up all He HAD as God; He did not give up what He IS as God. As a man, He was filled with the Spirit of God (Matthew 3:13-17). Sourced by the Spirit of God He became the demonstration of the very image of God. He is the first man to experience this since Adam and Eve. God was in Jesus sourcing His life, His death, and His resurrection (Acts 2:22-24). This would reverse everything mankind lost in the original sin of man. Jesus would be exalted to the right hand of the Father (Acts 2:33). The Father would give Him the Promise which is now poured out (Acts 2:33). You and I can enter into the same intimate relationship with God Jesus had; we can be sourced by the Father. The same nature of God living in Jesus can now live in us! Jesus was the individual used by God to accomplish this! He is God who made the sacrifice to become man!

My life melts in the awareness of such a sacrifice. I am driven to love in the expression of forgiveness now offered. My fears are gone; I have no desire to hide. These facts mean acceptance and change for my life. No wonder I am a Jesus pusher!!!

I am a Jesus pusher!!! Peter declared, "Therefore let all the house of Israel know assuredly that God has made this Jesus, whom you crucified, both Lord and Christ," (Acts 2:36). Jesus is God! The wonder of redemption is that He gave up what He HAD as God to become man. As a total man He was sourced by the Spirit of God. This is Peter's explanation of Pentecost. In this final statement Peter exclaims that even His position as both Lord and Christ is sourced by God. Notice these two ideas are totally inseparable. He cannot be Lord without being Christ. They cannot be separated in experience or in theology. The actual Greek text states, "kai kurion auton kai Christon." When translated literally it reads, "and Lord self and Christ." There is a double linkage of the two titles, Lord and Christ. This is done by the Greek word (kai) translated both. The same Greek word (kai) is then inserted between the two titles. Notice also the Greek word (auton) which is not normally translated. It is a pronoun of the "self." It is used to intensify the statement or emphasis. Jesus Himself is both Lord and Christ. He is not sometimes one and then the other. He is always both all the time.

We must not allow the separation of these two. Jesus cannot be my Christ (Savior) without being my Lord. Jesus will not save me from my sins, and allow me to maintain ownership of my own life. Salvation always places me in the Kingdom where the Lord reigns. I want to embrace Him as He is. He is worthy of this in my life. I am a Jesus pusher!!!

———————

Jesus PUSHER | 92

I am a Jesus pusher!!! Jesus ascended to the right hand of the Father. He received from the Father ownership of the Kingdom of God. The Greek word (Kurion) translated Lord means owner, possessor, and master. Jesus was sourced by the Father in establishing the Kingdom. Jesus ascended to the heavens and gave the Kingdom back to the Father in humble submission. Now the Father has announced that Jesus is King of the Kingdom. He has received this position from the Father. Notice how Peter explains this: "Therefore let all the house of Israel know assuredly that God has made this Jesus, whom you crucified, both Lord and Christ," (Acts 2:36). God the Father sourced Jesus as both Lord and Christ.

We must be careful of our evangelical language. Often we speak of Jesus as Savior (Christ); at another setting we mention His Lordship. Sometimes we have proposed the question, "If Jesus is your Savior (Christ) will you allow Him to be your Lord?" This suggests the Lordship of Christ in our personal lives is optional. This is absolutely impossible. They are not two categories. He is both Lord and Christ. Jesus cannot be other than He is. He is both! If I embrace Him, I cannot choose one or the other. He is worthy of my entire life at all times. I am totally surrendered to Him. I want all that He is in all that I am. I am a Jesus pusher!!!

Jesus
PUSHER | **93**

I am a Jesus pusher!!! The Lordship of Jesus is not a secondary or additional issue in our relationship to Him. It is a salvation issue. The difficulty in our understanding seems to be in the area of surrender. I can surrender all to Jesus now; but it is always what I know at that point in time. Surrender is never stagnant, but always expanding. As I grow in Christ my surrender must grow as well. Jesus reveals truth to me which expands my embrace of Him. This means I am totally surrendered today; I must also be totally surrendered tomorrow. My surrender must expand to truth revealed tomorrow. There is never a time I can be less than totally surrendered and be Christian.

The writer of the Book of Hebrews illustrated this truth. In describing Jesus, he said, "Though He was a Son, yet He learned obedience by the things which He suffered," (Hebrews 5:8). Bible scholars relate this statement to Jesus' experience in the Garden of Gethsemane. Jesus was never disobedient. He was always totally surrendered to the Father. However, in the garden, He moved into a situation never before experienced. His "total surrender of yesterday" must expand to embrace this new experience in order to be "totally surrendered today." This is the continual experience of our relationship with Jesus. There is no place of arrival. At the beginning of the relationship, Jesus is Lord; the continuation of the relationship means Jesus is Lord. If I am filled with the nature of Jesus, I will experience who He is! He is both Lord and Christ (Acts 2:36). I am a Jesus pusher!!!

Jesus PUSHER | 94

I am a Jesus pusher!!! Peter's concluding statement of the explanation of Pentecost acknowledged the Lordship of Christ. His insight stated, "God has made this Jesus, whom you crucified, both Lord and Christ," (Acts 2:36). This word was used in a variety of ways in Peter's culture. It was connected with royalty. Many of the emperors adapted the term "Lord" as their title. It was applied to the possession or ownership of something or someone. Even in this passage there is a progression in this Lordship. He became Lord! It is the sovereign authority of the Owner of all things (God, the Father) who has bestowed upon Jesus the ownership of the Kingdom of God.

He is not the owner because He is God (although He is). He is owner of the Kingdom because He is a man sourced by the Spirit of God. It was through this Spirit-sourced Man that life, death, resurrection, and ascension took place. The Father sourced the Kingdom through Jesus and now has made Him King, owner. He is not against me, but is coming to me sourced by the Spirit having made a way for me. He owns the Kingdom and invites me to enter. I am free to participate in the Spirit, the nature of the Kingdom. The Jews to whom Peter was preaching viewed Jesus as a criminal; they crucified Him. God views Jesus as Lord. Peter is calling them to change their view; they can enter the Kingdom. Perhaps it is better to state that the Kingdom can enter them. We can be filled with Him, the Lord of the Kingdom. No wonder I am a Jesus pusher!!!

Jesus PUSHER | 95

I am a Jesus pusher!!! Peter pointedly confronted the Jews of the Dispersion with the crucifixion of Jesus. All their lives they had dreamed of the coming Messiah. The Hebrew word "Messiah" is the equivalent of the Greek word "Christ." It literally means "the anointed One." In this sense "the chosen One." Their entire hope rested in the coming of this Deliverer. Every morning, the first words of the day would be "Could this be the day?" Every lamb offered on the sacrifice altar pointed to this hope. Christ would be a man; but a Man appointed by God to be the King of the Kingdom. Peter is crying out to them, "God has made this Jesus, whom you crucified, both Lord and Christ," (Acts 2:36).

Obviously they did not recognize Jesus as this Christ. They thought He was a fake and pretender. He was a bothersome human being deserving elimination. He was the brunt of their fun and mockery. They did not see anything worthwhile in Him. They crucified Him. How have you and I viewed Him? He has been the brunt of our profanity. His name is connected with every evil and bad thing that has happened to us. We stand before our crucifixion of Him and mock Him as surely as those of days gone by. He is the great Savior of the world; yet we refuse the personal salvation He offers us. He is love; yet we continue to hate. He is the revelation of eternal things; yet we are possessed with temporal things. He is the wisdom of God; yet we are dictated by our stupidity. We view Him as worthless. In the ancient days, He was at least worthy of crucifixion. We don't even have time or interest in that; we simply ignore Him as if He does not matter. Wait! This Spirit-sourced Messiah has become both Lord and Christ. The nature of the Father is ours through Him. We have a second chance! I am a Jesus pusher!!!

Jesus PUSHER | 96

I am a Jesus pusher!!! The outside God has just entered into one hundred and twenty people. It is called Pentecost (Acts 2:1-4). Peter is moved upon by the Spirit to offer explanation to over three thousand Jews. The opening statement of his explanation is Jesus of Nazareth, a Man (Acts 2:22). His closing statement is God has made this Jesus, whom you crucified, both Lord and Christ (Acts 2:36). Everything between these two statements continues to be about Jesus. Pentecost can only be understood in light of Jesus. He is the lens through which we must see everything God is doing. Each time we step outside of Jesus, we divide and destroy ourselves. When one highlights miracles, wonders, and signs (Acts 2:22) apart from Jesus, it produces sensationalism and racketeering. When death (Acts 2:23) is seen outside of Jesus, there is nothing left expect hopelessness. Life after death must be viewed through Jesus (Acts 2:24). If not it becomes ghostly and shadowy. The gifts of the Spirit apart from Jesus produce spiritual stars and performers. Jesus must be the determining factor of all things.

How can I adequately tell you how central Jesus is to everything? How can I convince you to embrace Christ as the center in every issue of your life? How can I cause you to visualize "Jesus is the answer" as more than religious jargon? There is absolutely nothing outside His person. He is my theology. He is my ruler by which I measure everything. He is my source which causes my life. I am a Jesus pusher!!!

Jesus PUSHER | 97

I am a Jesus pusher!!! There is a distinct contrast between Peter's opening and closing statement in his sermon explaining Pentecost. He begins by presenting *Jesus of Nazareth, a Man* to over three thousand Jews (Acts 2:22). He strongly speaks to this group alone. He refers to them as *you yourselves*. This is a translation of the Greek word "autoi' which is a reflective pronoun. It is a stronger focus than the normal pronoun. This message is directed to this specific group. The closing statement of his sermon is directed to *all the house of Israel* who must know Jesus is *both Lord and Christ* (Acts 2:36). He has moved from a specific group of Jews to every Israelite in all generations. Abraham, Moses, and all the prophets must know the truth about Jesus. This is verified by the far reaching extent of *the promise* (Acts 2:39). It reaches to the future generations of Israelites and to those *who are afar off* (Acts 2:39). They are the group who are *as many as the Lord our God will call* which includes us. We must know what God is doing in Jesus.

This informs us of the immensity of what is taking place in Jesus. This is not an issue to be dealt with only on Sunday morning. It demands the attention of everyone every moment. No one is to be left out; no situation must be experienced without its influence. No one can exclaim, "This does not apply to me." The world must know what the Father is doing in and through Jesus. Those of us who do know must dedicate all our energy, time, and money that those who do not know may know. "Know" is the key word! If one truly knows Jesus, how can he not be a Jesus pusher?!!!

———————

I am a Jesus pusher!!! Peter's Pentecost sermon begins with a verb which is contrasted with the verb of his closing statement. He begins by addressing a large group of Jews who must **know** (Acts 2:22). In the climatic sentence he addresses the entire world of all generations and the verb is **know** (Acts 2:36). While in the English translation these verbs may appear the same, they are the translation of two different Greek words. This creates the contrast.

The opening Greek verb (oido) means to perceive, understand, or grasp. It is expressed in the phrase "to see." Peter tells them of ***Jesus of Nazareth, a Man*** that they have known. They participated in His crucifixion. They did not think He was a vision, angel, or a ghost. They knew He was a man. Everyone is compelled to acknowledge Jesus on this level. History reveals this man called Jesus lived and was crucified. His teachings affect every world religion. He is an historical person. Who can deny ***Jesus of Nazareth, a Man***?

However, the final statement of Peter's sermons takes us to a new level of consideration. He is addressing the whole world; he is calling them to **know** (ginosko). It is a relational word. It is not data but actually embracing or experiencing. It is the Greek word used for the most intimate relationship in marriage. Everyone must know Jesus on this new level which is not just a physical relationship but a spiritual reality. Once you know Him intimately, you become a Jesus pusher!!!

Jesus PUSHER | 99

I am a Jesus pusher!!! I am a reasonably intelligent individual; I can master data. I can comprehend and figure out information. This kind of knowledge is all within my control. I can view **Jesus of Nazareth, a Man** (Acts 2:22) through the eyes of my knowledge. I can debate His actions and messages. I can set aside any claims He might impose on my life as unrealistic and unreasonable. I can study the law, the oral traditions of the elders; I can calculate His violations. I can justify my participation in the crucifixion. It may not be the best; but *it was expedient that one man should die for the people* (John 18:14). There are significant ramifications if Rome is aware of this radical. We must contain the situation or Rome may judge us all by Him. Isn't this reasonable?

Data on this level may indirectly affect my life, but it is not at the center of my life. Peter opens his message on Pentecost with this beginning level, but he closes with a call to an entirely different level (Acts 2:36). God, the Father, was sourcing Jesus. Through this sourcing, He established the possibility we could be sourced in the same way. Jesus was given a position of **both Lord and Christ** in this new realm of sourcing (Acts 2:36). Intimacy with Jesus in this new sourcing will affect my entire life. Relationship with my wife is changed; how I raise my children is different. This truth is so big it pulls me into its heart. It goes to the depth of my soul; it burns in my bones. This source becomes the controlling force of my very existence. It is Jesus! It is not Jesus as information, concept, or creed. It is Jesus as personal, oneness, and intimate. All of life is changed in Jesus. I am a Jesus pusher!!!

Jesus PUSHER | **100**

I am a Jesus pusher!!! One of the great sermons of the Bible is Peter's explanation of Pentecost (Acts 2:14-36). His final statement is, ***"Therefore let all the house of Israel know assuredly that God has made this Jesus, whom you crucified, both Lord and Christ,"*** (Acts 2:36). The Father sourced Jesus to produce an entirely new Kingdom, the Kingdom of God. It is within you; therefore, it is the same sourcing Jesus knew. He can now reign in our lives. This is not an attempt to convert you to a "belief system." We are not proposing an adjustment in your life style. No one wants to manipulate you by stirring your emotions so you will enlist. Paul cried, "I want to ***be found in Him, not having my own righteousness, which is from the law, but that which is through faith in Christ, the righteousness which is from God by faith; that I may know Him and the power of His resurrection, and the fellowship of His sufferings, being conformed to His death*** (Philippians 3:9, 10). I can actually know Him. Every aspect of who He is can be experienced. I can know Him as Lord; I can experience Him as Christ. I can be intimate with His person.

There is no other place to go. He alone provides the sourcing which is adequate for my life's situations. Every situation has been created by inadequate sourcing; I have lived out of myself. My track record reveals my failures; it demands a new source. Jesus is the provision of God, the Father, for me. He has been found abundantly adequate in every situation. I am a Jesus pusher!!!

Jesus PUSHER | 101

I am a Jesus pusher!!! This focus on Jesus gives me a desperate desire to "hear" Him. I am not concerned about hearing an audible voice. I want an intimacy with Him which is beyond verbal communication. Hearing an audible voice indicates separation from Him. The communication of the heart, His mind to my mind, is my desire. I want to be so sensitive to Him He can reveal His slightest desire.

Peter opened his explanation of Pentecost with **"Men of Israel, hear these words,"** (Acts 2:22). This Greek word (akouo) translated **hear** is used to describe a disciple's understanding or hearing with the ear of the mind (Matthew 11:15; John 8:43, 47; 1 Corinthians 14:2). It is used in the sense of "to give heed" or "to obey." It would require openness, a willingness to respond. This is not always easy. Luke gives us the end result of this appeal. **Now when they heard** (akouo) **this, they were cut to the heart, and said to Peter and the rest of the apostles,** "Men and **brethren, what shall we do?"** (Acts 2:37). The Greek word (akouo) translated **when they heard** is highlighted in the sentence. It is a participle (verb acting as an adjective). Since it is in the nominative case it modifies the subject, **they**. The focus is not on "what they heard" but upon "the act of their hearing."

The result of their hearing was **they were cut to the heart**. This is the difficulty with listening to Jesus. It is always like surgery. However, He does it with such care and tenderness. He becomes so intimate with me; He joins me in the suffering of the surgery. I must listen to Him! I am a Jesus pusher!!!

I am a Jesus pusher!!! I do not want to know data or information about Him. I do not want to know history or theology concerning Him. I want to hear His voice. I want to see His lips part. I want to grasp His expression of the deep things of His. I want to be so close I feel His breath on my check as He communicates His mind to my mind. This requires intimacy; all walls must be removed. Oh, is my heart ready to hear Him? Does the texture of my inner most being respond to His molding? If He wants to speak to me, what could stop me from hearing?

Jesus discussed this with the Jews of Jerusalem. They claimed Abraham as their father. If Abraham was really their father, they would respond as Abraham, seeking and open. But they had another father. Jesus asked them, ***"Why do you not understand My speech? Because you are not able to listen*** (akouo) ***to My word,"*** (John 8:43). He boldly told them that their father was the devil. He concluded by saying, ***"He who is of God hears*** (akouo) ***God's words: therefore you do not hear*** (akouo)***, because you are not of God,"*** (John 8:47).

If I hear and listen to His voice, I will be intimate with Him; I will know His thoughts. If I am intimate with Him, I will hear and listen to His voice; I will know His thoughts. Hearing and intimacy are closely related. They are the cause and effect of each other. I must know Him to hear Him; I must hear Him to know Him. "Jesus, whatever the consequences, speak to me!" I am a Jesus pusher!!!

I am a Jesus pusher!!! How can I know for sure I am hearing (akouo) the voice of Jesus? The answer is clearly stated at the end of Peter's sermon (Acts 2:14-39). ***Now when they heard this, they were cut to the heart, and said to Peter and the rest of the apostles, "Men and brethren, what shall we do?"*** (Acts 2:37). The subject of this sentence is "***they***." But Luke identifies them as the ones who ***heard this***. The ones who were in the act of hearing is the subject. The verb of the sentence is "***were cut*** (katanusso)." "Kata" is a prefix intensifying the root word. It means "from." "Nusso" means "to prick or pierce." This is the only time this word is used in the New Testament. "Piercing through" naturally takes place when one is "hearing" (akouo).

I cannot be intimate with Jesus, hearing His voice, without constantly being changed. If I want to remain as I am, I can be religious, but I must not hear Him. If I want to live undisturbed and unchanged, I must not be open to His voice. His very presence will pierce my heart; His light will confront my darkness. I will be shaken at the core of my existence when He speaks and I hear. This is the price of knowing Him.

But why should I resist? Every change He brings is for my benefit! He only speaks what is good for me. He is bent on making me like Him. Oh the wonder of being intimate with Him; He is changing me into his likeness. "Dear Jesus, pierce the depth of my being; leave nothing undisturbed. I am listening!" I am a Jesus pusher!!

Jesus PUSHER | 104

I am a Jesus pusher!!! I desperately want to hear the voice of Jesus! Not an audible voice, but the intent of His heart. Could He share His inner feelings and desires with me? The Jews of the Dispersion heard the Spirit of Jesus flowing through Peter. The truth went beyond argument and mere facts and pierced their hearts. Luke reports, *Now when they heard this, they were cut to the heart, and said to Peter and the rest of the apostles, "Men and brethren, what shall we do?"* (Acts 2:37). The subject of the sentence is "those who are hearing." The verb is the thorough piercing or pricking. The direct object receiving the action of this piercing is **the heart**. The Greek word (kardia) translated **heart** is common to us. The Old Testament focuses on the heart as the seat of the desires, feelings, affections, passions, and impulses. *For the life of the flesh is in the blood* (Leviticus 17:11). Obviously, as the blood circulates throughout the body, it comes from the heart and returns to the heart. The source of our life is found in the heart. This is the core of what makes us who we are.

This is where I want to know Him! Not in some casual or superficial way. Not in some religious way. I want to hear Him at the very core of my being. I want His Words to spill forth from my inner heart to affect every aspect of my living. I want all of life to be influenced by His speaking. Every pattern of action which is threatened by His voice must yield. I want to hear Him with the ears of my heart! I am a Jesus pusher!!!

I am a Jesus pusher!!! I propose this as if I have never gone against Him. The real truth is ***Christ Jesus came into the world to save sinners, of whom I am chief*** (1 Timothy 1:15). I am guilty of crucifying Him! The Jews of the Dispersion listened to Peter's explanation of Pentecost. His message highlighted Jesus; the One they had ***taken by lawless hands, have crucified, and put to death*** (Acts 2:23). ***Now when they heard this, they were cut to the heart, and said to Peter and the rest of the apostles, "Men and brethren, what shall we do?"*** (Acts 2:37). My heart resounds with this same question, for I am as guilty as they.

"What shall we do?" is not a cry for a list of rules or activities which will undo the situation. Let's call a committee meeting; let's develop a plan of action. This is not "***do***" in the sense of an action, performance, or accomplishment. There is nothing to "***do***" in this sense. What action could I "***do***" which would balance what I have already done? Good deeds do not cancel our bad deeds. How much money could I pay Jesus to cancel my debt? How much service is demanded? I debt is huge; I am so guilty!

"What shall we do?" There is absolutely nothing I can do. The matter is in His hands. He has come to me with the embrace of forgiveness. He embraced me with the warmth of one who is my Lover! He whispered the desire for intimacy with me! He restores me back to His dream for my life! No wonder I am a Jesus pusher!!!

I am a Jesus pusher!!! ***"What shall we do?"*** This question is asked three times in response to John the Baptist's preaching (Luke 3:10, 12, 14). In the conversion of Saul of Tarsus it is used twice (Acts 9:6; 22:10). A jailor is shaken into giving this response (Acts 16:30). The same question is asked by the Jews of the Dispersion (Acts 2:37). There is a distinction between those in Luke's account and those in the Book of Acts. When John the Baptist responded to this question, he required them to carry out specific activities. He gave instructions which applied to their particular situation. After Pentecost, the answer is always in terms of response.

The Greek word (poieo) translated ***do*** suggests the answer. It points you beyond an activity one does to make things right. It is the word used when trees ***bear*** fruit. Trees do not "do" fruit; it is the process of "poieo." Our understanding will be increased, if we translate the word as "respond." "Doing" is a focus on oneself. "Responding" is a focus on interaction with something or someone beyond oneself. Relationship with Jesus is never a "doing;" it is always a "responding."

I want intimacy with Jesus! I do not want a list of activities to accomplish. I want to embrace His person. I want to know Him on the level of the heart. I want to live responding to His every desire, flowing in His presence and fellowshipping with His person. I am a Jesus pusher!!!

Jesus PUSHER | **107**

I am a Jesus pusher!!! When the Jews of the Dispersion are **cut to the heart**, they cry out, *"What shall we do?"* (Acts 2:37). Peter does not give them a list of activities or sacrifices to do. He calls them to respond in the depth of their hearts. My guilt is beyond description or correction. There is nothing I can do! Could I simply respond to the love of Jesus as He embraces me in forgiveness?

This is surrender on a new level. The difficulty with emphasizing surrender is the natural tendency to slip into the "doing" aspect. I immediately consider "things to surrender." I often struggle with the difficulty of "taking it back." I present it to Jesus, but quickly take it back when I leave. The focus of surrender seems to be on me and how well I can "do" it. It is a focus on "self." Could I simply respond to Jesus, which allows Him to do in me what He desires? Only He can pry my fingers loose and release me. Even my surrender is not something "I do" it is a response to "His doing."

This is the basis of intimacy with Jesus. I only know Him in the embrace of His person when He is allowed to "do." I have attempted to do service for Him; I now want Him to serve through me. I have lived my life for Him; He wants to live His life through me. My ministry has not been pleasing to Him; He wants to minister through me. I have struggled, attempted, and tried; I am tired and have accomplished nothing. I will rest in Him who came to source me. I will respond to His doing. I am a Jesus pusher!!!

Jesus PUSHER | **108**

I am a Jesus pusher!!! I desire to step from a "doing" religion to a "responding" Christianity. I want to live in His presence and experience His action. I want my thoughts and movements to be in response to His sourcing and supply. Christianity has always been so difficult and tiresome. Is it because I have been "doing" it? Could I collapse in His arms and let Him do through me what I cannot do? Is this why His death on Calvary is really my death? It is death to all my doing. I will live in response to His person.

The Jews of the Dispersion cried out, ***"What shall we do?"*** (Acts 2:38). Peter did not give them a list of things to do. He spoke of response. They were to respond in repentance (Acts 2:38). It is a change of mind. Jesus had already accomplished this in them, for they were asking the question. Would they respond to this change? He encouraged them to ***be baptized in the name of Jesus Christ*** (Acts 2:38). This was not just a ceremony to experience. It was an embracing of Jesus who had already embraced them. Would they respond?

In fact, responding would allow them to ***receive the gift of the Holy Spirit*** (Acts 2:38). According to the passage (see Acts 2:33) Jesus poured out this gift in abundance upon them. The issue is one of response. Will they simply "receive?" I will respond to Him in this moment. All He is doing in my life, I will embrace. All resistance or hesitation is set aside. I want Him in His fullness. I am a Jesus pusher!!!

Jesus PUSHER | **109**

I am a Jesus pusher!!! When ***cut to the heart*** the Jews of the Dispersion cried out ***"What shall we do?"*** (Acts 2:37). Peter's answer was ***"Repent,"*** (Acts 2:38). This is not an activity to do but an attitude of response. The Greek word (metanoeo) consists of "meta" (denoting changing of place or condition) and "noeo" (to exercise the mind, think, or comprehend). Repentance is giving up a former thought to embrace a second thought.

The Spirit of Jesus revealed truth to these Jews through Peter's sermon. They had embraced the perspective of the leaders of Israel. Jesus must be eliminated for the sake of their traditions and law. They were content with their involvement in His crucifixion. Now the Spirit of Jesus has convinced them (changed their mind) and ***cut them to the heart***. Repentance is not an activity they will do, but a response to what Jesus revealed within them. Will they embrace Him?

This is the attitude in which I want to live! Jesus reveals; I respond to His revelation. This is a state of repentance. Repentance is not an experience one has or an activity one does. It is not something to go through, to accomplish. It is a state of intimacy with Jesus as I constantly respond to what He reveals to me. He constantly lifts me to new levels, changing my life for the better, and He enables me in new avenues of service. I will offer no resistance to His revelation. I am living in repentance. I am a Jesus pusher!!!

I am a Jesus pusher!!! Repentance is linked with *for the remission of sins* (Acts 2:38). The Greek word translated *remission* is "aphiemi." This Greek word does not focus just on the result or consequence of an action. It always includes the action itself. There is an action of repelling, releasing, or putting away. Repentance is giving up a former thought to embrace a second thought. This change of mind releases the full energy of Christ's sacrificial love to repel guilt from my life. Sin with all of its multifaceted fingers imprisoning me is literally pushed from me. I am released, delivered, or "aphiemi" from my sins.

This is not something I do; it is a response. In experiencing forgiveness, I do not receive a thing. It is always relational. Jesus literally comes to embrace me. Forgiveness is His attitude toward me; will I respond to it? If I do not respond (repent), then forgiveness is left incomplete. Jesus died on a cross to provide forgiveness; He arose from the dead so He could execute what He provided. He ascended to the right hand of the Father in order to receive the Promise of the Father. He poured out His Spirit so He could embrace me in forgiveness. All is provided. The only thing needed is "my response." Forgiveness is found in His embrace! I want Jesus! He is all I need! He is my peace, supply, rest, life, assurance, and forgiveness. All is found in Him. No wonder, I am a Jesus pusher!!!

Jesus PUSHER | 111

I am a Jesus pusher!!! Before Jesus was born, an Angel of the Lord appeared to Joseph in the night. He gave a clear cut mission statement concerning Jesus. He declared, *"And she will bring forth a Son, and you shall call His name Jesus for He will save His people from their sins,"* (Matthew 1:21). After Pentecost, Peter challenged the Jews of the Dispersion, *"Repent, and let everyone of you be baptized in the name of Jesus Christ for the remission of sins; and you shall receive the gift of the Holy Spirit,"* (Acts 2:38). At the heart of both of these statements is the issue of ***sins***.

Jesus is the context of both of these statements. His birth is central in the first; the outpouring of His Spirit is the focus of the other. Everything God desires for our lives is in Jesus. Everything intended in the eternal plan for our very creation is Jesus! Intimacy found in the Spirit of Jesus fulfills the love of God for us! Anything outside of Jesus is labeled "sin." Sin is not defined in terms of a deed; it is defined in how a deed relates to Jesus. If He does not source the deed, it is sin! The goodness of the deed does not justify it. The sincerity expressed within the deed does not make it righteous. The heart of the entire matter is Jesus. The Jews were not bad; they missed Jesus. They missed the true end and scope of their lives; they crucified Jesus.

I am opening my life to nothing but Jesus. He is the boundary for my existence. He will be the reference point of all my thinking and doing. I am a Jesus pusher!!!

———————

I am a Jesus pusher!!! Peter preached a strong sermon to a great crowd of Jews. His concluding statement was, *"Repent, and let every one of you be baptized in the name of Jesus Christ for the remission of sins; and you shall receive the gift of the Holy Spirit,"* (Acts 2:38). There are two main verbs in this statement. "*Repent*" is in the active voice; the Jews are responsible for this response. The Spirit of Jesus moved upon their lives revealing truth; they are now responsible for responding to this truth.

The second main verb is "*be baptized*." It is an imperative, a command. It is in the passive voice; the subject, the Jews, receives the action of this verb. This was startling to me! When the Jews truly *repent*, they will be acted upon by baptism. Clearly understand, baptism is a physical act which involves water. Paul compared this physical act of being covered with water to Jesus' burial. The act of coming out of this covering of water was likened to the resurrection of Jesus. Therefore, we are buried with Jesus and resurrected with Jesus in newness of life (Romans 6:4). There is a mystical aspect to this activity. While an individual may be responsible for the physical action of water baptism, the spiritual reality of this baptism can only be received as the Spirit of Christ acts upon the individual. The entire focus is our place in Jesus. He is the sphere in which we dwell; He is the seat in which we are positioned (Ephesians 2:6). It is in His embrace we experience all the blessings of God (Ephesians 1:3). Everything is about Jesus. I am a Jesus pusher!!!

.

I am a Jesus pusher!!! The Jews of the Dispersion were *cut to the heart* with the reality of their spiritual condition. Peter gave them these instruction, *"Repent, and let every one of you be baptized in the name of Jesus Christ for the remission of sins; and you shall receive the gift of the Holy Spirit,"* (Acts 2:38). The usual form of baptism is *into* (eis) *the name of the Father and of the Son and of the Holy Spirit* (Matthew 28:19). However, Peter changed the approach to *in* (epi) *the name of Jesus Christ*. This does not indicate the formula to be said over the individual. The debate between the two formulas misses the point of the passage.

The *name of Jesus Christ* is simply an expression referring to the person Himself. It is not a reference to something attached to Him, but to the entirety of what is contained in His person. This is not a baptism by the authority of Jesus Christ, but a baptism based upon the foundation of His very person. "Baptism" means to immerse, submerge, to overwhelm, or saturate. The Jews are to be submerged and saturated into the very person of Jesus! Jesus is the fulfillment of the law. He now will be the foundation of their lives. As the law dictated their actions, schedules, and perspective of life, they will be saturated in the Spirit of Jesus who will shape and form their lives.

I want to be submerged into Jesus. I want His Spirit to encompass my life and reshape all my living according to His person. I am a Jesus pusher!!!

––––––––––––

Jesus PUSHER | 114

I am a Jesus pusher!!! Three to five thousand Jews of the Dispersion listened to Peter's explanation of Pentecost. His instructions were very clear: *"Repent, and let every one of you be baptized in the name of Jesus Christ for the remission of sins; and you shall receive the gift of the Holy Spirit,"* (Acts 2:38). The Greek verb translated *be baptized* is singular in number. This fact is verified with the Greek word (hekastos) translated *everyone*. It is the idea of "each" or "separating or singling out." Peter is calling them to *repent*, giving up their former thought concerning Jesus to embrace a second thought. If this takes place, they will be submerged, immersed into Jesus. Each individual will be singled out by Jesus. They will experience intimacy with Him as He personally becomes the base of their lives.

In becoming a Christian, I did not simply join a group of people who have a certain belief system. I am not one name among many on a membership list. I am not just one more face added to a large crowd. I am a selected individual attached to Jesus. His love is powerful and amazing. When I experience it, it seems as if I am the only one He loves. My mother always testified of being the favorite of Jesus. God does not have any grandchildren. I am His son; He is my Father. The intimacy of the relationship is beyond description. The most profound truth of the Scriptures is "God loves me!" It is not a theology; it is the reality of my life. I am His and He is mine. I am a Jesus pusher!!!

I am a Jesus pusher!!! Peter did not preach without expecting response. He cried, ***"Repent, and let every one of you be baptized in the name of Jesus Christ for the remission of sins; and you shall receive the gift of the Holy Spirit,"*** (Acts 2:38). The third verb in this statement is a Greek word (lambano) translated ***shall receive***. It has two applications in the Scriptures. It expresses the emphasis of "to take, seize, lay hold of." It has the idea of force or violence. In Peter's statement, a new believer would aggressively want, desire, seek and long to receive. There is no resistance or hesitation. This is my attitude toward the fullness of Jesus.

A second application of this Greek word (lambano) is "to receive what is given, imparted, imposed, or to obtain." The focus is not as aggressive. It is passive with an emphasis on receptivity and openness. I recognize the pouring out of the Spirit of Jesus upon me. I am drenched in His presence. There is no force, no battle. I simply am swept away in His grace.

Both are true in our passage. I do not need to choose between them. My hunger for Him is satisfied. His fullness is mine. I sought Him; He found me. I ask Him; He answered. I knocked; He opened. My heart continues to aggressively seek; He continues to embrace and fill. What a Jesus! I am a Jesus pusher!!!

Jesus PUSHER | 116

I am a Jesus pusher!!! Isn't it amazing? God loves me so much; He makes promises to me! Listen to Peter's sermon, **"For the promise is to you and to your children, and to all who are afar off, as many as the Lord our God will call,"** (Acts 2:39). The main verb in the passage is the Greek word "eimi" which is a verb of being. Peter does not have to convince God to promise me. It is not wishful thinking. **The promise** is placed into a state of being. The promise has a life of its own. It is the life of the Holy Spirit. There are several things which verify this truth.

It is a CERTIFIED promise! In the Greek text, there is an article (the) before the word **promise**. This is a specific promise with specific content (see Acts 1:4; 2:33). It has to do with the Spirit of Jesus indwelling me. It is **the promise** in which all other promises are fulfilled. This promise has CONTENT. Peter begins his statement with "**For**" (gar). His previous statement was **"you shall receive the gift of the Holy Spirit,"** (Acts 2:38). This content is not described in quantity such as gallons or quarts. It is the wonder of relationship with a Person.

Another element is the CONTINUATION of the promise. As Peter boldly proclaims the wonder of **the promise** to the Jews, he definitely refers to the prophecy with which he began his sermon (Acts 2:16-21). This promise for me is the heart's desire of God for generations of time. Jesus is the fulfillment of it all. His Spirit fills me! I know Him! I am a Jesus pusher!!!

I am a Jesus pusher!!! Peter assures his congregation ***"For the promise is to you and to your children, and to all who are afar off, as many as the Lord our God will call,"*** (Acts 2:39). The Greek word (epangelia) translated ***promise*** comes from the Greek word (epangello) meaning "to announce." It is used only for the promises of God in the New Testament with only one exception (Acts 23:21). It has to do with "the thing promised or a gift graciously given." It is not a pledge secured by negotiation. Therefore it is contrasted with the Greek word (omnuo) which is an oath or pledge.

God does not need to swear by an oath; therefore we can force Him to keep His promises. The Greek word for promise appears fifty-two times in the New Testament. Every time it refers to God's promise to us. In the verb form it is always in the middle voice. Therefore, it is an expression of personal preference. In other words, God desperately wants to fulfill this promise. Everything God has done from the start of the Old Testament is to fulfill ***the promise***. We do not have a record of anything God ever did which is not about ***the promise***. His total focus of wisdom, energy, and exceedingly great power is about ***the promise***. He is driven by His love. His own heart becomes the very security of ***the promise***. ***The promise*** is a fulfillment of the love for me. He removed every obstacle keeping me from intimacy with Him. He is waiting on my response. ***The promise*** is mine. I am His! All He desires for me is mine. His promise is the fullness of the Spirit of Jesus. Jesus completes the promise of God in my life. What a Jesus! I am a Jesus pusher!!!

I am a Jesus pusher!!! The climax of Peter's sermon explaining Pentecost highlights ***the promise*** (Acts 2:39). The Greek word (epangelia) translated ***promise*** has a root Greek word (angelia) meaning "something announced." The Greek word "angelos" is the announcer or messenger. This is the root word for our English word "angel." The Greek word "evangelia" is the message of good things or the Gospel. You can see this cluster of words all refer to the message of truth found in the Person of Jesus. It is the "good news" of the Gospel.

In the New Testament, the usage of this Greek word (epangelia) can be gathered into three groups. The first group is the frequent references to God's promises to Abraham concerning an heir. Abraham would be the father of a people through whom the Messiah would come (Romans 4:13-16, 20). A second group is the usage of this Greek word (epangelia) used in reference to David's seed. Paul preached, ***"From this man's seed, according to the promise, God raised up for Israel a Savior – Jesus,"*** (Acts 13:23). The third group is ***the promise*** concerning the gift of the Holy Spirit (Acts 2:38, 39). 1:13). Jesus told His disciples that He often spoke with them about this ***promise*** (Acts 1:4). There are not three different promises. These are aspects of the same promise. The supreme goal of all God accomplished from Abraham to King David to the birth, death, resurrection, and exaltation of Jesus Christ is that He might pour His Spirit into our lives. Intimacy with Jesus is the focus of God's action. I am a Jesus pusher!!!

I am a Jesus pusher!!! Jesus is the fulfillment of all prophecy! In the Old Testament, there are three hundred and thirty-two verbal predictive prophecies concerning Jesus. A prophet actually proclaimed to a crowd of people each of these prophecies hundreds of years before they came to pass. Jesus fulfills every one of them down to the smallest detail. The possibility of one man fulfilling all of them is stated as "one out of eighty four with one hundred zeros after it."

Matthew writes an entire book to the Jews. He makes one consistent argument in behalf of Jesus as the fulfillment of prophecy. He front loads the first four chapters with prophecy. Seven times in these four chapters he stops his narrative to remind us; this is a fulfillment of prophecy. He mentions prophecy only six times in the rest of his twenty-four chapters. It is a reminder of what he heavily emphasized at the beginning. The concluding paragraph of his prophecy emphasis comes near the close of chapter four (Matthew 4:12-17). He uses prophecy to authenticate the person of Jesus. As one views prophecy through the person of Jesus, the plan of God for my life becomes clear! God's plan is Jesus. All prophecy points to Jesus, the fulfillment of the plan. The plan is now complete in Jesus. We are on a new level! We have shifted from expecting and waiting to embracing and experiencing. There is nothing more; it is all in Jesus. In Him I have all God wants for my life. I am a Jesus pusher!!!

Jesus PUSHER | **120**

I am a Jesus pusher!!! John the Baptist was the last of the Old Testament prophets. Jesus says that he was the greatest man who was ever born; however, *he who is least in the kingdom of heaven is greater than he* (Matthew 11:11). The progression of the Old Testament is traced through the prophets. It appears Moses was the first of this group. God told Moses, *"I will raise up for them a Prophet like you from among their brethren, and will put My words in His mouth, and He shall speak to them all that I command Him,"* (Deuteronomy 18:18). In every crisis moment in Israel's history God raised up a prophet. However, all of these prophets were progressing to *the Prophet* (John 1:19-21; John 6:14; John 7:40). *The Prophet* would be the fulfillment of all the prophecies of previous prophets. He is not only *the Prophet*, He is the performance of all prophecy.

John the Baptist, the last of the prophets, was put in prison; he would soon be beheaded. The focus is now turned to Jesus, *the Prophet* (Matthew 4:12). Jesus is all in all. We are no longer waiting for the fulfillment of prophecy; Jesus is here. We do not anticipate the unfolding of a plan; He is the plan. Paul cried, *"You are complete in Him who is the head of all principality and power,"* (Colossians 2:10). Our position is in Him; we rest in Him! We do not search for answers; He is the answer! I am a Jesus pusher!!!

I am a Jesus pusher!!! Many people are intrigued by prophecy. The investigation of the unfolding prophetic events and our location in that sequence is addictive. Prophecy is not about Jesus; it is Jesus! The ultimate theme of Old Testament prophecy is Jesus; but it was in the future tense. Matthew's Gospel account places us on a new level. Jesus is "present tense." The Pharisees and Sadducees had a very difficult time with the "present tense" Jesus. A strong financial contributor to the budget of the temple was the offering of sacrificial lambs. Each lamb was a testimony of the coming Messiah. It was prophecy in the future tense. If "The Lamb" is present tense, there would never be a need for further lamb sacrifices. The temple with all of its activities testified of the coming Messiah. If He is here, the significance of these activities and the temple would fade. The leaders of Israel chose a future tense Messiah rather than a present tense Jesus.

We face the same dilemma. We focus on what Jesus will do at the second coming. We sing songs of heaven, streets of gold and great mansions. There will be no more death, pain, or sorrow. What about the present tense embrace of Jesus in my life now? The way I am going to live as a result of the second coming is the way I am to live now filled with His presence. Sin will be banished then; will I allow His presence to banish it now in my life? Peace will reign then; will I allow Him to rule in peace in my life now? In a real sense, we are waiting for nothing. All I am experiencing in the intimacy of the present tense Jesus will simply manifest itself in fuller revelation in the future. He is here; I am His! I am a Jesus pusher!!!

I am a Jesus pusher!!! Jesus brought about a radical change. It is called the "New Covenant." The role of the Old Testament prophet was to prepare us for the coming of the Kingdom of God. The law was its structure. In miniature form Israel attempted to act out the Kingdom of God as prophesied. Their failures were embarrassing. When Jesus came the Kingdom of God was present. A great shift took place. It was the difference between a shadow and the real thing. Our King is now here!

It is true; there is prophecy in the New Testament about our future. Prophecy did not cease at the end of the Old Testament. However, in the New Testament its appearance radically changes. The Old Testament prophet would relay to us what God told him. His opening statement would be "The Word of the Lord came unto me." In the New Testament, the Spirit of Jesus speaks to every man individually. Even the Old Testament prophets spoke of the day when ***"No more shall every man teach his neighbor, and every man his brother, saying, 'Know the Lord,' for they all shall know Me, from the least of them to the greatest of them, says the Lord,"*** (Jeremiah 31:34). Jesus is the fulfillment of all the dreams of God for my life. Beyond Him there is nothing to be done or given. Every new thing to come will simply be the unfolding of His person in my life. If He is the essence of heaven and He is the "way," when I am in Him I am already there. There is nothing left to be accomplished which is outside of His person. I am to focus on Him alone. I must not get sidetracked from Him. I will allow no other subject to dominate my attention. I am a Jesus pusher!!!

Jesus PUSHER | 123

I am a Jesus pusher!!! John the Baptist was the last of the Old Testament prophets. Jesus is the first individual of the New Covenant. John the Baptist is the prophet who is foretelling; Jesus is the fulfillment of all he foretold. The shift from the Old Covenant to the New Covenant took place between these two individuals. The shift from John the Baptist to Jesus presents an awesome contrast. It is found in the message each delivered. John the Baptist was filled with the Spirit from his mother's womb (Luke 1:15). However, it was the special filling of the Old Testament for the purpose of a task. His message was to highlight the law. Israel must repent and become ready for the new thing God was doing in Jesus, the Kingdom of God.

Jesus was also filled with the Spirit of God (Matthew 3:13-17). But He was the first individual to experience the coming of the Spirit in the New Covenant (Acts 2:1-4). This indwelling of the Spirit would be power for a task, but also intimacy with God. The message produced from such a relationship would not just be words repeated as the Old Testament prophet. Jesus is the very *image of the invisible God* (Colossians 1:15). The Spirit of God flowed through Jesus to bring a revelation of the very heart of God. Jesus not only spoke the message of God, He was the message. What He spoke became reality in His living. The Spirit of God lived in Him in order to live through Him. This is a new day! I can be filled with the Spirit of Jesus in the same way. I am not one who proposes a theology about Jesus; I am to be one who experiences the life of Jesus who produces the image of Jesus through me. My life becomes a Jesus pusher!!!

I am a Jesus pusher!!! John the Baptist and Jesus were cousins. They not only had physical relationship through family, but also linkage in ministry. There is a strong comparison between the methods of both. Matthew refers to John the Baptist as one who **had been put in prison** (Matthew 4:12). This phrase is a translation of one Greek word, "paradidomi." "Para" is the prefix meaning "over to." The root word "didomi" means "to give." This Greek word (paradidomi) is introduced by Matthew because John the Baptist is a forerunner of Jesus. Matthew will use this same word fifteen times as a semi-technical term for the announcement of the cross of Jesus. John the Baptist did not forerun the miracles, preaching style, or organizational structure of Jesus. He foreran the cross style of Jesus.

As they made their way down from the Mount of Trans-figuration, the disciples asked Jesus concerning the forerunner. He promptly told them this forerunner had already come **and they did not know him but did to him whatever they wished**. John the Baptist did not resist, fight back, or rebel. It was the style of the cross. Jesus went on to say, **"Likewise the Son of Man is also about to suffer at their hands,"** (Matthew 17:12). It appears a pattern is established. Jesus calls His disciples to this same life style of the cross (Matthew 20:25-28). I want His heart to be mine so His style can be expressed through me. I want to know His mind so His thoughts can be visible in my life. I want His Spirit to indwell me so I am an expression of His attitude. I want my life to be a consistent Jesus pusher!!!

I am a Jesus pusher!!! There is an "unseen" world; it is just as real as the "seen" world. It has more authority and influence than our physical world. Our physical "seen" world is constantly responding to the spiritual "unseen" world. The tip of an iceberg is plainly seen projecting from the water. However, there is a massive amount of the iceberg not seen. The tip does not determine the activity of the iceberg; it is only an indicator of what is not seen. Could it be my physical existence is simply an indicator of the massive movement in the spiritual realm? The physical is a stage upon which the spiritual displays itself.

Jesus is the iceberg; we are allowed to see the tip of His activities for a few years. What took place in the spiritual realm was so explosive; it thrust itself into our physical realm. Stars began speaking to wise men. They came to Jerusalem. Surely the Jews, who were to be the physical avenue of the world's redemption, would know His location. These wise men searched the Scriptures; He was born in Bethlehem, five miles from Jerusalem. Not one Jewish leader went to see the "explosion of the spiritual into the physical." The physical realm responded with indifference. Herod, the King, declared war on the new revelation. His war contained deception (Matthew 2:8), anger (Matthew 2:16), and the destruction of baby boys (Matthew 2:16). I will not join them! I will embrace Jesus, the revelation of the "unseen" world. As the spiritual world moved through Him into my physical world, so I will allow Him to move through me. I welcome His controlling, spiritual presence to disturb my physical world. I am a Jesus pusher!!!

I am a Jesus pusher!!! A tremendous spiritual movement from the "unseen" world was taking place in John the Baptist. The spiritual movement of an Old Testament was now exploding into the days of the New Testament. It could no longer be contained. John was the final prophet of the Old Testament. There was no prophet for four hundred years. His message was prophetic. His methods, dress, and dwelling place testified; he was not a product of the Jewish schools. God was doing what He does best through the prophet. But John the Baptist was only the beginning of the explosion. He was to prepare the way for the full blown revelation of the spiritual world, Jesus!

Recognizing this new movement, the devil launched his forces as well. War was declared. This revelation of the heart of the spiritual world must not be seen. John the Baptist was beheaded through the demonic forces (Matthew 14:8-11). This was the indicator that Jesus should leave Judea and begin His ministry in Galilee (Matthew 4:12, 13). Galilee was in darkness; now they would see a great Light. They literally settled down and were sitting in the region of death; now the Light would dawn (Matthew 4:16). The physical stage of Galilee would know the performance of the Light of God, Jesus! Jesus came to me! In the midst of physical activities the spiritual reality of His being was revealed. I have embraced Him. I will sit no longer in the dark. I will allow the Light to reveal and transform me. I will be a child of the Light! I am a Jesus pusher!!!

Jesus
PUSHER | **127**

I am a Jesus pusher!!! There is a tremendous shift taking place in Jesus. We are moving from the Old Testament into the New Testament. The Old Covenant is now fulfilled in the New Covenant. The law of God is now completed in Jesus. Matthew gives us a physical illustration of it by presenting John the Baptist who is decreasing that Jesus might increase. John the Baptist is the last of the Old Testament prophets. Jesus is now *"the kingdom of heaven is at hand!"* (Matthew 3:2). This does not mean that the Old is destroyed by the New. Rather, the first is literally being fulfilled, completed, or brought into the second. When a young couple falls in love, they become engaged. It is a period of planning, adjusting, and developing relationship. When they enter into marriage, the engagement is gone. It has not disappeared for it is the basis of the marriage. All of its memories and influences are still there contributing to the marriage relationship. Engagement is gone, but not destroyed. It was an important period, but only as it contributed to marriage.

You and I live in the reality of the marriage. All of the Old Covenant is fulfilled in Jesus. The law with all of its requirements and the ceremonies with all of their activities come together in Jesus. I am His and He is mine! We are no longer dating; we are married. The intimacy of the fullness of the Spirit of Jesus now embraces my life. We are one. Jesus is my life! I am His and He is mine! I will not go back to duty, obligation, and commands; I will live in love, relationship, and intimacy. Jesus is my Lover! I am a Jesus pusher!!!

I am a Jesus pusher!!! When John the Baptist was imprisoned, Jesus left Judea to begin His Galilean ministry. He came to Nazareth, His home town. He preached in their synagogue, but found significant resistant among those He knew in the past. Their response was, **"Is this not Joseph's son?"** (Luke 4:23). They went to school with Him. They ran down the back alleys of Nazareth playing hide and seek. They were raised with the rumors concerning His real father. Now He comes to them as their Messiah. The scorn and ridicule of all the past years will not let them embrace Him. If they could have only seen Him as He really is! They would need to set aside their own cultural training, their personal opinions, and their prejudices. He came to Nazareth to give them a new revelation of Himself.

How often my culture and church tradition has shaped my opinion about Jesus. I have not seen Him as He really is. Jesus continually comes to my life with the revelation of Himself. All the false perceptions are overshadowed. He breaks through the hurts of my past to show Himself as true. I am discovering Jesus as He truly is. This is why I am a Jesus pusher!!! The chances are He is not as you may have thought Him to be. He wants to bring new revelation of Himself to you. This is not a theological adjustment, but an embrace of His person. Are you open to such a revelation? I am a Jesus pusher!!

I am a Jesus pusher!!! When Jesus came to Nazareth to minister, they viewed Him as *Joseph's son* (Luke 4:22). In their Old Testament framework, they wanted Him to do the same miracles among them He did in Capernaum. They thought in terms of the Old Testament self-sourcing. How could a carpenter's son source any miracle? He would have to prove it to them. The marvelous factor was not based in Jesus' heritage; it was based upon His source. In the synagogue, Jesus read from the Book of Isaiah: *"The Spirit of the Lord is upon Me, because He has anointed Me,"* (Luke 4:18). Everything Jesus did was sourced by the Spirit of God. Being Joseph's son did not source His activities.

As this passage unfolds the crowd from Nazareth was irritated to the degree they attempted to kill Him. If Jesus was sourced by *the Spirit of the Lord* should they not embrace Him as well? Was this the New Covenant beginning in Jesus? Could we also experience such a sourcing in our personal lives? Sign-seeking demands an individual prove who He is by His own resource. The New Covenant is an entirely different approach. If one is sourced by the Spirit, the power of the sourcing cannot be used as he desires. The sourced individual is not in charge but an instrument of the Spirit. If Nazareth truly wanted the movement of God, they would embrace Jesus who was sourced by the Spirit of God. The Spirit would reveal Jesus to them. I am embracing Jesus and the Spirit of God is marvelously revealing Jesus to me (John 15:26; 16:15). This is why I am a Jesus pusher!!!

Jesus PUSHER | 130

I am a Jesus pusher!!! Jesus proclaimed to His hometown, Nazareth, ***"The Spirit of the Lord is upon Me, because He has anointed Me,"*** (Luke 4:18). Then He proceeded to illustrate this reality by two examples from their Old Testament history. The first story concerned a widow from Zarephath (a Gentile city). Elijah, a prophet sourced by the Spirit of God, announced a three and one half year period without rain which produced a famine. He was instructed to go to this Gentile widow's home. She provided her last food for his meal. God sourced her bin of flour and jar of oil to never be empty (1 Kings 17:14). The second story concerned Naaman, a Gentile army commander, who had leprosy. He came to Elisha, the prophet sourced by the Spirit of God. Naaman followed the prophet's instruction and was healed.

These stories irritated the crowd in Nazareth until they attempted to kill Jesus. Their prejudice against Gentiles consumed their total attention. They missed the message of who Jesus was in their midst. My prejudices must not block His communication to my life. I must not twist His truth to fit my agenda. The glory of His presence must not be hindered by my personal convictions. I must not allow my theology (my personal reasoning) to keep me from His perspective. Everything I can produce must be set aside to allow Him to reveal and source my life. I must be a Jesus pusher because He has captured me; He is revealing Himself through me. I am a Jesus pusher because of Him!!!

I am a Jesus pusher!!! Upon the imprisonment of John the Baptist, Jesus moved His ministry to Galilee (Matthew 4:12, 13). It would have been politically correct to minister in Jerusalem, befriend the leaders of Israel, and become known in the temple. Jesus could have correctly claimed Judea as His home place; He was born in Bethlehem. But He did not; He went to Galilee. The Galileans were His people; He was raised among them. Their fishing and farming culture was His. He identified with their political struggles; He understood their economic circumstances. He spoke with their accent; He enjoyed their music. He was one of them!

I have this same personal connection to Jesus. He came from my hometown, speaks with my accent, and was raised in my environment. How can Jesus do this for all of us? A friend of mine shared with me this vision. Jesus was sitting on the throne of His Kingdom. My friend was sitting next to Him. My friend seemed so small; in fact, his feet stretched out straight on the chair as if he were a child. He asked Jesus, "Are we alone?" Jesus laughed and said, "No, there are millions of people all around." With a wave of His hand He corrected my friend's vision so all were seen. "Why are they not sitting beside you as I am?" was his next question. Jesus answered, "They are!" Let me assure you of your special connection to Him. He has your color of skin, your history, and knows your need. He is from your hometown. When He comes to where you are, He has come home! I am a Jesus pusher!!!

I am a Jesus pusher!!! Jesus ministered alongside John the Baptist for a brief period of time. When John was taken to prison, Jesus moved His ministry to Galilee. He loved the people of Judea. He wept over the city of Jerusalem. Jesus used the imagery of a hen gathering her chicks under her wing. This was His desire for them; but they would not (Matthew 23:37). He made them aware of judgment, but did it through tears and regret. They had the startling opportunity of embracing Him at His birth in Bethlehem; but they were indifferent. They soon lost their opportunity to know their King. He began His ministry among them, but quickly moved on to Galilee. One more time they lost their opportunity.

How many times has He has come to me? Has He wept over me, crying out with the desire to gather me to His protection? Has He whispered His message in my ear again and again? How many times have I resisted? How many chances have I already missed? I will miss them no longer! I am crying out to Him for deliverance from my indifference. I want the hard shell of my heart to become tender. I desperately desire to hear the whisper of His instruction in my inner heart. I will place all other voices on mute in order to hear Him alone. No other influence, no other agenda, and no other resource will be sought. He is my all in all! My heart is sensitive to His call. He embraces me. I am a Jesus pusher!!!

I am a Jesus pusher!!! Jesus left Judea in order to minister in Galilee (Matthew 4:12). There was a great need in Galilee. How could it be adequately described? The prophet states it as: *"The people who sat in darkness have seen a great light, And upon those who sat in the region and shadow of death Light has dawned,"* (Matthew 4:16). This is very strong Biblical language. It establishes contrasts. There is *light* and *darkness*; there is *light* and *the region and shadow of death*. The Jews in Jerusalem had an abundance of *light*. The scribes of the Scriptures and the temple with the very presence of God were among them. The great movements of God came to them. An angel appeared in the temple to Zacharias, the father of John the Baptist (Luke 1:8-25). Even the shepherds in this area saw the angels at the birth of Christ. Wise men from the East came to Jerusalem with the announcement. God had showered Judea with His *light.*

Now the *Light* is going to Galilee. Up to this time Galilee has been bombarded by *darkness*. The trade routes brought hundreds of people into their region spreading *darkness*. The prophet expands the contrast from *darkness* to *death*. The ultimate goal and result of *darkness* is *death*. But *Light had dawned*! Jesus has come! To every dark place of my life, He is the *light*. He did not send the *light* or describe the *light*. It is not a theology or meditation technique. He is the *Light*. I embrace Him and I see. All is exposed and I am well! I am a Jesus pusher!!!

Jesus PUSHER | 134

I am a Jesus pusher!!! Jesus received the news that John the Baptist was in prison. The projection was that he would be beheaded. Jesus immediately moved from Judea to Galilee to start a new ministry. In Galilee, He went down to His hometown Nazareth. But due to the negative reception there, He moved His home to Capernaum. One could project a lot of reasons why this took place. Was Jesus responding out of fear? Was He protecting Himself from hard times? Matthew is very bold in telling us the purpose of these decisions. He writes, *"that it might be fulfilled which was spoken by Isaiah the prophet,"* (Matthew 4:14). This is not an isolated statement. In the first four chapters of this Gospel, Matthew makes seven distinct references to prophecy. It is his pattern to stop in the midst of relating a story and refer to prophecy. Matthew is highlighting the purpose or plan God is accomplishing in this moment.

These events are not random or coincidence. From the Christmas story to John the Baptist to the Galilean ministry, Jesus is the focus of the plan. God is in charge and nothing will thwart the plan; Jesus is the plan. Things may look dark for Mary and Joseph as they flee to Egypt; but they are included in the plan, Jesus! John the Baptist may be depressed in a dungeon cell; but he is in the midst of the plan, Jesus! Do not question it! You and I are in the plan. Don't stray from the plan! This is why I am a Jesus pusher!!! He is the plan; He has included me. Don't miss the plan.

Jesus PUSHER | **135**

I am a Jesus pusher!!! The ministry of Jesus in Galilee was focused on the purpose of God. It is proven by the prophecy given by Isaiah hundreds of years before it happened (Matthew 4:14). God had a plan; Jesus is the plan! He is not like the owner of a large factory who employees hundreds of men. The owner will never meet these men; they are simply a means to an end. God's plan is Jesus; there is personal involvement in my life with Him. If this is not true, He could not be the plan. Jesus going to Galilee *fulfilled* (pleroo) what God prophesied through Isaiah. This Greek word paints the picture of an empty container. Content is placed into the empty container. The container is quickly filled, completed, or overflowing with the content. In this passage, the container is the dream in the heart of God. This dream is an intimate part of the very nature of God. To discard this dream would be to discard who He is. If this plan is not accomplished, He is left empty and unfulfilled. Jesus is found in the dream of the heart of God. Jesus is the plan.

If I miss Jesus, I miss everything that fulfills the heart of God. If I am not intimate with Jesus, I am not intimate with the heart of God. If I am not sourced by Jesus, I miss the righteousness of the heart of God. If I do not embrace Jesus, I miss the embrace of the heart of God. I must run to Jesus! There is no other place to which I can turn. In the person of Jesus I find my destiny, the plan. Jesus is where I belong; He is home! There is safety in Him; He is the haven of my soul! I am a Jesus pusher!!!

I am a Jesus pusher!!! God has an awesome plan. Jesus is the plan! Let me illustrate this with the young man who is desperately in love. His dream is not simply of a person to maintain his household; he could hire a maid for such a purpose. His plan is not just someone to "mother" his future children; he could hire a nanny. His wish is not just for companionship; he could secure an escort. At the core of his nature and being is all we conceive in marriage. It is all the above only with the cement of intimacy and oneness. It is not a plan he has which someone else can fulfill in his absence. Love demands the presence of the young man in the midst of the plan and dream. In fact, in a real sense, he is the plan.

Jesus is the plan and dream of God! The plan is not a project; the plan is not a venture. The plan is not an attempt or experiment. God does not have a plan apart from us. He descended from His throne to become one of us. Now we see that He is the dream and the plan. Everything God dreamed for us is found in Jesus. I am to be found in Him. In speaking of the fulfillment of the plan, Jesus said, ***"I am in My Father, and you in Me, and I in you,"*** (John 14:20). This is the ultimate of relationship. Love is fulfilled in oneness. While we may care for the house, watch over the children, and cook the meals, we are in the embrace of the One who loves us. We are in His plan. Jesus is the plan. I am a Jesus pusher!!!

I am a Jesus pusher!!! There are many great *"I am"* statements of Jesus. ***Jesus said to him, "I am the way, the truth and the life,"*** (John 14:6). ***Jesus said to them, "Most assuredly, I say to you, before Abraham was, I AM,"*** (John 8:58). Jesus said, ***"I am the bread of life,"*** (John 6:48). Jesus said to them, ***"I am the good shepherd,"*** (John 10:11). He also said, ***"Most assuredly, I say to you, I am the door of the sheep,"*** (John 10:7). In each of these statements, Jesus is stating who He is. But notice, it is a statement of who He is in connection with us. He is only the ***door of the sheep*** because we are His sheep. He is the ***way*** because I desperately need direction for my life. He is the ***truth*** because I am lost in confusion. He is the great ***I AM*** because there is no eternal life for me without Him. The fact of these various needs is my life does not create or cause them in Him. He is these things without me and before me. The fact I need eternal life does not make Him the great ***I AM***. He is the great ***I AM*** who created me in His image. Therefore, because of who He is, I can become. He is the ***way*** whether I exist or not. However, I was created by Him in His likeness; therefore, He is my ***way***.

God has a plan; it is Jesus. Everything that makes me the complete person I was created to be is found in Jesus. Therefore, Jesus is the plan for my life. Outside of Him there is nothing but chaos, destruction, and dismay. He is where I belong. I live in Him, the plan of God. I am a Jesus pusher!!!

Jesus PUSHER | **138**

I am Jesus pusher!!! Jesus moved His ministry from Judea to Galilee upon hearing John the Baptist was imprisoned. Matthew clearly states this was done ***that it might be fulfilled which was spoken by Isaiah the prophet*** (Matthew 4:14). The main verb of this statement (***fulfilled***) is in the subjunctive mood. This suggests the idea of "if" or "maybe." Matthew is highlighting the "choice" or "free will" of men; he is not undermining the certainty of prophecy. What God speaks is as certain as the very character and nature of God. Sometimes God speaks; therefore, it is true. But often God speaks because it is true. God speaks; worlds are created. But God also recognizes the responsibility of man. God speaks not to cause man's actions, but knowing man's actions. This is true for the Scriptures. Things are not true because they are in the Scriptures. They are in the Scriptures because they are true. God is speaking the Scriptures through His knowledge of all things. There is no doubt about the certainty of the Scriptures or prophecy.

This declares God's plan is secure. Jesus is this plan. The Jewish leaders can plot against Him; the Roman soldiers can crucify Him; John the Baptist can be imprisoned; you and I can disbelieve Him. It simply does not change the plan. The certainty of the plan does not rest upon my choice or response; it depends upon the character of God. Jesus, the plan, is the declaration of the character of God. He is the plan for my life; I will not miss Him. I am a Jesus pusher!!!

I am a Jesus pusher!!! Through the first four chapters of Matthew's Gospel account, he highlights prophecy seven times. Nearly every paragraph is explained in light of the prophetic pronouncement of the Old Testament. He explains Jesus' departure from Judea to Galilee, the beginning of a new ministry, as a result of *that it might be fulfilled which was* spoken by *Isaiah the prophet* (Matthew 4:14). It is startling that the main verb (*fulfilled*) is in the subjunctive mood. This suggests the idea of "if" or "maybe." Matthew is not proposing the uncertainty of prophecy. He is stating the element of choice for those participating within the fulfillment of the prophecy. Herod Antipas who imprisoned John the Baptist had a choice and is responsible for this action. Jesus was not forced to move His ministry to Galilee because of this prophecy. The citizens of Nazareth are responsible for their actions in attempting to kill Jesus (Luke 4:29).

In the circumstances of my life, I have a choice. It is true, God has a plan. Jesus is intimately involved in those plans; in fact, Jesus is the plan. He does not have a plan apart from us; He came to embrace us in the fulfillment of the plan. However, all of this is contingent upon my response to Him. Why would I not want to respond to Him? Everything outside of Him is death; it is in Him I find life. Jesus has a plan; Jesus is the plan; Jesus, the plan, indwells me. I am in the middle of the flowing plan of God in Jesus. I am a Jesus pusher!!!

———————

I am a Jesus pusher!!! Jesus moved His ministry to Galilee. The prophet Isaiah, quoted by Matthew, describes the people of Galilee. He writes, *"The people who sat in darkness have seen a great light,"* (Matthew 4:16). *"People"* is the subject of this sentence. *"Who sat"* describes them. The original prophecy (Isaiah 9:2) states, *The people who walked in darkness*. Evidently Matthew changed the word in order to increase the intensity of their condition. The conquering force of darkness had increased since the original prophecy. The Greek word (kathemai) translated *sat* is also used to refer to Jesus sitting at the right hand of the Father. It suggests the image of a person of great authority sitting in a place of great authority. Darkness so encompassed the people they are conquered by darkness and embrace it as their chosen desire. Never discount or treat lightly the impacting, controlling, dominating, inclusive force of sin. The imagery of *darkness* is very plain. Picture yourself in total darkness! All sense of direction is lost. The fright of the unknown paralyzes you from taking even one step. Every sound is terrifying. It is ultimate death. Perhaps seven hundred years earlier they were walking in darkness; now they are sitting.

Let us rush to the glorious news! They *have seen a great light!* Jesus came to them! No one else came. Not an abundance of supply or a team of experts came. Only Jesus came. He was the total answer to the great *darkness* that ruled their lives for hundreds of years. He is the light of God to my life. He is the ability to see. Wisdom and understanding are found in Him alone. He gives me direction. I have seen a great Light. I am a Jesus pusher!!!

I am a Jesus pusher!!! The prophecy of Isaiah describes the people of Galilee: ***The people who sat in darkness have seen a great light*** (Matthew 4:16). The verb of the sentence is ***have seen*** (eido). It means "to see" or "to perceive." There is an amazing interaction between this verb and the accusative (direct object) of the sentence, ***light***. ***Light*** is receiving the action of the verb. It is a contrast between people who are immersed in ***darkness*** and who now comprehend the ***great light***. The Greek word (mega) translated ***great*** expands the force of the ***light***.

The Greek word (phos) translated ***light*** comes from the root word "phao." It is also the root word for "phone," which is translated "to shine" or "sound." It is the basis for our word "telephone." It is the instrument through which a message comes. John the Baptist was the "phone" (***voice***) ***of one crying in the wilderness*** (Matthew 3:3). This concept of instrument is also contained in the ***light***. The ***light*** is the instrument by which you see your surroundings, but you do not see the ***light***. The ***light*** is actually ***life*** (John 1:4). It is the ***life***, which gives you the ***light***. Thus the ***life*** is the source of the ***light*** giving you the ability to perceive the ***life***. ***Light*** is an instrument by which the ***life*** embraces you. Do you embrace the ***light*** or does the ***life*** embrace you through the ***light***? Since Jesus is the ***light*** and the ***life*** it does not matter. It is HIM. I am a Jesus pusher!!!

I am a Jesus pusher!!! The sun produces the daylight. It is the revelation or instrument of its revelation. The daylight enables us to see our surroundings; it gives us life. Vitamins and nutrients are shared with us from the sun through the light. The sun, the source, gives us warmth through the light. How can one separate the daylight from the sun? They are inseparable! Jesus was filled with the Spirit; He is a Spirit-sourced Man. Jesus has ***departed to Galilee*** (Matthew 4:12). ***The people*** of Galilee ***who sat in darkness have seen a great light*** (Matthew 4:16). They are conquered, embraced, and overwhelmed with darkness. But the Father, through the Spirit-sourced Son, shined upon them. Revelation containing life, nutrition, and vision came to them; it is a new day!

The ***light*** came to them! They ***sat in darkness***. Does one see the ***light*** or does the ***light*** reveal itself? Does it actually force one into seeing? An individual can close their eyes, but the light is so great it forces its way through closed eyelids. Revelation will come; it cannot be stopped. Here is the promise: ***And the light shines in the darkness, and the darkness did not comprehend*** (overcome) ***it*** (John 1:5). I may be a Jesus pusher; but Jesus is His own pusher! He is revealing Himself; you cannot miss Him. He is pressing Himself upon your life. I am a Jesus pusher!!!

I am a Jesus pusher!!! "Prevenient grace" is the basis of all theology. It appears repeatedly in our studies. How could it not? It is so important. It may be necessary to speak of it every time we assemble. The meaning of "prevenient" is "going before." Another word for "grace" is "love." Therefore, prevenient grace is the love of God, which goes before any and every response of man. God initiates every encounter with Himself. He is after us! We cannot claim our discovery of God as a result of our effort. We did not learn, search, develop, or invent even the slightest knowledge of Him. Your first desire for God came from Him. He brought revelation to your life.

Seven hundred years prior to Jesus' ministry in Galilee, God spoke through a prophet. This prophecy is a revelation of prevenient grace. *The people who sat in darkness have seen a great light* (Matthew 4:16). They were overcome, submerged, and immersed in darkness. Absolute despair is the picture. Then Jesus, the *light*, came. God brought the *light*. No explanation is possible. This is "revelation." Man saw because Jesus revealed. Man heard because Jesus spoke. Man knows because Jesus imparted. The height of stupidity is to claim the right to stand before God as if we placed ourselves there. How could we earn the right? This self-pride is the epitome of the heart of evil. We fell into the depth of a pit; God has rescued us! We have strayed as sheep; the Good Shepherd has found us. We are the prodigal sons in the pigpen; the Father embraces us. Jesus comes to us! I am a Jesus pusher!!!

I am a Jesus pusher!!! ***The people who sat in darkness have seen a great light*** (Matthew 4:16). This refers to the people of Galilee. Jesus fulfilled the prophecy of Isaiah. But it is true of us all! Listen to the words of Paul to Titus, ***"For the grace of God that brings salvation has appeared to all men,"*** (Titus 2:11). The Greek word (epiphaino) translated ***has appeared*** is a combination of two Greek words. The first one presents the idea of "over," "upon," or "to." The second word means, "to shine." Paul portrays the idea of ***light***. This Greek word (epiphaino) appears first in the Greek text. Evidently Paul felt this was the most important part of his statement. God takes the initiative; He encounters every one!

No one can possibly miss the ***light***. ***The people who sat in darkness have seen a great light*** (Matthew 4:16). ***And the light shines in the darkness, and the darkness did not comprehend it*** (John 1:5). These statements establish the invincibility of the ***light***. The ***darkness*** cannot overcome the ***light***. This eliminates every excuse. No one can plead ignorance. No one can plead only one chance. The ***light*** continually shines. The ***light*** is shining even now in the ***darkness*** into which you and I may have wandered. This ***light*** is Jesus. He is our Way Out! I am a Jesus pusher!!!

I am a Jesus pusher!!! Matthew describes the ministry of Jesus in Galilee. It is a quote of Isaiah, the prophet, ***"The people who sat in darkness have seen a great light,"*** (Matthew 4:16). Consider yourself in a room of absolute darkness. A simple match is struck. It cannot be missed. No one can exclaim, "I did not see it!" Matthew highlights the word "***light***" with an adjective. It is the Greek word (mega) translated **great**. If the smallest **light** must be seen, how could the **mega light** be missed? In the great Book of Romans, Paul establishes this clearly. He declares, ***"What may be known of God is manifested in them, for God has shown it to them. For since the creation of the world His invisible attributes are clearly seen, being understood by the things that are made, even His eternal power and Godhead, so that they are without excuse,"*** (Romans 1:19- 20).

There is a revelation (***light***), which comes "to us" and is "in us." We not only know from the outside; we know from the inside. Everyman has this ***light***. While this is true in general, it is also true in particular. We are included in the revelation of God through Jesus from without and from within. Why would we not respond to the revelation of Jesus? To resist Him is to resist everything that is good for us. All barriers are removed; all excuses are set aside. I am embracing the One who is truth. I am a Jesus pusher!!!

———————————

I am a Jesus pusher!!! Matthew is very clear; Jesus is the *light*. Jesus *departed to Galilee* (Matthew 4:12). He is the fulfillment of the prophecy quoted from Isaiah, *"The people who sat in darkness have seen a great light,"* (Matthew 4:16). They saw Jesus! There is such an abundance of Scripture testifying to this truth. *In Him* (Jesus) *was life, and the life was the light of men. And the light shines in the darkness, and the darkness did not comprehend it.* (John 1:4-5). *That was the true Light, which gives light to every man coming into the world* (John 1:9). Jesus proclaimed Himself to be this *Light. Then Jesus spoke to them again, saying, "I am the light of the world. He who follows Me shall not walk in darkness, but have the light of life"* (John 8:12).

The *light* for every crisis is Jesus. When Jesus referred to Himself as the *light of the world* (John 8:12), He was *in the treasury, as He taught in the temple;* (John 8:20). The temple treasury was the outer court, the court of the women. It was the conclusion of the feast of Tabernacles. At that feast the Jews celebrated the illumination of the Temple. A massive series of candelabras were placed in the middle of this court. For one week a great stream of light would shine out continuously. This commemorated the pillar of fire that led Israel during the wilderness wanderings under Moses. As Jesus entered the court of the women, the light had just been extinguished. The candelabra were still in place, but they gave no light. Jesus declares that He Himself is *the light of the world* that will never go out. He is your *light*! I am a Jesus pusher!!!

Jesus PUSHER | 147

I am a Jesus pusher!!! ***The people who sat in darkness have seen a great light. And upon those who sat in the region and shadow of death, Light has dawned*** (Matthew 4:16). Jesus was going to Galilee to establish a new ministry. The people of this area are described as "sitting" in a place. It is not described in physical boundaries such as ***the land of Zebulun and the land of Naphtali*** (Matthew 4:15) even though this was their physical location. It is described as ***the region and shadow of death***. The Greek word (chora) translated ***region*** usually refers to an uninhabited or sparsely settled land in contrast to cultivated area or cities. In our passage this refers to a dwelling place over which there is a ***shadow of death***. It is a dwelling place (abstract), which is not a place (concrete)! This does not mean it is not real, but it is not a description of a physical place.

In the Scriptures, there is a spiritual reality in our lives, which is referred to as a place. I cannot physically remove myself from this place. In other words, if I physically relocate, I simply take my spiritual place with me. I do not move in and out of this spiritual dwelling. It is like a gigantic bubble surrounding me at all times. It is the very atmosphere of my being. It is my "spot." Often, I thought my personal problems were caused by my physical location; in reality, they are a result of my spiritual place. Jesus invades my spiritual dwelling; He is the ***light***! I give Him the right of way in my dwelling place. I am a Jesus pusher!!!

I am a Jesus pusher!!! The Galilean ministry of Jesus is described as a ministry in the ***shadow of death*** (Matthew 4:16). Death is actually personified. A shadow is the darkness cast upon a place by a body raised between it and the light. In this passage ***death*** is Satan who is blocking the light. The people of Galilee missed the light intended for them from the Old Testament. They dwell in ***darkness***.

Have you ever been totally frustrated with someone? It is so obvious to you that they are in a place of darkness. They cause their own ruin and destruction. How could you explain it to them? It is not about intellectual information or data. It is about a dwelling place. Their ***light*** is being blocked. They live in the ***shadow of death***.

The Gospel is the good news! ***Light has dawned*** (Matthew 4:16). The Greek word (anatello) translated ***has dawned*** is used nine times in the New Testament. It is used six times in connection with the sun. It has the idea of "springing up." Jesus departed from Judea and came to Galilee to begin His ministry. This is described as the ***light*** springing up in the spiritual place of darkness. Satan stood between the people of Galilee and the light. Jesus out maneuvered him. Jesus, the ***light***, comes to my dark place! I am a Jesus pusher!!!

I am a Jesus pusher!!! ***From that time Jesus began to preach and to say, "Repent, for the kingdom of heaven is at hand,"*** (Matthew 4:17). ***Jesus*** is the subject of the sentence. The main verb is the Greek word (archomai) translated ***began***. The Greek word (tote) translated ***that time*** is an adverb meaning "after that." ***Jesus began*** after His departure from Judea, going to Galilee. The verb (archomai) comes from the root Greek word (archo) meaning, "to be first." It most often refers to political rank or power. Our main verb is in the middle voice expressing the internal heart of Jesus beginning something new in Galilee.

The emphasis is blaring! Jesus responds to His heart's cry for the people of Galilee. The sophisticated, wealthy, legalistic, and narrow Jews of Jerusalem repeatedly refused the ministry of John the Baptist and Jesus. They did not embrace the introduction of the Kingdom of Heaven. In contrast, the people of Galilee, ***who sat in darkness,*** had such great need. Their great distress caused them to cry out. In which group am I? Jesus sees my need! I am open to Him! He comes to me! His heart's cry is for you as well! Could we respond together? I am a Jesus pusher!!!

I am a Jesus pusher!!! ***From that time Jesus began to preach and to say, "Repent, for the kingdom of heaven is at hand,"*** (Matthew 4:17). Matthew gives content to the ministry Jesus ***began*** in Galilee with two additional verbs. They are in the infinitive mood and are used as adverbs. ***Jesus began to preach and to say***. The first statement is a broader approach to the content while the second statement points directly to the content of the quotation.

The Greek word (kerysso) is translated ***to preach***. In the New Testament "preaching" plays a major role in the spreading of the Gospel. It is used sixty-one times as a verb. It is fundamentally a declaration of an event. It is contrasted with the idea of teaching (edidasken). Preaching is the statement of certainties, not the proclamation of possibilities. It is not to argue, reason, dispute, or convince by intellectual proof. A keen intellect can bring counterargument to all or any of these. It is the proclamation of what is, truth. Preaching is not information about Jesus; it is the revelation of Jesus. Preaching contains the mystical movement of His very person. Other subjects can lectured; the Gospel must be preached. It contains an anointing, which is His very presence. Regardless of speaking skills, techniques, or knowledge, preaching is not experienced without Him. He said, ***"I am the way, the truth, and the life,"*** (John 14:6). We are literally confronted with Him through preaching! I am a Jesus pusher!!!

I am a Jesus pusher!!! *From that time Jesus began to preach* (Mathew 4:17). Adequate preaching must be permeated with authority. According to Matthew, Jesus preached with great authority. At the close of the Sermon on the Mount, he records, *And so it was, when Jesus had ended these sayings, that the people were astonished at His teaching, for He taught them as one having authority, not as the scribes* (Matthew 7:28-29). Jesus' authority came from the Father through the Scriptures. The scribes mixed their declarations of the Scriptures with their own traditions and interpretations. This reduced their presentations to their own opinions; it produced great division and arguments. In the Sermon on the Mount, Jesus presented to them the fullness of the Scripture. In fact, He proclaimed the fulfillment of the Law and the Prophets (Matthew 5:17-20). This great sermon was the proclamation of the content's fulfillment. A brilliant mind, talented persuasion, or skillful debate, were not the basis of His preaching. Jesus was saturated in the Father through the Scriptures.

Jesus, after being raised from the dead, shared with two of His disciples. *And beginning at Moses and all the Prophets, He expounded them in all the Scriptures the things concerning Himself* (Luke 24:27). He based His entire life on the Scriptures. He believed in the validity of the first five books of the Old Testament. This was the basis of His authority. As Jesus shared the Scriptures with these two disciples their hearts burned within them (Luke 24:32). I want Jesus to share His Word with me. Does my heart burn? I am a Jesus pusher!!!

I am a Jesus pusher!!! Matthew gives us insight into the core of Jesus' preached message. ***From that time Jesus began to preach and to say, "Repent, for the kingdom of heaven is at hand,"*** (Matthew 4:17). "***To preach***" is the broad view of His message. The Greek word (lego) translated "***to say***" is the narrow view of the content. It is an adverb giving content to the main verb, ***began***. It paints the picture of laying things together or to collect. Jesus' preaching was a discourse where significant words are linked together. It is ***"Repent, for the kingdom of heaven is at hand."***

The foundation of repentance is the nearness of the Kingdom. The Greek word (gar) translated ***for*** is a causative particle. It is placed after one or more words in a clause to express the reason for what was previously presented. The call is to ***repent***. The reason for such a response is ***the kingdom of heaven is at hand***. One does not repent and the Kingdom comes. The Kingdom comes; we must respond by repentance. This is the Biblical order! Jesus, the King, comes to my life; I am drawn to the response of repentance. I could resist; why would I want to? All the provisions of the Kingdom are contained in Jesus. I can repent and embrace it all in Him. What a privilege! I am a Jesus pusher!!!

I am a Jesus pusher!!! The message of Jesus was *"Repent, for the kingdom of heaven is at hand,"* (Matthew 4:17). The Kingdom of Heaven is presenting itself to you. You should respond by repentance. Paul gave the same message. He writes, *"I beseech you therefore, brethren, by the mercies of God, that you present your bodies a living sacrifice, holy acceptable to God which is your reasonable service,"* (Romans 12:1). The basis of his presentation is very clear. *"Therefore"* links this statement to the previous verses. These verses highlight the great mercies of God (Romans 11:30-36). This is the Biblical order! God pours out His mercy upon us; we respond by presenting ourselves to Him as *living sacrifices*.

No wonder Paul writes, *"Or do you despise the riches of His goodness, forbearance, and longsuffering, not knowing that the goodness of God leads you to repentance?"* (Romans 2:4). One does not receive the goodness of God after he repents; rather one receives the goodness of God and is moved to repentance. Repentance does not cause Jesus to reconcile with us; rather reconciliation is all around us calling us to repentance. Repentance is the natural response to the love of God, which is embracing us this moment! Jesus has come to us; will we respond? I am a Jesus pusher!!!

———————

I am a Jesus pusher!!! Peter preached a sermon explaining the Pentecost event. It brought such conviction three thousand Jews were converted to Jesus. This group joined the one hundred and twenty disciples to form the early church. Luke gives us a description of the state of this group as they developed into the body of Christ (Acts 2:40-47). The emphasis in this statement begins with "subtracting" (Acts 2:40). He quickly shifts the emphasis to "addition" (Acts 2:41). In other words, the new converts were removed from one group and added to another group. Each group is clearly defined, but the greater description is the group to which they are added.

The language of "subtracting" and "adding" is consistently used in the New Testament. Paul declares, ***"He has delivered us from the power of darkness and conveyed us into the kingdom of the Son of His love,"*** (Colossians 1:13). "Light and darkness," "love and hate," "Kingdom of God and Kingdom of this world," and "truth and deception," are used to highlight "subtraction" and "addition." There is not a third or fourth group! There are only two groups. We are either in the Kingdom of God or the Kingdom of Satan. We either walk in light or we walk in darkness. We cannot serve two masters (Matthew 6:24). I want Jesus as my Master! I am a Jesus pusher!!!

I am a Jesus pusher!!! Peter preached a sermon explaining the Pentecost event (Acts 2:14-39). His entire explanation is Jesus! What God, the Father, did in and through Jesus, He now wants to do in and through us. The Jews of the Dispersion **were cut to the heart** for they had crucified Jesus (Acts 2:37). Peter did not give the final "amen" and then leave; he stayed and continued to clarify the spiritual truth. Luke writes, **"And with many other words he testified and exhorted them,"** (Acts 2:40). The first word in the Greek text (heteros) is translated **other**. This highlights the additional discussion. Peter answered their questions and constantly brought them back to Jesus. It may have been a lengthy time.

Peter **testified** during this dialogue (Acts 2:40). The Greek word (diemarturato) is the root word for "testify" with a prefix (dia), which intensifies the witness. It expresses a pleading with them. He told them his experience with Jesus. He denied Jesus three times; yet Jesus forgave him. Would He not do the same for them? Peter **exhorted** during this dialogue (Acts 2:40). This Greek word (parakaleo) comes from "para" (to the side of) and "kaleo" (to call). It means to aid, help, comfort, or encourage. It is in the imperfect tense expressing "kept on exhorting." Peter could not keep silent about Jesus. They must embrace Him. The subject of Peter's sermon, his testimony, and his exhorting was Jesus. He was a Jesus pusher!!!

I am a Jesus pusher!!! After Peter's sermon explaining the Pentecost event, **with many other words he testified and exhorted them, saying, "Be saved from this perverse generation,"** (Acts 2:40). Eugene Peterson renders this verse in The Message: **He went on in this vein for a long time, urging them over and over, "Get out while you can; get out of this sick and stupid culture!"** The heart of his appeal is **"Be saved."** This Greek word (sozo) is used fifty-four times in the Gospels. It is used fourteen times to describe deliverance from disease or demon possession; twenty times its usage is connected with the rescue of physical life from some impending peril or instant death. Spiritual salvation is the emphasis of the remaining twenty times.

The tone of its usage is the atmosphere of severe and serious peril. Demon possession, crippling disease, instant death, and spiritual damnation are all pending. As these monsters draw close, one must escape in order to survive. This Greek word (sozo) translated **Be saved** is the act of that escape. Peter makes it abundantly clear in his declaration: Jesus is our only salvation! There is no other to which we can turn. There is no certainty in the strength of others. No other provision is adequate. We have one single chance to escape. Jesus is the answer whatever form the peril of doom takes! It is not too late. Jesus can rescue! I am a Jesus pusher!!!

I am a Jesus pusher!!! Peter **testified, and exhorted them, saying, "Be saved from this perverse generation,"** (Acts 2:40). The urgency to escape the pending peril is captured in the Greek word (apo) translated **from**. It expresses motion and change of location. It states the separation of a person or an object from another person or an object with which it was formerly united but is now separated. The Message by Eugene Peterson gives the correct emphasis, **"Get out while you can; get out of this sick and stupid culture!"**

The main verb of this call is **Be saved** (sozo). It is in the imperative mood, making it a command. It has an assumed subject of "you." However, it is in the passive voice. This means the subject is NOT responsible for the action of the verb, but is receiving the action from another source. In this statement, it is called a "Divine Action!" It is not stated in the verse, but is assumed due to all Peter preached. There is no emphasis in this verse to save oneself. We cannot reprogram our thought process. We cannot resist the culture in which we are raised. Family connection and religious practices have shaped our lives. We are a part of **this perverse generation**. If we cannot save ourselves, how will we be saved? Jesus is the answer! Will we allow Him to do for us what we cannot do. He made us aware of our need; He provides the understanding of the answer; He expresses His love and desire to save us. He has done everything up to this point. Will we let Him complete the task? Jesus is our salvation!!! I am a Jesus pusher!!!

I am a Jesus pusher!!! Peter preached Jesus to the Jews of the Dispersion (Acts 2:14-39). They stood guilty before the truth concerning Jesus. They were a part of *this perverse generation* because they crucified Jesus. There was only one issue; it is Jesus. The content of Peter's sermon was about Jesus. The *many more words* he shared with them was about Jesus. When Peter *testified*, the content was about Jesus. He *exhorted* them about Jesus. His call to *repent* (give up a former thought to embrace a new thought) was focused on Jesus. He urged them to be baptized into Jesus. This is all about Jesus.

This identical scene plays again in our lives. Jesus has come to us! We must escape from the group, the culture, and the influence, which masters and dominates us. I would cry out to you, *"Get out while you can; get out of this sick and stupid culture!"* It may be a drug culture, an alcoholic culture, a materialistic culture, or even a religious culture. The call of the Gospel is to be subtracted from that influence and be added to another influence. Come from the Kingdom of Darkness and enter the Kingdom of Light. What is wrong with the culture? It is how it relates to Jesus! We must embrace Jesus. Whatever our focus, it must now be overshadowed with the sight of Jesus. Whatever controls our lives must now be subjected to Jesus. The direction in which we are going must now be the Way, Jesus. Jesus is our one chance! I am a Jesus pusher!!!

I am a Jesus pusher!!! What a day of ministry it was for Peter. *And with many other words he testified and exhorted them, saying, "Be saved from this perverse generation,"* (Acts 2:40). There is a strong emphasis of "subtraction" in this challenge. They must be removed from what controls them. Their culture, religious traditions, and self-protection have pushed them to crucify Jesus. Peter urges them to be removed from this control. But this is only half of the story. They were to be subtracted from one group in order to be added to another group. Luke writes, *"Then those who gladly received his word were baptized; and that day about three thousand souls were added to them,"* (Acts 2:41). Eugene Peterson, in The Message writes, *"That day about three thousand took him at his word, were baptized and were signed up."*

Luke gives only one verse expressing the "subtraction." However, he spends the rest of the paragraph (Acts 2:41-47) describing the "addition." Christianity is not a mere correction of some activities in our lives. It is completely beyond a token attendance to a different organization. There is a *"signing up"* taking place. It is a change in location from one group to another group. "Jesus" is our new location. We change our focus to Him. What motivates us is now Him. Jesus is the all encompassing driving force of our lives. I am "signed up." I am a Jesus pusher!!!

———————

I am a Jesus pusher!!! Peter spent much time with the Jews of the Dispersion. After an entire sermon, he testified, exhorted, and clarified their need. ***Then those who gladly received his word were baptized; and that day about three thousand souls were added to them*** (Acts 2:41). What a description of these new converts! They are ***those who gladly received***. It is a translation of the Greek word "apodechomai." "Apo" is the prefix, which means "from." The main Greek word is "dechomai," which means "to take or to receive." It is in the middle voice, which focuses on their personal preference. It helps to form the subject of the sentence. This verb is only used seven times in the New Testament. Exclusively Luke uses it. Luke uses this word six times to express the joy and openness of those who welcome a person or a group of persons.

However, in our passage, Luke uses it to focus on receiving ***his word***. What a moment it was in the lives of these Jews. The devastating reality of their guilt was followed by the message of forgiveness. Jesus was the content of ***his word***. Everything they missed, they could now possess in Jesus. Everything they had pushed out of their lives, they could now embrace as theirs in Jesus. God's plan as fulfilled in Jesus could be their experienced. Love, peace, forgiveness, and the fullness of the Spirit of God is now theirs in Jesus. No wonder they embrace this word with gladness! It is the good news of Jesus. What a privilege to bear news of victory. I am a Jesus pusher!!!

I am a Jesus pusher!!! The report of the evangelism after Pentecost is amazing. ***Then those who gladly received his word were baptized; and that day about three thousand souls were added to them*** (Acts 2:41). The Greek word (logos) translated ***word*** is very suggestive. It is the Greek word strongly used for Jesus (John 1:1). Whether or not Luke had this in mind as he wrote this verse could be debated. However, there is absolutely no doubt the content of Peter's preaching is Jesus. Every detail describes Jesus. The call of the message demands a response to the person of Jesus. Their treatment of Jesus was the guilt of the listeners. The connection between the ***word*** (logos) and Jesus is clear.

We must return to the contrast of two Greek words. The Greek word "phone" is translated "voice" (Matthew 3:3), "sound" (John 3:8), and "noise" (Revelation 6:1). "Logos" is translated ***word***. "Logos" is the rational thought of the mind. "Phone" is the instrument through which the "logos" is delivered. Biblical scholars from the earliest days contrast John the Baptist, the "phone," with Jesus, the "Logos!" John was ***the voice*** (phone) ***of one crying in the wilderness*** (John 1:23), but Jesus was emphatically declared to be the ***Word*** (Logos) ***that was with God and was God*** (John 1:1). The highest privilege is for you and me to be the "phone" giving expression to the "Logos" who is within us! I am a Jesus pusher!!!

I am a Jesus pusher!!! The content of Peter's explanation of Pentecost to the Jews of the Dispersion is Jesus. Luke records, ***Then those who gladly received his word*** (logos) ***were baptized; and that day about three thousand souls were added to them*** (Acts 2:41). The connection between the ***word*** (logos) and Jesus is clear. Biblical scholars consistently contrast "logos" with "phone." "Phone" is the Greek word translated "voice." It is the instrument giving expression to the rational thought or idea, which is "logos." A "word" is something even without a "voice." A "word" in the heart is truly a word before it is spoken and even after the speaking is completed. A "voice" is a meaningless sound, an empty cry, unless it also is the vehicle of a "word." When they are united communication takes place.

There is a sense in which the "voice" precedes the "word." The sound strikes the ear before the sense is conveyed to the mind. Although the "voice" precedes the "word," the "voice" is not really before the "word." The "word" is always before the "voice." When we speak, the "word" in our hearts must precede the "voice on our lips. The "voice" is the vehicle by which the "word" in us is transferred and becomes a "word" to others. In the act of accomplishing this, the "voice" passes away, but the "word" planted in the hearts of others and in the speaker remains. Peter is filled with the ***Word*** (Logos). He becomes the "voice" (phone) of that ***Word***. I want my life to be the "voice" (phone) of Jesus, the Word (Logos). I am a Jesus pusher!!!

I am a Jesus pusher!!! After Peter's explanation of Pentecost, Luke writes, ***Then those who gladly received his word were baptized; and that day about three thousand souls were added to them*** (Acts 2:41). According to Peter's instructions, they were to ***be baptized in the name of Jesus Christ*** (Acts 2:38). This was very significant for the Jews who actually participated in crucifying Jesus. It would require a complete change of mind (repentance). If a Jew received baptism in this Name, he was excluded from all communication with his countrymen. It would mean renouncing Judaism, and all the political advantages connected with it. The Jewish family life revolved around the local synagogue. They would no longer be welcome in such a gathering. This would affect their jobs and economy. The cost of embracing Jesus was very high!

Is Jesus of greater value than all these other items? Not just a single item is being considered, but all issues connected to Jewish living are brought together. Is He of greater value than my culture, family life, political advantages, economy, and personal life? Is He of more value than my physical comfort and safety? Were the martyrs of the early church wasting their lives on worthless issues of religion? All who truly experience Jesus testify of His extreme value! They too become Jesus pushers!!!

Jesus PUSHER | 164

I am a Jesus pusher!!! In response to Peter's sermon, **that day about three thousand souls were added to them** (Acts 2:41). The Greek word (prosetetheesan) translated **were added** is very strong. This word is used to signify the act by which cities, towns, or provinces change their masters, and put themselves under another government. Peter is calling these Jews to transfer from one ruler to another. Three thousand people left the scribes, Pharisees, and Jewish traditions in order to place themselves under the teaching of the apostles. They embraced Christ as the promised and only Messiah.

Let's thoroughly grasp what this suggests. This means more than making some improvements. It is not ceasing certain deeds and beginning others. You can come to church and work on adjusting your attitude without being **added**. All of us can use some help in our family relationships. None of us are perfect and are open to instruction. But the call of Jesus is far beyond this procedure. It is a line drawn in the sand. It is stepping from one group to another. It is the changing of Kingdoms. It is about being **added** (prosetetheesan). Jesus is now going to be the Ruler in my life. He alone shall dominate and dictate. He is worthy of this position. In fact, it is the only position He can occupy. I am a Jesus pusher!!!

I am a Jesus pusher!!! Jesus is so attractive to me. What is it about Him that causes my entire being to respond? The consistency of His nature reassures me. His holiness pulls me to goodness. His love embraces me and will not let me go. His wisdom challenges me to know more. His attitude draws me to all that is positive. His emotional stability presents me with a foundation for stable living. His wholeness assures me that I can be complete in Him. The light of His countenance brightens my life. His resurrected life allows me to live in Him. His complete serenity brings rest to my soul. The boundaries of His arms will not let me stray. His crucifixion assures me of His love. His reigning Lordship tells me nothing can harm me. His authority over all things shrinks all obstacles. His generous heart gives me all I can ever need. His penetrating eyesight gives me guidance. His amazing discernment erases confusion. His shared power gives me confidence in every situation. His grace and mercy embrace me in every failure. Why does He attract me? I was made for Him! I cannot live without Him; why would I want to try?

I am a Jesus pusher!!! The protection of His presence is greater than a big brother. His guidance for my daily living gives clarity to all my actions. His insight allows me to see the need of those who are hurting. His tender mercy blocks all revenge as it spill through my life. His uncomprehending forgiveness so startles me that I share it with others. Hatred becomes impossible in light of His presence. I live in peace! I am a Jesus pusher!!!

———————

I am a Jesus pusher!!! I am not the only Jesus pusher. The early church believers were focused on Jesus. They stepped from the traditions of the scribes and Pharisees to the **apostles' doctrine** (Acts 2:42). This means they moved from crucifying Jesus to embracing Him! It was actually a "state of being." Luke writes, **"And they continued steadfastly in the apostles' doctrine and fellowship,"** (Acts 2:42). The first Greek word (eimi) translated **"they"** is actually "they were." In the first person it is "I am." It is in the imperfect tense expressing the concept of "keeping on." This is not a new series of activities, the study of a new philosophy, or the adopting of new religious ceremonies. This is a new spiritual location, a state of being. Jesus is the new location.

How can one actually dwell in Jesus? This terminology is used repeatedly in the New Testament. We are actually "in Christ." We are also told again and again that Christ is in us! This is the wonder of a relationship so close it can only be expressed as "in." His actual nature dwells within us; in response to His presence we become in Him. What drives Him now drives us. We take on the mind of Christ! It is described as "oneness," "children," and "bride." We are intimate with Jesus! I am a Jesus pusher!!!

Jesus PUSHER | **167**

I am a Jesus pusher!!! The early believers found new life in Jesus. In this new location, **they continued steadfastly** (Acts 2:42). This phrase is a translation of the third Greek word (proskartereo) in the sentence. It is a participle in the nominative case. Thus it modifies the subject of the sentence, **they**. The root Greek word (kartereo) means "to be strong, steadfast, firm, to endure, hold out, or to bear the burden." The prefix (pros) means "to." This implies motion toward something. Luke gives content to the subject of this sentence. This group (**they**) persists, endures, and never wavers. The verb is "**were**," which is a state of being. They absolutely will not wander from this state of being. Their new location is Jesus and they will not be distracted!

How is this new location described? Paul declares every spiritual blessing is found **in Christ** (Ephesians 1:3). We are actually chosen **in Him before the foundation of the world** (Ephesians 1:4). We are adopted **as sons by Jesus Christ to Himself** (Ephesians 1:5). We are made **accepted in the Beloved** (Ephesians 1:6). It is **in Him we have redemption through His blood** (Ephesians 1:7). On and on the list progresses! In this state of being, in relationship with Jesus, these are all natural ingredients of being in the very being of Jesus. No wonder I am a Jesus pusher!!!

I am a Jesus pusher!!! The early believers changed their location. They were now located in Jesus. Luke writes, ***And they continued steadfastly in the apostles' doctrine and fellowship, in the breaking of bread, and in prayers*** (Acts 2:42). One must not view this list as a series of activities. They were in a "state of being," which is Jesus. Now he describes various aspects of this new location. The first one is ***apostles' doctrine***. The Greek word (didache) translated ***doctrine*** can be translated "teachings." The single function of the apostles was to ***give witness to the resurrection of the Lord Jesus*** (Acts 4:33). This was not a testimony to the doctrine, concept, or idea of the resurrection of Jesus. It was a verification of the actual resurrected person of Jesus. In other words, they were constantly presenting the living Jesus. He is alive and you can know Him. He is your dwelling place.

It is one thing to learn about Jesus, it is another thing to learn Jesus. Their teaching was not ideas but presence. Our desire is not to highlight facts, but to embrace Truth. Jesus said, ***"I am the way, the truth, and the life,"*** (John 14:6). Religious slogans do not help me in my crisis; I need someone greater than I am to intervene in my behalf. I need Jesus! I must embrace Him; He must embrace me. I am a Jesus pusher!!!

I am a Jesus pusher!!! The early Christians **continued steadfastly in the apostles' doctrine** (Acts 2:42). This is the first item on the agenda of their activities. At first you might think they simply had classes on theology taught by the apostles. However, the role of the apostles is specifically stated for us. In selecting an individual to replace Judas as an apostle, the early church established criteria. It was determined that the replacement must have accompanied them **all the time that the Lord Jesus went in and out among us, beginning from the baptism of John to that day when He was taken up from us** (Acts 1:21-22). The criteria was for the purpose of becoming **a witness with us of His resurrection** (Acts 1:22). It was not enough to experience the resurrection appearances of Jesus; they must know those appearances in the context of His life. A person could not correctly testify of His resurrection unless they experienced His crucifixion. No one understands His crucifixion unless they see the style of the cross in His daily living.

Therefore, the entire doctrine of the apostles focused on the person of Jesus! These Jews had crucified Him. Now they spent their time in the unfolding revelation of His person. "Who Jesus is" bombards them daily through the teaching of the apostles. It would be safe to state that they were saturating in the Person of Jesus. He was their curriculum. They were students after Him! Paul cried out, **"that I may know Him and the power of His resurrection, and the fellowship of His sufferings, being conformed to His death,"** (Philippians 3:10). I am a Jesus pusher!!!

I am a Jesus pusher!!! The early disciples ***continued stead-fastly in the apostles' doctrine*** (Acts 2:42). "Saturation in His person" was contained in this teaching. However, "saturation in His Word" was also present. The Greek verb (proskartereo) translated ***they continued steadfastly*** emphasizes this. They did not attend a three-day seminar or meet for Wednesday evening Bible Study. Searching the Scriptures to see Jesus was a continuous daily practice. All their lives, the Law determined their living. Now Jesus became the lens through which they viewed the Law. The Living Word brought new life to the Written Word. They had saturated in the Scriptures in the past, but did not find Jesus (John 5:39). Now they knew Him; the Word came alive to them.

It is amazing! The moment you discover Him, you find Him everywhere in His Word. The revelation of His person becomes consistent. This is a proper discipleship program. Here is the curriculum. Every occasion must find Jesus through His Word. Every sermon must be an exposure of Him through His Word. I must saturate in Jesus through His Word. He speaks to me through His Word. He is the "Word!" He is not written material or stale ideas. He is the Living Person who is directly speaking to me through the Written Word. The Word is alive because He flows through it. In His embrace, I hear Him speak and understand. ***"They continued steadfastly!"*** I am a Jesus pusher!!!

———————

I am a Jesus pusher!!! The Jews of the Dispersion experienced Jesus! They crucified Jesus; now they embraced Jesus. What is more important, Jesus embraced them. ***They continued steadfastly in the apostles' doctrine*** (Acts 2:42). The apostles were eyewitnesses to the life and resurrection of Jesus. They were able to open the Scriptures and reveal Jesus to the new converts. I want a church focused on the Word. If it is just focused on the Bible, the Written Word, it becomes doctrine, rules, and concepts. We must saturate in Jesus through His Word. It is amazing! The moment we discover His Person, we find Him everywhere in His Word. The revelation of His person becomes consistent. This is a correct discipleship program. Here is the curriculum. Every gathering of the church will consist of seeing Jesus through His Word. Every sermon is an exposure of Jesus through His Word.

The traditions and laws of the Old Testament caused the Jews of the Dispersion to participate in the crucifixion of Jesus. Now they were added to and relocated in Jesus. They began to see their traditions and laws through the eyes of Jesus. The Old Testament became a living organism in the presence of Jesus. They understood Jesus through His Word; they understood the Word through Jesus. What a revelation! I am a Jesus pusher!!!

I am a Jesus pusher!!! The early believers were filled with the Spirit of Jesus. They lived in this dwelling place, state of existence. Jesus was their new location. ***And they continued steadfastly in the apostles' doctrine and fellowship*** (Acts 2:42). These were not two activities in which they participated. They were expressions of the "state of being." The Greek word (koinonia) translated ***fellowship*** is very significant in the early church. He is not discussing the activity of "hanging out," "potluck suppers," or "an evening in the new gym." Involved in this Greek word is ***fellowship*** with a purpose. The idea of "partner" quickly comes to the forefront. For instance, Luke gives us insight into the linkage between Peter, James, and John. He refers to James and John as ***partners*** (koinonos) ***with Simon*** (Luke 5:10). These men were ***partners*** in fishing. They had several boats, nets, and equipment. They shared the work and the profits. They were business partners.

The Bible only considers two kinds of partnerships! There are only two possibilities for your life. You are either a partner with Satan, fulfilling his dreams, engaged in his enterprise or you will be in partnership with Christ. There is no third category. The concept of neutrality does not exist. There is not even a half and half. Jesus pulls us into His very nature. We are not workers on the assembly line. We are sons in the main office. We are not errand boys accomplishing assigned tasks. We are His partners! I am a Jesus pusher!!!

Jesus PUSHER | 173

I am a Jesus pusher!!! The early believers are described as **continued steadfastly in the apostles' doctrine and fellowship, in the breaking of bread, and in prayers** (Acts 2:42). The aspect of **the breaking of bread** is connected to the Lord's Supper. All would agree the Lord's Supper is entirely focused on the crucifixion of Jesus. He commanded us to remember this. As He broke bread and gave it to His disciples, He said, **"Take eat; this is My body." Then He took the cup, and gave thanks, and gave it to them, saying, "Drink from it, all of you. For this is My blood of the new covenant, which is shed for many for the remission of sins,"** (Matthew 26:26-28). However, the very fact Jesus instituted this with all the disciples present bespeaks the community of believers. The cross of Christ is planted in the midst of my personal life and in the midst of my relationship with you. The early converts were saturating in the teachings of the Scriptures (**in the apostles' doctrine**) and involved in business with the Father and each other (**fellowship/** koinonia). They were also consistently viewing their lives and their relationships in light of the cross (**in the breaking of bread**).

Eating a meal together in light of the death of Jesus determines my relationship with you. It must involve PARDON. I must forgive you in the same manner and the same depth He forgives me! How has Jesus forgiven me? His forgiveness is without condition or reservation. It is lavish, extravagant, and in abundance. It is forgiveness before I even ask. There is no hesitation in Jesus forgiving me. If I do not forgive my brother in the same manner, a wall is erected which stops me from receiving the flow of forgiveness (Matthew 6:14-15). I am wholeheartedly embracing the forgiveness of Jesus! I am a Jesus pusher!!!

I am a Jesus pusher!!! Luke lists four conditions of the early church (Acts 2:42). They are not just activities but each is a "state of being." One of these is *"in the breaking of bread."* This refers to having a meal together including "communion at the Lord's table." Eating a meal together in light of Jesus' cross determines my relationship with you. It must involve PROVISION. I must meet your needs in the same manner He has met my needs. Paul wrote, **Blessed be the God and Father of our Lord Jesus Christ, who has blessed us with every spiritual blessing in the heavenly places in Christ** (Ephesians 1:3). **For in Him dwells all the fullness of the Godhead bodily; and you are complete in Him, who is the head of all principality and power** (Colossians 2:9-10). Such thoughts nearly take one's breath away. The description of the provision is found in the words **every** and **complete**. In fact, He is the provision. There is absolutely nothing I need outside of Him. I must meet your needs in the same manner He has met my needs. I am an extension of His presence in your life. I am the visible image of His invisible presence. He wants to flow through me that He might meet the needs of your life. I must abide in your presence with the same attitude He has because He is my attitude. I must view you in the same manner in which He views. I am a Jesus pusher!!!

Jesus PUSHER | 175

I am a Jesus pusher!!! The early church experienced **the breaking of bread** together (Acts 2:42). There is strong evidence this experience included "The Lord's Supper," remembering Jesus' cross. Eating together in the midst of the cross also involves PROSCRIPTION. This is the act of proscribing; it means to denounce or condemn. I must judge you as He has judged me at the cross. He assumed all my judgment within Himself that I might experience all His righteousness. My judgment was exchanged for His righteousness. **For He made Him who knew no sin to be sin for us, that we might become the righteousness of God in Him** (2 Corinthians 5:21). He knowing the depth of all that I deserve embraced it in its completion. Without hesitation, condemnation, or conditions He joined me in my need that I might embrace His solution.

How quick am I to condemn you? It is as if I just wait to find something in your life to judge. Jesus said, **"Judge not, that you be not judged. For with what judgment you judge, you will be judged; and with the measure you use, it will be measured back to you** (Matthew 7:1-2). If His Spirit sources me, how He sees you is how I see you. There is no judgment. I embrace Him and you. I am a Jesus pusher!!!

———

I am a Jesus pusher!!! The community of believers lived at the table *"in the breaking of bread,"* (Acts 2:42). I must see you in light of His death for me! However, I must see you in light of His death for you! This immediately involves PARDON. I must forgive you in relationship to how He forgives you. Our self-sourcing always inspires the question, "How far do you take this? How often or how much am I required to forgive?"

In the pagan world it is get the other person before they have a chance to get you. And you most certainly must never forgive. The Jewish world demands that you do to another exactly what they have done to you. An eye for an eye is correct procedure. Of course, you forgive only after you have had your revenge. Peter considers himself very generous in proposing, *"Lord, how often shall my brother sin against me, and I forgive him? Up to seven times?"* (Matthew 18:21). Forgiving seven times is very extravagant. However, there is a limit. You will always have those who push the limit; therefore you can withdraw your forgiveness from them. Jesus' answer was, *"I do not say to you, up to seven times, but up to seventy times seven,"* (Matthew 18:22). In the Old Testament context *seventy times seven* means infinity. How should I forgive you? The answer is "Jesus!" I am to go as far as He went for you. He went all the way to the cross. Evidently there was no limit; He never said, "It is enough." In light of His cross I must forgive you in the same manner He forgives you. How could I do less and be an extension of His presence to you? I am a Jesus pusher!!!

I am a Jesus pusher!!! As the early believers gathered together for **the breaking of bread** they shared "The Lord's Supper" (Acts 2:42). They ate together in light of the cross of Jesus. This involved PROVISION. In other words, I must meet your needs in the same manner that Jesus met your needs on the cross. There seemed to be an undisputable principle displayed from the cross. Your needs had priority over Jesus' needs. Your concerns took priority over His concerns. The difficulty in embracing the cross is the lack of personal advantage. There is no angle, no hidden agenda. There is no sales pitch. It is a call to lose your life as He did. In fact, it is His call, **"If anyone desires to come after Me, let him deny himself, and take up his cross, and follow Me,"** (Matthew 16:24).

Another difficulty in embracing the cross is there is nothing beyond it. Isn't there the resurrection? Yes, but only as you stay on the cross. In other words, the cross is not something to go through or endure until it is over. Biblically I must take exception to a favorite song of the Evangelical Church, "The Old Rugged Cross." We will not exchange the cross for a crown. The cross is the fundamental principle of the eternal Kingdom of God. We do not go beyond it. It is only as I come to the cross and stay there that I live. Heaven will be heaven because of this. The needs of others have priority over our personal needs. This will make heaven on earth. It is the style of the cross. I am a Jesus pusher!!!

I am a Jesus pusher!!! The early church joined together in the meal at the cross (***in the breaking of bread***). This means I must see you in light of His death for you. This involved PROSCRIPTION. Here at the cross, I must judge you as He judged you. We all marvel at the crucifixion event. While one of the criminals being crucified with Jesus was criticizing, the other rebuked him. He said, ***"Do you not even fear God, seeing you are under the same condemnation? And we indeed justly, for we receive the due reward of our deeds; but this Man has done nothing wrong." Then he said to Jesus, "Lord, remember me when You come into Your kingdom,"*** (Luke 23:40-42). This is a perfect time for Jesus to condemn, judge, and testify for law keeping. He simply says, ***"Assuredly, I say to you, today you will be with Me in Paradise,"*** (Luke 23:43).

When is it proper to condemn? In the Gospels, the only time Jesus offered words of judgment and condemnation were to condemn, judgmental religious people. Evidently condemnation must only be given to condemnation; judgment must only be pronounced toward those judging. I want to live in the death of Jesus; I want to see you through His death; I want to allow His life to flow through me to you. I am a Jesus pusher!!!

I am a Jesus pusher!!! Luke speaks of the early church as *they continued steadfastly* (Acts 2:42). This statement actually highlights a "state of being." It is not a series of activities. He lists four activities: *doctrine, fellowship, breaking,* and *prayer*. The success of these early Christians was not in doing these activities, but their spiritual state of being which caused them to do the activities. The idea of *they continued* is used often in connection with *prayer*. Before the Pentecost event, *these all continued with one accord in prayer* (Acts 1:14). It is used six times in the Book of Acts. In three of these cases, it is in reference to *prayer* (Acts 1:14; 2:42; 6:4).

Paul encouraged us to *"Pray without ceasing,"* (1 Thessalonians 5:17). The Greek word (adialeiptos) translated *without ceasing* is an unusual word. It is only used four times in the New Testament. It does not mean continually in the sense of every day, before each meal, or every morning. It is defined as uninterrupted, without intermission. It is what we call "practicing His presence." It is a Divine awareness. Intimacy with Jesus captures your mind and heart until you live moment by moment in unity. His influence is constantly guiding your decisions, thoughts, and attitudes. Is this possible? He is great enough to capture your life! I am a Jesus pusher!!!

Jesus PUSHER | 180

I am a Jesus pusher!!! The early believers participated *in prayer* (Acts 2:42). Exactly what were these early Christians doing when there is a reference to prayer? What is the content of "praying" in their context? The Greek word translated *prayer* in our verse (Acts 1:14) is in the noun form. It is used thirty-seven times in the New Testament and nine of those are found in the Book of Acts. The verb form of this same word is used sixteen times in the Book of Acts. As you work your way through this book it appears they are always in a state of prayer. I was amazed to find this Greek word only used eight times as a noun in the Gospel accounts. Each of these occurrences relates to Jesus. Even more amazing, the verb form of this word is used forty seven times in the Gospel accounts. Each time it refers to what Jesus does or is and is used in the words of Jesus to others. In other words, in the Gospels the disciples never one time participate in the act of *prayer*.

If this is true, the early church entered into a new experience. For the first time they participated in what Jesus taught them in the Sermon on the Mount (Matthew 6:5-15). Jesus ascended to the right hand of the Father and they now pray in His name. Opening before them is a new era of communication between God and man. Were they aware as they prayed that Jesus went behind the veil for them in the Holy tabernacle not made with hands? He at that moment made intercession for them (Hebrews 7:25). What a privilege to live in His presence! I am a Jesus pusher!!!

I am a Jesus pusher!!! We discovered the early believers were constantly in prayer (Acts 2:42). Matthew also used the Greek word (proseuchomai) translated **prayers** when recording Jesus' cleansing of the temple. Jesus gave explanation for His dramatic actions by stating, *"It is written, 'My house shall be called a house of prayer,' but you have made it a den of thieves,"* (Matthew 21:13). Notice, the temple was neither a house of "intercession" nor a house of "supplication." It was a house of "prayer." It was not just a location where men asked for something. It was a place of sacrificial offerings, worship, cleansing, and activities related to relationship with God. It would be like calling your home a "house of marriage." Everything connected with marriage is contained within that house. Eating, crying, laughing, resting, planning, dreaming, and loving all occur in this house. It is a place where two lives intersect.

Prayer is not about the position of the body or the tone of your voice. It is about all the activities and aspects, which pertain to intimacy with Jesus. It is conversations with Him and about Him. It is worship and singing, eating and knowing He provided it, and each moment "practicing His Presence." You are living in Him. Life is found only in Jesus. I am a Jesus pusher!!!

Jesus PUSHER | 182

I am a Jesus pusher!!! What did you do today? I spent the whole day in prayer! Do you mean you missed work? Oh, no. I went to work, picked up the kids, and ate supper with my family. But it was all prayer! There was a continuous interaction with Him. I constantly felt and experienced His influence. I found myself in continual worship. My fellowship and interaction with Jesus was moment by moment.

Perhaps you think this is impractical. How could such a strong discipline be maintained? Even when I am on my knees in prayer, my mind wanders. Luke wrote about the early church, ***"And they continued steadfastly in the apostles' doctrine and fellowship, in the breaking of bread, and in prayers,"*** (Acts 2:42). The main verb of the sentence is the Greek word "eesan," which is not translated into the English sentence. It is a state of being! This describes prayer, not as an activity at a set time, but a flow in the lives of the believers. This is why I am a Jesus pusher. He is not a religious activity, ceremony, or belief system. He is a Person who indwells me! There is no aspect of life that does not know His presence and influence. He is unrelenting in strengthening and sourcing my life, enabling me. He does not give me peace and joy; He is my state of peace and joy. My days and nights are filled with Him. I do not want to experience any activity in which He is not present. I am a Jesus pusher!!!

———————

I am a Jesus pusher!!! The early disciples experienced "prayer," (Acts 2:42). They did not only have established periods of prayer, but the reality of Jesus' presence engulfed their lives. They lived moment by moment in His influence. Prayer in this sense ceases to be an activity, something you do or sessions of requesting. It becomes who you are! Prayer as an activity creates guilt. How many hours a day is enough to pray. How can one hour a day in prayer satisfy my heart's longing for Him every moment? Is three hours a day sufficient? Don't I have to devote all of my time to prayer? How can I do this? Prayer has to cease being an activity I partake in; I must "be" prayer. I must be so consumed with Him that He is included in all things. He can even be in my distractions.

We understand this clearly in relation to ourselves. We have lived with ourselves for years. We totally involve ourselves in all we do. We constantly maintain fellowship with ourselves. We go to bed at night and awaken in the morning with ourselves. We never make a decision without involving our own opinion. One man said, "Everywhere I go, I go to, and spoil everything!" I never have a moment when I am not aware of "me." Will I allow Jesus to be this real in my life? Can He be as much at the heart of my life as I am? He will make me the person He created me to be! I need Him. I am a Jesus pusher!!!

I am a Jesus pusher!!! Luke writes concerning the early believers, ***"Now all who believed were together, and had all things in common,"*** (Acts 2:44). The Greek word (echo) translated ***had*** plays a dominate role in Christianity. There is another Greek word used for possessing materialism. This word (echo) is relational and focuses on spiritual things. It announces that Christianity can be characterized positively as a "religion of having."

There is a long list with Scriptural references describing the various spiritual aspects we have in Jesus! In John's account of the Gospel, it is stressed repeatedly that we have (echo) eternal life presently. This elevates the richness of living in Jesus from the realm of hope to the realm of present possession. We have God's love (John 5:42), peace (John 16:33), grace (John 17:13), light (John 8:12), and life (John 5:40). There is something greater than all of these. We can actually "have" Jesus! He is ours and we are His! The reason we have all of the spiritual necessities listed above is because we have Him. These are all byproducts of His presence. This means there is a singular need in my life; it is Him. It is understandable He can have me; but I am startled, amazed, and overwhelmed to understand that I can have Him. He is all that I need! There is nothing more or less than Him. In Him I have everything; for He is everything! I am a Jesus pusher!!!

I am a Jesus pusher!!! Christianity is often called "A Religion of Having!" Luke described the early church as "having" (echo) ***all things in common*** (Acts 2:44). Are you surprised to learn that you belong to God? He has total rights to your life. Jeremiah referred to Israel as God's possession (Jeremiah 10:16). The prophecy of Isaiah was based on this great truth. ***But now, thus says the Lord, who created you, O Jacob, and He who formed you, O Israel: "Fear not, for I have redeemed you; I have called you by your name; you are Mine,"*** (Isaiah 43:1).

This is a vital truth in the New Testament. Paul wrote, ***"Or do you not know that your body is the temple of the Holy Spirit who is in you, whom you have*** (echo) ***from God, and you are not your own? For you were bought at a price; therefore glorify God in your body and in your spirit, which are God's"*** (1 Corinthians 6:19). We are His! Tommy and his father worked diligently to make a toy sail boat worthy of their local lake. Tommy was so excited on the day they first launched that little boat. Many wonderful days followed when he enjoyed sailing his boat along the shore. One day the wind caught the sails and the boat moved beyond Tommy's reach. He lost his boat. Several days passed by. Then one day as he walked past the local pawnshop, he saw his boat. He must buy it back. He worked for weeks to earn enough money to buy it back. Tommy accomplished the task and hurried to the pawnshop. With the boat in his hands he exclaimed, "You are mine twice. I made you and I bought you back!" You twice belong to Jesus. He made you; He bought you back! I am a Jesus pusher!!!

———

I am a Jesus pusher!!! The Greek word (echo) translated "**had**" is relational (Acts 2:44). It does not refer to physical, materialistic things. The Scripture presents the proposition that we belong to God. Jesus is our Creator and our Redeemer. He made us and He bought us back. However, it is absolutely incomprehensible that we can possess God. In the Old Testament, the Levites were to have God as their possession. All of the other tribes were given land, but not the Levites. God was their inheritance (Deuteronomy 10:9). The Book of Psalms proposes, '**O Lord, You are the portion of my inheritance and my cup,**" (Psalms 16:5).

In the New Testament, John writes, "**Whoever denies the Son does not have** (echo) **the Father either; he who acknowledges the Son has** (echo) **the Father also,**" (1 John 2:23). "**Whoever transgresses and does not abide in the doctrine of Christ does not have** (echo) **God. He who abides in the doctrine of Christ has** (echo) **both the Father and the Son,**" (2 John 9). Because Jesus created and redeemed us He owns and possesses us. We own and possess Him because He gives Himself to us! He reconciled us to embrace us. We are His; He is ours! Now I belong to Jesus; Jesus belongs to me! I am a Jesus pusher!!!

Jesus PUSHER | 187

I am a Jesus pusher!!! The early believers experienced possessing God! This is highlighted in a Greek word (echo) translated **had** (Acts 2:44). If God owns and possesses us because He made us and bought us back, can we claim the same about Him? Our embrace of Him is not based on what we have done or merited; He has given Himself to us! The story of the Book of Acts flows from Pentecost, the outpouring of the Spirit of Jesus. It was a gift. He gave Himself to us. The promise is *"and you shall receive the gift of the Holy Spirit,"* (Acts 2:38).

The proper understanding of a *gift* is very difficult for us. Our culture thrives on "doing," "performance," and "accomplishment." Even a gift is given because the receiver is worthy. Jesus has us because He created and redeemed us. We have Him because He gives Himself to us. Between "created" and "redeemed" there is huge failure on our part. It is the redemption that makes us worthy! We have not performed, earned, or merited such favor. He gives the generous gift of Himself. In our unworthiness, we have wanted inferior gifts from Him. We desired thing, solutions, and power. We should have wanted Him. He alone satisfies the heart. Why would we look beyond? There is nothing else but Him. I am a Jesus pusher!!!

I am a Jesus pusher!!! Christianity is known as a "Religion of Having!" Jesus has me; I have Jesus. I have Him because He gives Himself to me. The New Testament consistently presents the reality of demon possession. It is clear that no individual has demons; they have him. We do not own them; they possess and own us. Unlike Jesus, the Devil never gives himself to us. When did the Devil ever sacrifice in your behalf? When did He every pour himself out for you?

Jesus promised, ***"And we know that all things work together for good to those who love God, to those who are called according to His purpose,"*** (Romans 8:28). Did the Devil ever make such a promise to you and keep it? The heart of Jesus is the cross. He constantly bleeds, suffers, and dies for you. Has the Devil even for one moment made such a jester? Jesus has! Any right thinking person would shun the devil and everything connected to him. He does nothing but destroy every good thing in life. Jesus risks everything and gives Himself to me. He is always working for my best. He builds, strengthens, and empowers. He is trustworthy; He is always the same. Coming to Him is like coming home. I am safe in Him. He has given Himself to me. I am a Jesus pusher!!!

———

I am a Jesus pusher!!! It was said of the early church, ***"Now all who believed were together, and had all things in common, and sold their possessions and goods, and divided them among all, as anyone had need"*** (Acts 2:44, 45). The crucial issue in Christian stewardship is ownership. The devil is cunning and he would never attempt to keep us from giving of our materialism. He could never convince us that we do not owe Jesus. Instead he shifts the focus from "ownership" to "amount." If Jesus owns everything, the question is "How does Jesus want me to distribute it?" If I own everything, the question is "How much do I need to give?"

The underlying assumption of this last question is that I own everything I have. Jesus is worthy and requires a set amount for Himself. How much do I need to give Him? The Old Testament Law required a tithe (ten percent). If I give more, I feel very generous. I compare myself to others who give less. If I am wealthy, I may give less than a tithe and still give more than others. But Jesus is not concerned about "how much!" His concern is "ownership!" I have Him and He has me. In this tight, intimate relationship of His fullness He owns everything. He gives Himself to me; I give myself to Him. He is worthy of all. I am a Jesus pusher!!!

I am a Jesus pusher!!! Jesus finished his last public message (Matthew 23). He left the temple with His disciples. He suddenly stopped short just before the exit. He quickly told His disciples to hide; evidently something great was about to happen. Then a little old lady came waddling into the temple. She was humped shouldered; her robes were wrapped tightly around her. She went to the offering box looking carefully to be sure she was alone. Reaching into her robe she produced a small coin purse. She snapped it open, turned it upside down, and hit it on the bottom. All the money fell out; it was two coins. In one motion she tucked the coin purse away and departed.

Jesus exploded with excitement. He exclaimed, "Did you see that? It was great!" The disciples were confused. They were amazed when Sadducees floated several hundred dollar bills into the offering plate. This poor widow only gave two coins. Jesus explained, "You missed the truth. It was not how much she gave; it was how much she kept!" (Luke 21:1-4). She gave all. The amount was insignificant. She kept nothing, but gave total ownership to God. Jesus is worthy of all. If ownership is His, I am simply distributing according to His directions. This removes the struggle of amount. I give my total self to Him; He gives Himself to me. In this intimate relationship, I own nothing. I am His! I am a Jesus pusher!!!

———————

I am a Jesus pusher!!! Jesus' confrontation with the Rich Young Ruler bothers most of us (Matthew 19:16-22). The main issue is the final command of Jesus to this young man, *"If you want to be perfect, go, sell what you have* (huparchonta) *and give to the poor, and you will have* (echo) *treasure in heaven: and come, follow me"* (Matthew 19:21). Our main concern is "amount!" Is Jesus requiring him to give everything away? Jesus struck a blow at the very heart of the young man's spiritual condition. It was an ownership problem. He was searching for life. Materialism owned him and he was lifeless. Jesus called for the title of his life to be transferred to Him. Life would be found in Jesus.

Notice in Jesus' statement, the Greek word regarding material possessions is different than spiritual treasures. You cannot have materialism like you have Jesus. Material things possess you; you do not possess them. Jesus gives Himself to us for our betterment. When He has us, we have Him. In this relationship life comes together in unexplainable richness. It is an ownership issue. In giving the ownership of our lives to Him, we receive all He is. The Rich Young Ruler gave the ownership of his life to materialism; he was still searching for life. We cannot possess Jesus without Him possessing us. Oh, I want to be His. I am a Jesus pusher!!!

Jesus PUSHER | 192

I am a Jesus pusher!!! In the early church, the believers **had all things in common** (Acts 2:44). In fact, **they sold their possessions and goods, and divided them among all, as anyone had need** (Acts 2:45). Communal living is suggested by some. In the context of this verse that would be practically impossible. Over three thousand individuals were added to the church (Acts 2:41). These individuals did not live in the same house or even the same area. The Scripture reveals an amazing generosity among the believers, but not everyone sold everything. Many people maintained their homes for they ate together on various occasions (Acts 2:46).

Jesus was now their possession; and they were His possession. This greatly affected how they treated their materialism. They realized everything was under His control. The story is told of several families during a great revival who felt they should give their homes to the church. The wise pastor received those homes and immediately asked each family a key question. Would you live in this house belonging to Jesus? Would you maintain the upkeep and pay the utilities? They must realize Jesus might send someone their way that they were to help; after all it is Jesus' house. We do not own material things; they own us. We must yield ownership of ourselves to Jesus. He gives Himself to us; in Him we have all things. I am a Jesus pusher!!!

Jesus
PUSHER | **193**

I am a Jesus pusher!!! The early believers cared for the needs of others. Luke says they *"sold their possessions and goods, and divided them among all, as anyone had need"* (Acts 2:45). It is an ownership issue. If Jesus owns me, He gives Himself to me. I have the heart of Jesus! I am possessed with His concerns. The key issue is *"as anyone had need."* The Greek word (chreia) translated **need** expresses the idea of necessity. Jesus expressed the same attitude in the Sermon on the Mount. The Old Testament Law allowed for an attitude of revenge, *"an eye for an eye and a tooth for a tooth."* But Jesus called for the attitude of "meeting the need." *"If anyone wants to sue you and take away your tunic, let him have your cloak also. And whoever compels you to go one mile, go with him two. Give to him who asks you, and from him who wants to borrow from you do not turn away,"* (Matthew 5:38-42).

There is no hint of meeting certain requirements in any of these statements. No one hesitates thinking they might be enabling. They are simple statements of the heart of God within the believer. There is no goal to reach. Intimacy with Jesus is experienced. We are one with His desires. This is how we respond because we are filled with Him. I want His heart! I want to know Him so well I am like Him. I am a Jesus pusher!!!

———————————

I am a Jesus pusher!!! Luke begins to give content to the life lived among the early believers. ***Now all who believed were together, and had all things in common, and sold their possessions and goods, and divided them among all as anyone had need. So continuing daily with one accord in the temple, and breaking bread from house to house, they ate their food with gladness and simplicity of heart*** (Acts 2:44-46). The phrase ***with one accord*** seems to state an important aspect of the state of being in which the believers lived.

The unity of the believers often becomes the dominant concern in the church. But this unity is always a byproduct of unity with Jesus. The unity under discussion is unlike any other unity among any other groups. The Greek word (homothumadon) translated ***with one accord*** is actually a compound word. The first word is "homo" which means "one and the same." The second word is "thumadon" which is temperament or mind. It has to do with passion or heavy breathing. In other words, this is not a casual unity. There is intensity in this unity. There is something going on which is so gigantic it has captured them all. It is Jesus! He captured them. The apostles taught them about Jesus; their fellowship centered on Jesus; they ate together, which involved the Lord's Supper; they prayed in intimacy with Jesus. Everything was about Him! Division comes from a lack of His person. He alone can bring unity. I am a Jesus pusher!!!

I am a Jesus pusher!!! *So continuing daily with one accord in the temple* describes the daily activities of the early believers (Acts 2:46). There was a great unity among them. Luke makes this same emphasis before the Pentecost event. While they waited together in Jerusalem for the coming Promise, they *all continued with one accord in prayer and supplication, with the women and Mary the mother of Jesus, and with His brothers* (Acts 1:14). The resurrected Lord created this. He was with them for forty days of *infallible proofs* (Acts 1:3). He captured them; He spent this time *speaking of the things pertaining to the kingdom of God* (Acts 1:3). Their imaginations were filled with the wonder of what it would be like to be filled with the same life that Jesus possessed. Jesus must have restated all the parables of the Kingdom. They saw the truth through the eyes of the resurrection. This was so huge everything else became secondary. This resurrected Jesus mastered them. They were *with one accord* (together with heavy breathing) as they waited for the fullness of the Spirit.

Now Pentecost explodes into their lives! They are filled with the Spirit of Jesus. If they were in unity before, it is intensified and increased now. They are absolutely riveted to Him. They can speak of nothing else. He is the center point of their thinking. They have time for nothing else. All other issues become non-essential in comparison. Their minor differences do not matter. They have one drive and one passion. They are "together with heavy breathing" in Jesus. I am a Jesus pusher!!!

Jesus PUSHER | 196

I am a Jesus pusher!!! The statement *"with one accord"* is used ten times in the Book of Acts. It is an emphasis on unity. *The believers were together* (Acts 2:44). The Greek words (epi, to, auto) translated *together* is proceeded by the Greek word (en) translated *were*. It is a verb of being. This verb is the imperfect, third person plural of "eimi." The disciples were in a state of being placing them in a location. They were constantly coming together. They were not drawn to a religious service of entertainment or to a series of fun activities. It was not organizational loyalty; they did not come together out of tradition or family upbringing.

This is not a message to create guilt because you do not come to the services of the church. The issue is not "if" you come; the issue is "why" don't you want to come? What is lacking within you? Why don't you crave the worship, corporate moving of the Spirit of God, linking with other believers, and the revelation of the Word? Why would this not be a high priority? Why would this not be your first choice? It is not a physical activity issue; it is a "spiritual fellowship with Jesus" issue. He brings us together! I am a Jesus pusher!!!

———————

The apostle Paul illustrated the unity of the believers as the "body" of Christ (1 Corinthians 12:12-31; Ephesians 4:1-16). One member of the body does not reject another member of the body. The foot is not the hand and yet it is part of the same body. The ear is not rejected from the body because it is not an eye. Paul cries, *"That there should be no schism in the body, but that the members should have the same care for one another. And if one member suffers, all the members suffer with it; or if one member is honored, all the members rejoice with it. Now you are the body of Christ, and members individually"* (1 Corinthians 12:25-27).

Luke described the early church as **continuing daily with one accord in the temple** (Acts 2:46). Keep the focus. This is a state of being; they were drawn together due to this state. They linked together seeking the revelation of the resurrected Lord. They focused their energies on the enterprise of the heart of Christ. They poured out their lives through their relationship in the cross style. They were continually practicing His presence. Why would you not be drawn to this? The entire reason behind Paul's illustration is the oneness of each member of the body under the control of the head. Jesus is our Head. The unity, enterprise, and passion all come from Him. Because I am intimate with Him and you are intimate with Him, we are intimate with each other. This draws us **together** (Acts 2:44). I am a Jesus pusher!!!

I am a Jesus pusher!!! ***"The believers were together, and
had all things in common,"*** (Acts 2:44). ***"So continuing
daily with one accord in the temple,"*** (Acts 2:46). Let me
remind you of the Greek word (homothumadon) translated **with
one accord**. It is a combination of two Greek words. The first
Greek word (homou) means "together." The second Greek word
(thumos) means "passion" or "heavy breathing." There was an
attitude of passion and enthusiasm for Jesus permeating all of
their personal relationships.

Let me remind you the Greek word (koinos) translated
common is used here in the sense of what concerns all. The
believers were together in a community. Their attitude and
practice was not based on economic theory. There was no legal
socialization. Their partnership in the enterprise of Christ expressed their loving fellowship and renouncing ownership in order
to help others. No one can give without relinquishing the right to
keep. Only one thing can break the bondage of ownership in
any area of our lives. We must experience His enterprise. What
a church this must have been! But the focus is not on activities;
they are a byproduct of their involvement in Jesus. All of these
activities of the early church were about their passion for the
heart of Christ. Or was it the very heart of Christ who gave them
this passion? We must come back to Him! He must capture us!
He is our new location! I am a Jesus pusher!!!

I am a Jesus pusher!!! Luke describes the atmosphere expressed in the fellowship and unity of the early believers. It is significantly compounded when one thinks of the increasing numbers involved. They went from one hundred and twenty (Acts 1:15), to three thousand one hundred and twenty (Acts 2:41), to an abundance of more than eight thousand (Acts 4:4). It is a marvelous testimony to the power of Jesus within the believers.

They ate their food with gladness and simplicity of heart, praising God and having favor with all the people (Acts 2:46-47). These words occur only in the language of the Bible and the Church. Luke describes a joy encompassing the whole person and radiating from him. The Greek word (aggaliasis) translated ***gladness*** is a forceful word. It contains the idea of inner joy, but also carries with it the outward expression. It might be translated "exultation" which is "to rejoice greatly" or "to be jubilant." The Greek word (aphelotes) translated ***simplicity*** is only used one time in the New Testament. It carries the emphasis of "smooth." It is the picture of a plowed field with no rocks or obstacles in it. In our passage, this description is connected to the hearts of the believers. There was no obstacle in the inner lives of these believers. It has to do with purity of intention and sincerity. Jesus alone can cause this. I am a Jesus pusher!!!

I am a Jesus pusher!!! Luke describes the early church as *"having favor with all the people"* (Acts 2:47). Persecution would come soon enough. However, the ordinarily normal Jewish person found the lives of the believers blessed and attractive. The Greek word (charis) translated *favor* means "grace." They shared the abundant grace of Jesus experienced by all believers within their community. They were guilty of crucifying Christ; but the resurrected Jesus filled them. They experienced total forgiveness and the fulfillment of their lives. This same grace was expressed in their daily lives to the extent it affected all of their surroundings.

In the Greek language there are two different Greek words translated "good." One Greek word (agathos) describes a thing as good. However, the Greek word (kalos) means something is not only good but it also looks good. It has a winsome attractiveness about it. The indwelt presence of Jesus brought loveliness to the lives of the believers. There are many people who are good but they are hard. They would never do wrong or hurt you, but they do not draw others to them. As this new body of Christ was formed, the presence of the Spirit of Jesus drew the community to them. Only Jesus can do this in our lives. I want Him to affect my family and community through me. I am a Jesus pusher!!!

Jesus PUSHER | **201**

I am a Jesus pusher!!! I am a great lover of theology. The word theology comes from two Greek words which are connected to each other. This compound Greek word is a combination of "Theo" and "logos." "Theo" is translated "God" and "logos" is translated "word." Therefore, theology is "words about God." It is great to discuss great ideas about God. Each of us develops his own conclusion. There are some of us who spend our entire life engrossed in these ideas and concepts about God. We learn to debate these ideas, sharpening our perspective, and become very stubborn about our conclusions.

Then God became flesh and upset everything. Christmas is not just a theological earthquake to be included in our classroom discussions. It is the entrance of a person of God into my life structure and plans. Suddenly Joseph and Mary are disturbed with the presence of a third person. He is really the second person of the Trinity invading their territory. Jesus, who is God, has come! The established patterns of life are set aside. The rituals they have always followed are disrupted. What do I do now? This is the question of the hour. I cannot respond to Jesus like I have responded to "my theology." He wants to participate in the flow of my actions and thoughts. He wants to give me His mind. Jesus is born! It is Christmas! I am a Jesus pusher!!!

I am a Jesus pusher!!! This is the amazing truth about the Christmas narratives. No one involved in these stories is concerned about theology. The setting of the Christ child's birth is not a theological classroom. This is real life drama. The dreams of this couple are not out of the ordinary. They want to establish a home, have children, and raise those children among family and friends. Joseph saved the necessary money; he paid the dowry. He is making improvements to his house, adding an extra room in anticipation of their firstborn child. Mary is learning new recipes and gathering the necessary items to equip the kitchen. They are not struggling with the "existential" existence of man. They are filled with the events of life. Christmas is the story of God entering the realm of man's living!

We are very good at departmentalizing our lives. We push religion off to one day a week, isolating it from our jobs, recreation, entertainment, and friends. You can do this with "religion" but not with Jesus. God planted Jesus in the midst of the everyday lives of Joseph and Mary. It is equally true with us! Christmas is the story of Jesus being born in us. The New Covenant will come through the cross; Jesus will fill us with His Spirit. All of life will now be empowered and affect by Him. What a privilege. It is Christmas. I am a Jesus pusher!!!

I am a Jesus pusher!!! Joseph is in a moral dilemma. His situation is turned upside down. The marriage plans are ruined. Embarrassment comes crushing into his friendships. He has to make decisions about issues he should never experience. God confronts his theology. He is a just man. This means he does what he is required by the Old Testament law and ceremonies. He comes to a conclusion about Mary. He cannot possibly marry her because that would be an admission that he is the father of her child when he is not. He cannot participate in her sin. According to Jewish law, he should escort her to the magistrates at the city gates. They will pronounce the verdict of guilty; she will be stoned to death. But he just cannot bring himself to do such a thing. Jesus has disrupted his traditions.

I quickly establish my religious traditions. I set certain times when I go to church; I pray routinely at set times. I establish a pattern for reading the Bible. I am comfortable in my traditions. But it is Christmas! Jesus is born in the midst of my traditions. His presence creates unusual dilemmas not answered by my traditions. He goes beyond my set patterns and calls me to His life! Will I let Him be born in me this Christmas? I am a Jesus pusher!!!

I am a Jesus pusher!!! There was a man by the name of Abram. He was living in the Ur of Chaldean; this is where his father settled. He conducted his business from a small shop he built. He sold silver statues of foreign gods. One day Jehovah tapped him on the shoulder and told him to go on a journey. He would not tell him where; but at the end of each day when they met at a sacrifice altar, He would give him new direction. This was the plan of God who would enter into the flesh at Christmas time.

In Abram's life, this was not a theological discussion. It was not about a new god who would join the rest of the silver statues he supplied to the people. This was the plan of Jesus. Jesus interrupted Abram's life, disturbed his materialism, upset his home, and determined his future. It is the evidence of Jesus intersecting the life of a man.

Be assured He will do this in your life as well. Santa Claus comes for a brief moment and we can continue as we were. He joins us in our traditions and establishes patterns of life. But not Jesus! When Jesus is born, stars begin to speak. Wise men ride on camels for two years to discover the truth of His person. Kings are disturbed and angered. Baby boys are killed. Mothers and fathers will never be the same. A young family flees into exile in Egypt. Reputations are at risk. No one will ever be the same again. How can it be any different in our lives? I am a Jesus pusher!!!

I am a Jesus pusher!!! Joseph was a ***"just man"*** (Matthew 1:19). This indicates he lived according to the acceptable requirements of his present religious age. Within the structure of this righteous observance, Joseph is struggling with how to respond to the coming of Jesus in Mary's womb. According to proper Jewish law, she should be stoned to death. To the other extreme, he could marry her; however, Jewish righteousness would never allow such a thing. Joseph would be admitting to everyone that he is the one who committed sin with her. There was no way his righteousness would allow him to embrace her in marriage.

But there is a new righteousness that comes with Jesus. His arrival marked a fulfillment of the law. This fulfillment is "love!" What argument is there against Paul's great statement: ***"For all the law is fulfilled in one word, even in this: 'You shall love your neighbor as yourself,'"*** (Galatians 5:14). Has not Jesus come to take us beyond the righteousness of the Old Covenant and bring us into the love rightness of the New Covenant? Laws would not accomplish this; love cannot be legislated. It must come from a changed heart. Is this why Jesus came? Can He change my nature from a legalistic and judgmental individual to one who embraces the total will of God, love! I am a Jesus pusher!!!

I am a Jesus pusher!!! Joseph calculated his position of right-eousness and came to an acceptable compromise. Mary is with child. Joseph is deeply aware that he is not the father. He will give her a private divorcement. It is the best answer in light of the fact there is no right answer. How can this situation be "undone?" There is no way out. This is the only thing his "righteousness" can tolerate and justify. It is the righteousness of the Old Covenant. If he forgives and marries her, he admits his guilt in her sin.

If Joseph is to follow the call of God from an angel of the Lord in the night hour, he must set aside his concept of the Old Covenant righteousness. He must embrace the New Covenant righteousness of love. Can he simply love Mary and accept her as she is? Can he embrace the child to be born as his own? Can all walls of prejudice and bitterness be broken down? Can he be redemptive through obedience to God's call? Jesus cannot survive in Joseph's life in the Old Testament righteousness. If Joseph maintains the Old Testament righteousness, the plan of God for redemption will be aborted. To respond to the Christ child is to respond to righteousness on a new level. It is the mind of Jesus! I am a Jesus pusher!!!

I am a Jesus pusher!!! God placed His entire redemptive plan in the hands of one man's response. If Joseph did not listen to the angel's instructions and obey, the life of the Messiah was at risk. Joseph must set aside his concept of righteousness learned from the Old Testament and embraced the new call. This became clearly defined again and again in the ministry of Jesus to Israel. Jesus could not survive the sacrificial system of the Old Testament. The leaders of Israel were so entrenched in their ceremonies. The fingers of these ceremonies reached into the financial structure of their culture. Millions of dollars revolved around the offering of sacrificial lambs. Position, power, and political offices were dependent upon the Old Testament righteousness. If the leaders of Israel were to embrace Jesus they would need to surrender the Old Testament sacrificial system now fulfilled in Jesus. Embracing Jesus would be to embrace a new righteousness.

Our righteousness of "doing" fits comfortably into the Old Covenant righteousness. It feeds our egos, massages our pride, and gives us value. We can overcome our depressions; we can even control our anger by soothing it with a sense of pity for those who are not as good as we are. If Jesus becomes my righteousness, it will change everything. My righteousness will be found only in Him not my accomplishments. Can I make such surrender? I am a Jesus pusher!!!

I am a Jesus pusher!!! The birth of Jesus called Joseph to a new level of righteousness. Jesus could not survive in the Old Covenant righteousness. Joseph responded to the call of God to embrace, forgive, and redeem. The leaders of Israel did not respond in such a manner; they crucified, killed, and hated. Jesus moves us from the righteousness of exterior to interior.

We recognize it again and again in our own relationships. We want to dwell in the "eye for an eye and tooth for a tooth" structure of righteousness. It seems fair to us. But Jesus came! He is saying, ***"You have heard that it was said to those of old,"*** (Matthew 5:21). He continues to say, ***"But I say to you,"*** (Matthew 5:22). Six different times He gave this contrast in the Sermon on the Mount. He contrasted "not murdering" in the Old Covenant with "not hating" in the New Covenant. He continued with "not committing adultery" in the Old Covenant with "not lusting" in the New Covenant. He even spoke of "divorce for any reason" in the Old with "forgiveness and love" in the New. In the Old Covenant an individual's word was dependent upon the object of his oath. In the New Covenant you must just be honest? Have integrity! His presence explodes my sense of righteousness to a new level. It is His mind and heart. Will I allow Him to be born in me, to birth a new righteousness of love? I am a Jesus pusher!!!

I am a Jesus pusher!!! At Christmas Jesus, the babe, entered into the lives of a young couple. He was not a new theology or philosophy; He was a new revelation of God. If embraced, He would change everything. The Old Testament traditions would be altered. Even Joseph's perspective of righteousness would not be the same. One can adjust theology to fit a life style; one can rationalize a philosophy. But Jesus cannot be adjusted. He has come.

The call of Christianity is not the call of a set theology; it is a call to intimacy with God through Jesus. Christianity cannot be mere ritual ceremonies; it is relationship with a person. To reduce the Christian faith to legalistic activities is to violate the very love expressed through the coming of Jesus. Worship experiences on Sunday morning cannot substitute for being sourced by Jesus all week long. The God of the Holy of Holies who was isolated from His people has torn the veil. The temple that once housed God in our town has now become the body of Christ. You are His temple. As Jesus came to dwell in the womb of Mary, so He now wants to indwell your life. He wants to unite with your mind and heart. This is far greater than religion; this is Jesus. I am a Jesus pusher!!!

I am a Jesus pusher!!! Jesus entered into the life of Joseph and Mary in a practical manner not just a religion. In fact, Joseph is called to a new and full revelation of God in his life. For over four hundred years, there was no revelation of God. No bushes burned; no prophets spoke. No one saw any handwriting on the wall; no angels were reported. Joseph's entire concept of God was contained in the Old Testament Scriptures. It was all hearsay. He had learned and heard about God, but he did not know Him. Joseph believed in Jehovah God with all of his heart. It was demonstrated in the rituals and ceremonies he maintained. He was ***a just man*** (Matthew 1:19). He knew the stories behind each of the Feast Days of Israel. He knew God delivered, but he did not know the God *who* delivered.

Now God entered into the flesh; it was their flesh. Mary was with child. Joseph would actually live with God. He would provide for God. He would participate in all God was going to do. Jesus ushered in the New Covenant. It was a new revelation and relationship with God. Man could actually be filled with God. The God of Mount Sinai came to unite with man in intimacy. God would become one with man. Jesus is this revelation. What an opportunity we have to know God! I am a Jesus pusher!!!

I am a Jesus pusher!!! Joseph was betrothed to Mary. But she was found with child. Joseph believed in God; his revelation of God would be the God of Mount Sinai. God came in thunder and lightning. The people trembled and shrunk back in terror. The prophetic line was established. It was better for one man to risk speaking to God than for the entire nation to be lost. God was judgmental. He had certain demands and punished those who broke His rules. He was a killer of men, women, and children. He was a God to fear. You did not want to get on His bad side. God is omniscient; you cannot fool Him. He hides in the Holy of Holiness and no man dares enter there. He commands the stoning of adulterers; He destroys nations who are His enemies. This is the revelation of God in the mind of Joseph.

Can you imagine how startling it was for Joseph? He actually helped deliver God into the world in a stable of an inn located in Bethlehem. He held God as a helpless babe in his hands. He would help teach Him to read, play ball, and work. He would teach Him the carpenter trade so God could follow in his footsteps. He hugged God and put Him to bed at night. Joseph actually provided for God! How can this be? This is an unbelievable revelation of God. This God is Jesus. He became one with us! I can know Him. I am a Jesus pusher!!!

Jesus
PUSHER | **212**

I am a Jesus pusher!!! Joseph was in a moral dilemma. He was betrothed to Mary who was now with child. Joseph is not the father of the child; what should he do? Can he accept the angel's announcement? God has actually invaded their world. Not just in an earthly sense but personally. They must deal face to face with God.

Is it any less radical for us? God actually looks like my brother! In fact, this is what He calls me (Hebrews 2:11). God has become one of us! Someone cried, "One like us, one with our skin has made it to the right hand of the throne!" Now we see how God really feels. He does not hate His enemies but says, ***"But I say to you, love your enemies, bless those who curse you, do good to those who hate you, and pray for those who spitefully use you and persecute you,"*** (Matthew 5:44).

But this new revelation goes beyond activities. It is a revelation of how God can indwell man; it is a revelation of God actually living His life through man. It is a revelation of the dream God has for me! He wants to be born in me. It is a revelation of the imparted life of God that can come to every man. This will radically change my approach to life. I must embrace Him in the power of His presence and know His life in me! I am a Jesus pusher!!!

I am a Jesus pusher!!! Peter and Andrew, two brothers, are busy ***casting a net into the sea*** (Matthew 4:18). The net was probably about nine feet in diameter, and the two brothers were skilled in its use. The Greek term for this particular net was "amphiblestron." It is related to our English word "amphibious," which is an adjective describing something related to both land and water. It is so named because the persons using the net would stand on or near the shore and throw the net into the deeper water where the fish were. This was not a hobby on the weekend or an enjoyable Saturday morning of "going fishing." ***They were fishermen*** (Matthew 4:18). The Greek word (halieos) translated ***fishermen*** is used only a few times in the New Testament. It means one whose occupation is catching fish.

The call of Jesus upon the lives of these two men is a call to repent. They must give up a former thought which in this case is their occupation. That is what occupied their time. It was the support of their family; it was their way of life. It was in their thinking and life's plan; they were comfortable and familiar with fishing. They invested in it; it was their security. This is not a call to professional ministry; it is a call to Jesus being their life. He now wants to be all that fishing has been in their lives. It is the same for you. I am a Jesus pusher!!!

Peter and Andrew were fishing. As the story expands, there are two other brothers, James and John also fishing with their father, (Matthew 4:21). This is not only their occupation but has been their way of life from birth, their heritage. These two sets of brothers are called upon to embrace a second thought. This second thought will be an absolute, radical change at the core of their existence. Jesus calls them to repent, *"Follow Me, and I will make you fishers of men"* (Matthew 4:19). This is an allegory connecting their present and future vocations.

It is, however, very important to notice, this is not just the embrace of a new vocation. One might leave his fishing business and become a full time disciple without following Jesus. Repeatedly Jesus will call people to *"Follow Me!"* But outside of this situation He never called them to be *fishers of men*. If the former thought is "fishing for fish" and the second thought is being *fishers of men*, surely this call will take place again and again in Galilee. Joining ourselves to Him results in an adjustment to our lives' central focus. The former thought is for the survival of us. We work for us; we plan for us; we prepare for us. Our vocation is for us. We only work to support us. Who will work hard if they do not need the money? Jesus calls us to embrace a second thought. It is Him! When He becomes the second thought, He gives us a new focus in our vocation. It is for others. This is what He will do within us. This is His responsibility; our responsibility is to respond in repentance. I am a Jesus pusher!!!

I am a Jesus pusher!!! Jesus calls His disciples. There are several different recorded aspects of the call. These may be referred to as stages or phases of God's call on our lives. It establishes a pattern for the unfolding maturity God wants us to experience. Wherever we are in the journey, it compels us forward. The first step is A CALL TO FAITH. It is amazing how God orchestrates the events in our lives to bring us to Himself. John the Baptist was standing with two of his disciples (John 1:35). He witnessed to them concerning Jesus. They immediately followed Jesus and spent the entire day with Him. There was wonderful sharing, teaching, and fellowship during that day. It was so impacting that Andrew, one of those disciples, ran to find his brother, Peter. *And he brought him to Jesus* (John 1:42). On the very next day Jesus *found Philip and said to him, "Follow Me,"* (John 1:43). Philip shared with Nathanael. All of these encounters took place in Judea. These men went with Jesus to Galilee and experienced the first miracle (John 2:1-12).

The Scriptures record, *"and His disciples believed in Him,"* (John 2:11). They became disciples based on their faith. Again and again the Scriptures describe the action of faith as "invoking the activity of the second party." These men desperately wanted to change Israel, but knew they could not. The empire of Rome had overpowered them. The corruption and chaos within their Jewish traditions pressured them. There was only one hope. The Messiah must come. He alone could do what they could not do. It is here in this encounter with Jesus, they realize He is the One to act in their behalf. They believed; do you? I am a Jesus pusher!!!

Jesus PUSHER | 216

I am a Jesus pusher!!! The first call of the disciples was A CALL TO FAITH. After experiencing Him, the Scriptures states, *"and His disciples believed in Him,"* (John 2:11). This is essential for being a Christian disciple. We attract people to the church because of our care and love. They become a part of our fellowship and enjoy the activities. They receive the benefits of being a part of the church. But there must be an encounter with Jesus. They must realize the desperate need of their own lives and circumstances. The pattern of defeat, the awareness of the emptiness, and their guilt for their own sins cripples them. They must embrace Jesus through faith (invoke the activity of His Person).

Has this happened to you? This is not an advanced state but a beginning step. It is here that you must start. If you miss this you nullify all other aspects of the call of Jesus on your life. If you attempt to build a Christian life without this, it is a house built on sand (Matthew 7:24-29). This is not an experience to get through but a base upon which everything else will rest. Everything in Christian experience flows through the response of faith. This is the blood that flows through the veins of the Christian. He is always invoking the activity of the Second Party. I cannot; but Jesus can! I will let Him! I am a Jesus pusher!!!

I am a Jesus pusher!!! Peter and Andrew and several others encounter Jesus in Judea. They believe in Him; they become His disciples. Their second encounter with Him is in Galilee. John the Baptist was in prison; Jesus goes to Galilee to begin His ministry. He establishes His headquarters in Capernaum (Matthew 4:12-13). Jesus is walking by the Sea of Galilee. In the Greek text the name "*Jesus*" is not present. The subject is actually "a third person, singular, pronoun (He)." The Greek word (peripateo) translated *walking* is a verb. It is a participle used as an adjective for "He." Jesus was always "walking around." It was His method of ministry (Matthew 9:35).

As He walked by the Sea of Galilee, He saw the same disciples He met in Judea. They had returned to their fishing. Since these disciples responded to the first stage of His call, He decides to renew and strengthen the call. He said, *"Follow Me, and I will make you fishers of men"* (Matthew 4:19). The Greek word (poieo) translated "*I will make*" is in the active voice. This means the subject of the sentence is responsible for the action of the verb. It is in the future tense. Obviously this has not happened to the disciples until this moment. Jesus asks the disciples to join Him for the purpose of allowing Him to form them into something new. What they have been is not what they will be! Oh, the wonder of His plans for you. Will you let Him form you? I am a Jesus pusher!!!

I am a Jesus pusher!!! While walking by the Sea of Galilee, Jesus confronts Peter and Andrew again. He calls these fishermen, ***"Follow Me, and I will make you fishers of men"*** (Matthew 4:19). He wants to ***make*** (poieo) them into something new. What they are is what they know. What they know is their present security. It is comfortable. It may not always be pleasurable; but it has the feeling of certainty. The disciples are quite willing and even anxious for the Roman domination to end. They are willing for their situation in Galilee to be different. They readily see the need for change all around them, but they do not yet comprehend the needed change must come in them. At this moment they have no way of visualizing Jesus forming them into the moving force that will utterly change the world in seventy years. They will indeed become ***fishers of men***. Their response must be "faith!" They must invoke the activity of the Second Party. Will they trust Him to reform them?

Paul vividly describes this formation for us (2 Corinthians 3:7-18). His illustration is the face of Moses. The presence of God planted the glory of God in Moses' face. The children of Israel demanded a veil to cover it. But when we turn to the Lord, ***the veil is taken away***. We stare into the very glory of His person; we ***are being transformed into the same image from glory to glory, just as by the Spirit of the Lord*** (2 Corinthians 3:18). We cannot possibly do this; will we let Him? It is by faith. I am a Jesus pusher!!!

———————

I am a Jesus pusher!!! Another phase of Jesus' call is focus. The disciples encountered Him in Judea. They believed He was the Messiah. Jesus called them again in Galilee while they were fishing. He would form them into something new. Evidently they continued to fish and share in His ministry in Galilee. One day down by the Sea of Galilee the crowds pressed Jesus. Peter and the other disciples had fished all night and caught nothing. As they were cleaning their nets Jesus encouraged them to go fishing again. They resisted, but Jesus insisted. As they responded they caught so many fish their net was breaking (Luke 5:1-11). They called for another boat; both boats were filled with fish until they began to sink.

When Simon Peter saw it, he fell down at Jesus' knees, saying, "Depart from me, for I am a sinful man, O Lord!" (Luke 5:8). This was a crucial time in Peter's life and in the other disciples as well. It is an absolute step in the call of God upon our lives. It is inevitable that as one response to the presence of Jesus "self-revelation" will take place. It was not that Peter had committed some sinful act and Jesus caught him in the midst of it. He had been responding to Jesus in faith. At various times he followed and experienced moments of excitement in his faith. It is here his focus on himself becomes very apparent. This issue will not be settled in this encounter. But it has started. The revelation of self-centered focus will come again and again until Peter is broken. Is it any different with us? I am a Jesus pusher!!!

I am a Jesus pusher!!! ***When Simon Peter saw it, he fell down at Jesus' knees, saying, "Depart from me, for I am a sinful man, O Lord!"*** (Luke 5:8). Peter was an experienced fisherman supporting his family. He had fished all night and caught nothing (Luke 5:5). If he could not catch fish, no one could. He knew all the methods of fishing and all the best places to catch fish. Jesus, a carpenter, came along to give instructions on fishing. Peter resisted and wanted to dismiss the idea as ridiculous Jesus pressed him. Peter's self-sourcing was revealed by the miracle of two full boats filled with fish. It was a lesson designed for him. It was a call to faith, invoking the activity of Christ only.

This experience made such an impact that the disciples responded. ***So when they had brought their boats to land, they forsook all and followed Him*** (Luke 5:11). They could no longer be part time followers. All their excuses about family responsibilities, finances, and their fishing business were set aside. Their focus must be on Jesus and Jesus alone! The Greek word (aphiemi) translated ***they forsook*** means "to dismiss" or "to let go." There is a strong sense of repel or push away. It was not taken from them; but by an act of their will they pushed everything else aside to focus entirely on Jesus. Will you do the same? I am a Jesus pusher!!!

I am a Jesus pusher!!! After the disciples' initial response in faith, they went back home to their fishing. Jesus came by the shore of Galilee and encountered this same group again. He called, *"Follow Me, and I will make you fishers of men"* (Matthew 4:19). He gave them a beginning vision of what following Him would look like. In the next phase of the call the disciples, after fishing all night and catching nothing, had cleaned their nets, and were going home for some much needed rest. Jesus insisted they go fishing again. Reluctantly they went out into the deep and let down their nets. They experienced the greatest catch of their fishing experience. When they returned to shore, Jesus said, *"Do not be afraid. From now on you will catch me,"* (Luke 5:10). Here was a glimpse of the larger vision of following Him.

Now the disciples follow Jesus fulltime. The prayer meeting is called to pray for the laborers needed to accomplish the great harvest. As they pray, Jesus springs to His feet to announce the answer to their prayers. He is going to send them! This is not new; He proclaimed this consistently in the call. This is the practical aspect of "following Him." There is no way for the call of God to come to fruition in our lives without our enlistment in the harvest or fishing for men. To be joined to the heart of Jesus is to be joined to evangelism. Are you responding? I am a Jesus pusher!!!

———————————

I am a Jesus pusher!!! Whatever the call of Jesus upon your life, it will result in "evangelism." This was true with Isaiah in the Old Testament. He was the right hand man of King Uzziah; but the king was dead. Everything he counted on and built toward was now gone. In a state of dismay Isaiah came to the temple. The vision of God in His holiness was disarming. Isaiah saw himself and cried out, ***"Woe is me, for I am undone. Because I am a man of unclean lips, And I dwell in the midst of a people of unclean lips, For my eyes have seen the King, the Lord of hosts"*** (Isaiah 6:5). Isaiah's focus was changed forever. Once God cleansed him, the call came loud and clear, ***"Whom shall I send. "And who will go for Us?"*** (Isaiah 6:8). How could Isaiah not go, having seen God and himself?

The disciples were praying to the Lord of the harvest to send labors. Their prayers are answered. Jesus is sending them. He immediately empowers them. They are raised from disciples to apostles (Matthew 10:1, 2). They become "sent ones!" Jesus takes the power contained within Him and transfers it to His disciples. Everything they need to accomplish the task is now theirs. Jesus does not look for men with talent, education, or aggressive personalities. He wants men who will be totally His and live by faith. He desires men who will invoke His activity in their behalf. The call of God is upon us. How will we respond? I am a Jesus pusher!!!

I am a Jesus pusher!!! Let the words of Jesus echo in your mind! *"Follow Me!"* He captures you by His presence. You see His miracles. You realize your own personal inability to affect a change in the governmental system of your land. Your nation must be re-established; you are the people of God. God has promised for generations of time that a Messiah will come. You are convinced Jesus is the One. Now, He calls you to join Him. What a privilege!

There are actually three Greek words (deuto opiso mou) translated *"Follow Me."* The first Greek word (deuto) is an "interjection." It is like "hey," "hello" or "look out." These kinds of words are not spoken casually or without intent. This first Greek word (deuto) literally means "come" or "come here." The second Greek word (opiso) means "after." In this context it means "behind me." The third Greek word (mou) is the personal singular pronoun, "me."

The standard pattern for the selection of disciples was that the would-be disciple requested to follow a teacher of his choice. In our passage, Jesus inverts this procedure and asks these men to follow Him. This call is not intended to be an imperative. It is an invitation or an encouragement. These two factors are amazing elements of the Gospel. He comes to us! Without demand He invites us! Are you responding? I am a Jesus pusher!!!

———————

Jesus comes to you; He invites you. These two factors are found throughout the parables of Jesus. The Parable of the Wedding Feast depicts the Kingdom of Heaven as an invitation to a great occasion (Matthew 22:1-14). As you read the story, you become aware of the persistent encouragement of this invitation. The King has great plans in which he desires your participation. The Parable of the Workers in the Vineyard tells us of a landowner ***who went out early in the morning to hire laborers for his vineyard*** (Matthew 20:1). Even the Parable of the Sower is the story of one who comes and plants the seed into the soil of our lives. We are to respond to the movement of the Sower (Matthew 13:1-9).

Even in the earlier encounter of the disciples with Jesus, He took the initiative. When John the Baptist testified to them concerning Jesus, they began to follow Him; Jesus took the initiative and drew them into His fellowship (John 1:37-38). Jesus took the lead when he called Matthew, the tax collector (Matthew 9:9). It was an invitation. Listen to the words of Jesus, ***"You did not choose Me, but I chose you and appointed you that you should go and bear fruit, and that your fruit should remain,"*** (John 15:16). Listen to the words of the Apostle Paul, ***"Just as He chose us in Him before the foundation of the world that we should be holy and without blame before Him in love,"*** (Ephesians 1:4). Jesus comes to you; Jesus invites you. I am a Jesus pusher!!!

I am a Jesus pusher!!! Jesus extends the invitation, ***"Follow Me,"*** (Matthew 4:19). The disciples came with their own dreams and presuppositions. Jesus lived with them for three years and attempted to overcome their traditional expectations of an earthly kingdom. If they had only listened and grasped the significance of this early invitation from Jesus. He promised much more than a simple earthly change of government. Their faith needed to expand; His activity will be the shaping of their lives.

Wasn't this ingrained in every discipleship attachment? Coming after a teacher meant to begin to be like Him, follow his teaching, and imitate his person. There was a formation, which must to take place in the life of the disciple. He would not be the same at the close of disciple program. He would join the master as one person and leave the teaching of the master a different person. While this would be true with any teacher and disciple, Jesus offered an entirely different level of change. Jesus came to live within them at Pentecost. In this new relationship, they began to grasp the depth of this formation. They must enter into this relationship through faith (invoking the activity of the second party). They must place themselves in His hands to shape them as He saw fit. What a privilege! I am a Jesus pusher!!!

I am a Jesus pusher!!! Jesus calls, **"Follow Me, and I will make you fishers of men."** The Greek word (poieo) translated **I will make** is at the very heart of the statement. They are to follow Him and allow Him to "make them." The goal of "making them" is that they become world changers. None of this will happen unless His hands shape and form them. **"I will make"** (poieo) is in the active voice. This means the subject (Jesus) is responsible for the action. This discipleship linkage will be like no other in existence. They will not be shaped by learning information or new lessons. They will not be developed by new habits and styles of discipline. Jesus Himself will shape their lives. His indwelt person sources them.

"I will make" (poieo) is in the indicative mood. This means it is a simple statement of fact. This is neither a suggestion nor a hopeful statement. If they accept His invitation nothing will be able to stop this formation. **"I will make"** (poieo) is in the future tense. This is not what the disciples are at this moment; this is a view of what they will be. This is not a focus on the past; it is not about examining, adjusting, or understanding the effects of previous experiences. This endeavor is a new plan, their possible future. This is the turning of a corner and going in a new direction. This formation is in spite of the shape of the past. Will we place ourselves in His hands for such a radical formation? I am a Jesus pusher!!!

I am a Jesus pusher!!! Jesus sounds a call to the disciples, *"Follow Me, and I will make you fishers of men,"* (Matthew 4:19). We understand the depth of this call in a way they did not. Jesus invited this group to travel with Him on a journey. It is a journey through the cross, resurrection and ascension. He will be exalted at the right hand of the Father and pour out His Spirit. The formation Jesus proposes will ultimately take place by the empowering of the Holy Spirit. The disciple and the teacher will become one in a way no other disciple and teacher have ever done. In this beginning stage, Jesus invites them to *"Follow Me!"* This formation soon moves from "following" to "indwelling." It is amazing to discover the emphasis of the Gospel after the crucifixion. After the cross we are never again told to "follow" Jesus. At this early stage the disciples could easily follow the physical Jesus. After the crucifixion and throughout the Pentecost events God changes the picture. Jesus indwells them. They cannot follow Him for He is within them. The indwelt Spirit moves them; they are sourced. The formation happens from within them.

They have no choice in the formation. They do have a choice in becoming a disciple. Many others did not follow Him (John 6:60). The formation is without choice. It is inevitable (impossible to avoid or prevent)! They are being formed into His likeness. I am a Jesus pusher!!!

I am a Jesus pusher!!! Ichthyology is the branch of zoology focused on the study of fish. Jesus called His disciples. *"Follow Me, and I will make you fishers of men,"* (Matthew 4:19). The focus of the call is *"I will make you fishers of men."* The focus is not upon success; it is not upon materialism. He does not propose the establishment of educational facilities presenting a philosophy of successful living. He is not suggesting a successful career in the ministry. The establishment of a prestigious church denomination is not the goal. They are to be fishermen of men.

If you accept this statement, the ultimate goal of the Jesus' formation in your life is to make you an evangelist. The ultimate purpose of His death is not to get you to heaven, but to enable you to participate in saving souls. His resurrection is not so you can live comfortably in mansions in the sky; it is that you might rescue people. He did not come to bring peace but to wage war for the purpose of snatching the prisoners of war from the hands of the enemy (Matthew 10:34). From His own lips He states the purpose of His coming. *"For the Son of Man has come to seek and to save that which was lost"* (Luke 19:10). The angel announced to Joseph the purpose of the birth of Christ, *"And she will bring forth a Son, and you shall call His name Jesus for He will save His people from their sins"* (Matthew 1:21). Even at His death, He rescues fallen man (Luke 23:43). Even after His resurrection, He has a call for His disciples. *"Go therefore and make disciples of all nations, baptizing them in the name of the Father and of the Son and of the Holy Spirit,"* (Matthew 28:19). What a privilege to unite with Him! I am a Jesus pusher!!!

I am a Jesus pusher!!! Jesus said, *"Follow Me, and I will make you fishers of men"* (Matthew 4:19). From the beginning of Jesus' life to the end of His earthly presence, the call is evangelism. How can this be ignored? If we accept His call, He forms us. He does not form us into holy saints to be displayed in the final museum of the sky. His dream is not of a nice group of people developing professional music programs to praise His name. His cry is to win our world! To miss this is to miss Him!

Let us be very plain! The call of Jesus is to "follow Him." The call is not to become *fishers of men*. Don't lose the focus of the call. If the call is to become *fishers of men*, we will revert to training sessions. Our emphasis becomes techniques and the development of skills. Those with the most outgoing personalities, natural born salesmen, become the stars of the group. Though we applaud those who are effective, we must not lose sight of the call! The call is to *"Follow Me!"* In being joined to Him, I become like Him because His nature envelops me. What drives Him begins to drive me; His love becomes my love. The way He thinks is the way I now think. He becomes so engrained into my being that He is forming me. If we have not become *"fishers of men,"* then we are not following. This is not optional; it is inevitable! It is not the goal; the goal is to be formed by Him. What a privilege. I am a Jesus pusher!!!

I am a Jesus pusher!!!

He said to them, "Follow Me, and I will make you fishers of men" (Matthew 4:19). On a dangerous seacoast where shipwrecks were frequent, a crude little life-saving station was built. A few devoted crewmen kept a constant watch over the sea with no thought for themselves. After a while the station became famous. Some of those who were saved wanted to become a part of the work. They felt a larger, nicer place would be more appropriate as the first refuge of those saved from the sea. So they replaced the emergency cots with hospital beds and put better furniture in the enlarged building.

Soon the station became a popular gathering place for its members to discuss the work and to visit with each other. They hired professional crews to do the work on their behalf. One day a large ship was wrecked off the coast, and the hired crews brought in many boatloads of cold, wet, half-drowned people. The beautiful new club was terribly messed up. At the next meeting there was a split in the club's membership. Most of the members wanted to stop the club's lifesaving activities altogether, being unpleasant and a hindrance to the normal social life of the club. Other members insisted on keeping lifesaving as their primary purpose, but they were voted down and told that if they wanted to save lives they could begin their own station down the coast somewhere.

As the years went by, the new station gradually faced the same problems the old one had experienced. It, too, became a club, and its lifesaving work became less and less of a priority. The few members who remained dedicated to lifesaving began another station. History continued to repeat itself; and if you visit that coast today you will find a number of exclusive clubs along the shore. Shipwrecks are still frequent in those waters, but most of the people drown. Jesus still calls! I am a Jesus pusher!!!

———————

I am a Jesus pusher!!! Evangelism is the heart of God! Those who are intimate with Him and share His nature are possessed with the passion to win the world. John Knox cried out to God, "Give me Scotland or I die!" Wesley burned with the conviction that the world was his parish. Jesus' parting words to His disciples as He ascended was concerning evangelism. He said, ***"But you shall receive power when the Holy Spirit has come upon you; and you shall be witnesses to Me in Jerusalem, and all Judea and Samaria, and to the end of the earth,"*** (Acts 1:8). Matthew records the only resurrection appearance of Jesus by appointment. It contains the "Great Commission." It provided moment by moment marching orders for every believer. He instructed, ***"Go therefore and make disciples of all the nations,"*** (Matthew 28:19).

In Jesus' first encounters with His disciples He called them to the focus on evangelism. Was there a possibility the disciples misunderstood the call? He spoke to them in their language. He described the heart of His intent with the symbol of their common work. He called them to ***"catch men!"*** (Luke 5:10). As they spent their time catching fish, they will now spend their time being ***"fishers of men!" Then He said to them, "Follow Me, and I will make you fishers of men"*** (Matthew 4:19). He calls us!! I am a Jesus pusher!!!

I am a Jesus pusher!!! In Luke's account, Jesus gives a strong focus to the actual content of being *fishers of men*. The entire statement is: *"Do not be afraid. From now on you will catch men"* (Luke 5:10). Guilt is an awful condition that imprisons the spirit of our being until we accomplish nothing. It creates a fear within the individual. This fear proclaims that the individual is inadequate. Peter just experienced a moment of revelation. All this time he had relied on his self-sourcing. This principle of life controlled every aspect of his living. Even his fishing business was dependent on his personal ability. In this moment of time, he saw the extreme lack and inability of self-sourcing in comparison to the wonder of what Jesus could do through him. It was illustrated to him through the one ability he could not question, his fishing. They had *toiled all night and caught nothing* (Luke 5:5).

Jesus calls Peter to return to fishing. Peter was the fisherman, not Jesus. What Jesus asked was against all of Peter's self-sourcing. In obedience, Peter discovered a resource far beyond his self-sourcing. Their net was so full it was breaking. Peter embraced his guilt. He immediately asked Jesus to leave. The sinfulness of his nature could not tolerate the purity of the flow of Spirit-sourcing. Jesus began His call with, *"Do not be afraid,"* (Luke 5:10). Keep responding Peter. The Spirit-sourcing takes him to a whole new level of living. The answer is not in a "departing Jesus" but an "embraced Jesus." Don't be frightened from responding to Jesus! I am a Jesus pusher!!!

I am a Jesus pusher!!! If fear is conquered, if response dominates, one can **catch men**. The Spirit of God will produce this in your life. "Catching men" is an INGREDIENT; it is not an activity. Jesus does not call the disciples to a new vocation; this is not a career move. He does not call them to develop new skills; this is not a program to learn evangelistic techniques. Jesus does not encouraging them to enroll in a crash course to help Him build a large following for His ministry. The very substance of "following Him" is to **catch men**. It is the nature of being Spirit-sourced.

This is plainly presented in the grammar structure of Jesus' statement. ***"Do not be afraid. From now on you will catch men"*** (Luke 5:10). The subject and verb of the second sentence is the Greek word (eimi) translated ***you will***. This verb means, "to be." It is used repeatedly as "I am!" It is a state of being. It is in the indicative mood, "a simple statement of fact." There is no attempt to present an argument. It is in the second person; it is singular, meaning ***"you."*** It is in the future tense; therefore, it is translated ***will*** instead of "am." This is the destiny, purpose, and focus of a Spirit-sourced person. The fullness of the Spirit of God downloads the heart of God to the believer. Jesus' focus becomes ours. We cannot help ourselves; we are intimate with Jesus. I am a Jesus pusher!!!

I am a Jesus pusher!!! Jesus said, *"Do not be afraid. From now on you will catch men,"* (Luke 5:10). The Greek word (zogreo) translated *catch men* is a participle in the nominative case. This is a verb giving content to the subject. It acts as an adjective. The subject becomes a "catcher of men!" In other words, *catching men* is a state of being in which you will be in the future. This is a repeat of the statement Jesus gave to His disciples just before His ascension. *"But you shall receive power when the Holy Spirit has come upon you; and you shall be witnesses to Me in Jerusalem, and in all Judea and Samaria, and to the end of the earth"* (Acts 1:8). *"You shall be"* (Acts 1:8) is a translation of the same root word as *'you will'* (Luke 5:10). The disciples were going to "be witnesses" not "do witnessing." This state was to be fully realized through the fullness of the Holy Spirit's sourcing.

It must be stated again and again that *catching men* is not a result of talent, personality type, or developed skills. We are not discussing one aspect of being a Christian. This is Christianity. This is not an activity for that group of people who are most suited for such involvement. This is the heart and soul running through everyone who is possessed with the Spirit of Jesus. It is not a specialty; it is the normal! It is a basic ingredient. It is the sourcing of Jesus in our lives. I am a Jesus pusher!!!

———————

I am a Jesus pusher!!! Present within the call of Jesus is INEVITABILITY. It is not optional. Jesus spoke clearly; they would become *fishers of men* when the followed Jesus. He said, *"Follow Me, and I will make you fishers of men"* (Matthew 4:19). "Following Him" was understood as attaching oneself to Jesus. It was a submitting to His teaching and philosophy of life. The moment this takes place Jesus is enabled to *make you*. You will become the product of His creative embrace. The natural result of such a Spirit-sourcing is *fishers of men*.

There is a contrast established in the phrase used in Luke's account. Jesus said, *"Do not be afraid. From now on you will catch men"* (Luke 5:10). The Greek word (zoogreo) translated *you will catch men* suggests a contrast with their fishing business. This Greek word is a compound word. It comes from the Greek word (zoos) translated "living." In addition, the Greek word (agreuoo) is added; it means "to catch or take." This word means, "to take alive." In relation to war, it is used for taking prisoners alive instead of killing them. In relation to fishing, the entire purpose and end result of the disciples will change. The contrast is "catch to life" or "catch to death." Up to this time they caught in order to kill; now they will catch in order to impart life. Do you see that "catching" is inevitable? There is no choice regarding the "catching." However, there is a choice involved in the "catching." If we are driven by self-sourcing, the "catching" is to death. If we are driven by Spirit-sourcing, the "catching" is for life. Jesus is "life." I am a Jesus pusher!!!

Jesus PUSHER | 236

I am a Jesus pusher!!! The angel descended; the earthquake shook the ground; the stone of the Jesus' tomb was rolled away (Matthew 28). The guards fainted for fear; the two ladies trembled in the presence of the angel. Mary Magdalene and the other Mary ran to tell the news of the resurrection. After reviving, the guards ran into Jerusalem to report the news of this event. Both the believers and the non-believers were filled with passion. The ladies ran to the disciples to tell the story of Jesus' resurrection. The guards ran to the leaders of Israel and *reported to the chief priests all the things that had happened* (Matthew 28:11).

Both groups were compelled to communicate. What the guards shared brought death. The leaders of Israel paid a bribe for the lie to be told. What the ladies shared brought life; the disciples responded by keeping the appointment in Galilee Jesus had made with them. The Great Commission was given to them. In seventy years they won their entire world to God. Life came to their world. *Catching men* is inevitable. We are evangelizing our world. We all have an influence upon those around us. Someone is following us; they will become like us. We are either "catching to life" or "catching to death." It is inevitable. I want my life to bear the influence of Jesus' presence. I am a Jesus pusher!!!

I am a Jesus pusher!!! INDIVIDUALITY is an important concept. The culture of Galilee was made of both farming and fishing. *And Jesus walking by the Sea of Galilee, He saw two brothers, Simon called Peter, and Andrew his brother, casting a net into the sea; for they were fishermen* (Matthew 4:18). The call to join Him was especially designed for fishermen. He spoke their language; He appealed to their understanding in the context of their daily lives. He designed this call for the individual to whom He was speaking.

What does this mean? Is Jesus only calling fishermen? Perhaps I am a *vinedresser* whose entire experience is related to vineyards. Jesus designed a parable just for me (Matthew 21:33-40). He spoke my language and called me to the responsibility of my personal vineyard. What if I am a shepherd? Jesus spoke directly to the shepherding culture of His day (Matthew 18:10-14). In the Parable of the Lost Sheep, the heart of the Father is expressed in the language of a shepherd. I need to get my staff in order to be used by the Father in my world. Perhaps I am a simple housewife trying to balance the financial budget of my household. Jesus speaks directly to me in the Parable of the Lost Coin (Luke 15:8-10). Maybe I am simply a father who cares for his family. Does Jesus not call me to join the Father's heart for His lost sons? Who could misunderstand the Parable of the Lost Son (Luke 15:11-32)? Whatever your culture, career, or situation in life, Jesus calls you! He designs a message in your language; He shapes His call to your scene. Jesus is calling you! I am a Jesus pusher!!!

I am a Jesus pusher!!! ***Then He said to them, "Follow Me, and I will make you fishers of men,"*** (Matthew 4:19). The "central message" of the Word of God focuses directly on the "central mission" of the people of God. Wait! Isn't the focus of the Scriptures on the "mission of God?" Indeed! However, there is no way to distinguish between the "mission of God" and the nature of God; this nature of God produces through the people of God the actions of God. Therefore, the true people of God express the passion and heart's desire of God. It is clearly expressed as "evangelism."

If the church misunderstands, denies, or ignores this passionate mission, it ceases to be the church. This mission is clearly dispelled throughout the Old Testament and into the New Testament. God has only one plan in which every event of history finds its place. He focuses His energy to redeem fallen mankind.

Every recording in the Old and New Testaments contribute to redeeming the world. It begins with God calling, ***"Where are you?"*** (Genesis 3:9). It continues throughout the entire Bible to ***and the Spirit and the bride say "Come!" And let him who hears say, "Come!" And let him who thirsts come. Whoever desires let him take the water of life freely*** (Revelation 22:17). Jesus is this love action; He is God acting His heart! Embracing Jesus is to be encompassed with redemption and to redeem! I am a Jesus pusher!!!

———————

I am a Jesus pusher!!! ***Then Jesus said to them, "Follow Me, and I will make you fishers of men,"*** (The mission of evangelizing the world is only ours because it is His. God took the entire initiative in this. ***"For God so loved that He gave,"*** (John 3:16). ***But God demonstrates His own love toward us, in that while we were still sinners, Christ died for us*** (Romans 5:8). He initiated this before the foundation of the world (Ephesians 1:4). It is His eternal dream, His design, and His drive. He selected a remnant called the Church to be the vessel to accomplish His plan. He calls us to partner with His Divine desires. ***The Lord is not slack concerning His promise, as some count slackness, but is longsuffering toward us, not willing that any should perish but all should come to repentance*** (2 Peter 3:9). He made provision for all. His love desires it. He planned it. Everything is in place for it to happen.

Let me ask you how you view your involvement in the church? Is the dream of your life focused on how to redeem your world? For what do you cry? What upsets you? Is your tiredness a result of the one thing that beats in the heart of God? Every situation and every person must be seen in view of how can I be the redemptive force of God in this hour? Could I boldly say, "If this is not true for you, you have missed the impact of the Gospel of Matthew and especially this initial call to His disciples?" Jesus is calling you! I am a Jesus pusher!!!

I am a Jesus pusher!!! ***Then Jesus said to them, "Follow Me, and I will make you fishers of men,"*** (Matthew 4:19). The element of CONTINUALLY is present in this call. The promise of Jesus is one of being engaged continually in evangelism. Jesus boldly presents the call to evangelism to two disciples. There is no mincing of words, no allurement with rewards, and no glamorizing the task. There is no time element attached. It is not an assignment for a period of time or until retirement. In fact, it is not a call to do something, but to become something. The continuity of evangelism is stressed.

Day by day, week after week, month upon month, and year after year His Spirit will actively flow through us for this purpose. Up to this time, they embraced Jesus as the Messiah. They followed Him as time would allow in their busy fishing schedule. Things are going to change, if they are to remain in relationship with Him. Matthew's account places emphasis on the future tense. Jesus said, ***"Follow Me, and I will make you fishers of men"*** (Matthew 4:19). Luke's account instead of the future indicative stresses the duration aspect of the call. ***And Jesus said to Simon, "Do not be afraid. From now on you will catch men"*** (Luke 5:10). "Catching men" will be the continuing involvement of our life. This is a result of the flow of Jesus within the believer. What a privilege! I am a Jesus pusher!!!

I am a Jesus pusher!!! ***Then He said to them, "Follow Me, and I will make you fishers of men"*** (Matthew 4:19). There is COMPLETENESS about the call of Jesus. Evangelism is not one part of Christianity emphasized whenever this aspect is needed. It is the summary focus of the throbbing heart and soul of the entire Gospel. Jesus is not calling His disciples to "do" evangelism, but to "be" witnesses. ***"I will make"*** is an expression of the creative flow of the Spirit of Christ within the believer. This call is fulfilled in the promise of Christ just before His ascension, ***"But you shall receive power when the Holy Spirit has come upon you; and you shall be witnesses to Me in Jerusalem, and in all Judea and Samaria, and to the end of the earth"*** (Acts 1:8). This statement opens with the declaration of the power to accomplish it. Jesus boldly declares the aspect of what the disciples will "be" rather than what they should "do." He closes with where this shall be accomplished.

Do not be fooled into thinking that "***fishers of*** men" is one aspect to be emphasized during special seasons of the Christian calendar. Often we are presented with various aspects of the Christian faith. No single aspect should be considered more important than the other. For instance, there is the activity of tithing. This is an important aspect of Christianity as one considers his financial obligation to the church. However, this is not the "whole" of Christianity. Other aspects would include Bible reading, prayer, and worship. All of these are important. Notice we did not include "witnessing!" It is not one of the aspects of Christianity; it is Christianity. This is who we are in intimacy with Jesus. Jesus must declare Himself. I am a Jesus pusher!!!

I am a Jesus pusher!!! ***Then He said to them, "Follow Me, and I will make you fishers of men"*** (Matthew 4:19). Jesus told the disciples that He would "***make***" them witnesses. He is not speaking to the development of skills or the acquiring of information. He refers to the essence of their "being!" Academic facts can be memorized by anyone. There are four spiritual laws and specific Scriptures, but this does not constitute the witness (***fishers of men***) He describes. There are facts about Jesus we all can know; but when those facts become truth we embrace Him for He is the truth. Jesus becomes the focus. The Biblical concept is that we experience the facts of Jesus until we are gripped with the person of Jesus. When we are gripped with the person of Jesus we "become" a witness.

We think that as Christians we must follow a specific list of activities: Bible reading, prayer, church attendance, tithing, and Christian service. If we include "witnessing" in our list it only applies to a few. We pride ourselves in the accomplishment of a few activities; they compensate for the lack of "witnessing." But this is not a proper view. Being ***fishers of men*** is not one of the many duties; it is the essence of being Christian. This is what I am going "to be" in Christ! He must be seen through my life. I am a Jesus pusher!!!

Jesus PUSHER | 243

I am a Jesus pusher!!! ***Then He said to them, "Follow Me, and I will make you fishers of men"*** (Matthew 4:19). There is a vast difference between doing evangelism and being a witness. One is about my action; the other is about what is acting upon me. One is about what I proclaim; the other is about what is being declared through me. One is about the facts I speak; the other is about the truth being seen through my life. One can be explained in terms of training, ability, personality, or talent; the other is all about Jesus being seen. One is speaking about Jesus; the other is about Jesus' speaking as He lives through me. One is about effort; the other is about relaxing and surrendering. One is about trying and duty, while the other is love, passion, and His life.

"I will make you" is a bold and explicit part of the statement of Jesus. Let me remind you ***"I will make"*** is a translation of the Greek word "poieo." It is in the active voice; this proclaims Jesus, the Speaker, responsible for the action of this verb. This is the same Greek word used for "trees bearing fruit." We will become ***fishers of men*** because the creative flow of the Spirit of Jesus will "bear" this within us. It will be the fruit of His creative ability! Aren't we involved? Aren't we doing something? We most certainly participate, but we are resourced. This is not about our talent, our ability, or us; it is about Him and His greatness. He demonstrates Himself through the individual who is available (***follow Me***). I am a Jesus pusher!!!

I am a Jesus pusher!!! ***Then He said to them, "Follow Me, and I will make you fishers of men"*** (Matthew 4:19). This fulfillment is clearly seen in the Book of Acts. Within seventy years the early disciples won their world to Jesus. They did not do it through memorized phrases or communication skills. It was not done by educational achievements (Acts 4:13). It was accomplished by an indwelt Life becoming their living. They were acted upon and responded to that action. It was about "being, not about "doing!"

Henry Stanley, a reporter, was anxious to achieve in the journalistic realm. He was given the opportunity to go to Africa for an exclusive interaction with David Livingston, the great missionary. He would be allowed to live with him and give an eyewitness account of his missionary work. When he returned to the United States his friends had a welcoming party for him. Each one was anxious to hear the details concerning life with David Livingston. After all of those weeks of living with this great missionary, Henry Stanley stated one thing, "If I had been with him any longer, I would have been compelled to be a Christian, and he never spoke to me about it at all." David Livingston was a life consumed with the essence of Jesus. The creative life of the vine is present in the branch; it has the bark of the vine and bears the fruit of the vine. Everything about the branch becomes an expression of the vine. There is not anything about the branch that has not come from the vine. No wonder Jesus cries, ***"For without Me you can do nothing,"*** (John 15:5). I am a Jesus Pusher!!!

I am a Jesus pusher!!! Far too often our evangelism exists within certain boundaries. If I am a pastor of a church, my evangelism exists within the realm of my church associations. If I teach a Sunday school class, my evangelism is focused on Sunday morning in a classroom. As a missionary my evangelism is focused on a particular geographical section of the world. If I participate in "jail ministry," that becomes the boundaries of my evangelism. However, as one views the statement of Jesus there is no suggestion of boundaries. ***Then He said to them, "Follow Me, and I will make you fishers of men"*** (Matthew 4:19). There seems to be no limits placed on the call. It is so open ended.

Would early Christianity become a sect of Judaism? Would the old prejudice limit the evangelism of their new faith? Would these early disciples develop a Christian faith within the legalism of the Jewish laws? After His resurrection before His ascension, He met with them at an appointed time in Galilee at the mountain (Matthew 28:16). He stated "the completeness of the call" by eliminating every other emphasis. There was no other focus. He highlighted "the condition of the call" by saying, ***"All authority has been given to Me in heaven and on earth"*** (Matthew 28:18). "The circumference of the call" is clearly stated as He cries, ***"Go therefore and make disciples of all nations"*** (Matthew 28:19, 20). Jesus focused their vision on ***all nations***. The old wine skins of Judaism could not contain the new wine of the indwelling of Jesus! Jesus is for everyone. I am a Jesus pusher!!!

I am a Jesus pusher!!! He spent forty days with them in a resurrection appearance. How desperately they needed the *infallible proofs* of this time. The climax to this teaching would be His parting words, *"But you shall receive power when the Holy Spirit has come upon you; and you shall be witnesses to Me in Jerusalem, and in all Judea and Samaria, and to the end of the earth,"* (Acts 1:8). This verse is so specific. *"... in Jerusalem, and in all Judea and Samaria, and to the end of the earth"* (Acts 1:8). If Jesus had only pointed *to the end of the earth*, the disciples would have focused on the remote regions and lost sight of their neighbors. If He only said *in Jerusalem*, they would have stayed in their Jewish organizational structure and settled to be a sect. He gave a clear call to their demonstration of His life to their world.

It included the religious organization that crucified Jesus; it reached out and engulfed the Samaritans. It was to be a complete demonstration of the life of Jesus all the time to everyone. There were to be no limits to the demonstration Christ's Christ through the disciples. It was fulfilled in the Book of Acts. The disciples demonstrated the life and power of Christ to the crippled beggar (Acts 3:6) and to the rulers (Acts 4:5). It took place through Philip for a man from Ethiopia, (Acts 8:27) and those who persecuted the disciples of the Lord, (Acts 22:20). There were no limits to the demonstration of Jesus through the lives of the disciples. Am I a disciple? I am a Jesus pusher!!!

———————

I am a Jesus pusher!!! ***Then He said to them, "Follow Me, and I will make you fishers of men"*** (Matthew 4:19). Jesus was determined to win the world. He received this focus from His Father, ***"For God so loved the world that He gave His only begotten Son, that whoever believes in Him should not perish but have everlasting life"*** (John 3:16). A Christian is filled with the nature of God; would not this same passion be expected?

When do I have the right to exclude someone from the witness? When do the circumstances become such that I have an excuse for not demonstrating Him? When does the other person say the words or do the thing exempting me from giving them Jesus? When does the other person have the color of skin or economic status creating a barrier not allowing Jesus to be seen in me? If you can turn the demonstration on or off, then you have ample evidence to know it is not His demonstration, but your own! Certainly He is not in control.

I am brought again to my knees in absolute submission to Him. Oh, for my life to be a demonstration of His person because He comes to live through me. Oh, for this demonstration to be so consistent, it will cover my entire world at all times. I am a Jesus pusher!!!

Jesus PUSHER | 248

I am a Jesus pusher!!! ***Then He said to them "Follow Me, and I will make you fishers of men"*** (Matthew 4:19). As you know, the Word of God is very strong concerning the focus on being rather than on doing. The New Covenant is dramatically different from the Old Covenant. The Old Testament was a focus on law accomplished through the resource and discipline of each individual. However, Jeremiah prophecies of a new day, ***"Behold, the days are coming, says the Lord, when I will make a new covenant with the house of Israel and with the house of Judah...I will put My law in their minds, and write it on their hearts; and I will be their God and they shall be My people,"*** (Jeremiah 31:31, 33).

Instead of the outside law of God condemning me when I fail, it is to be a motivation within me. Jesus fulfilled the law (Matthew 5:17). He indwells us through His Spirit; He is the resource by which the law is accomplished! The will of God is not that which I do, but it is a response to the flow of the Spirit of Jesus within my life! Obviously this does not mean there is no action of doing. It is a change from my self-action to my responding to the resource of the Spirit. The New Covenant produces more doing than under the Old Covenant. The Spirit of Jesus sources me. I have moved from "doing" to "responding." I am a Jesus pusher!!!

———————

I am a Jesus pusher!!! ***Then He said to them, "Follow Me, and I will make you fishers of men"*** (Matthew 4:19). Jesus calls them to "be" ***fishers of men***. We are reminded of this truth repeatedly in the study of the early disciples' calling. He will be responsible for making them this. The creative flow (poieo) will bear this fruit in their lives. This new experience will not be the product of an academic study or a development of a new set of skills. They will not go through a series of lectures and take a test. It will be a direct result of the Spirit of Christ living within them.

What about their participation? What is the response required from them? Matthew gives us two beautiful statements at the end of each encounter. Peter and Andrew respond to Jesus. ***They immediately left their nets and followed Him*** (Matthew 4:20). James and John had a similar response. ***And immediately they left the boat and their father and followed Him*** (Matthew 4:22). There seems to be three aspects of the response. They "***immediately***" respond to Jesus. "***They left***" highlights their attitude of surrender. They "***followed Him***" shows their attention and focus on Jesus. I want this to be my response. I am a Jesus pusher!!!

I am a Jesus pusher!!! Matthew records the response of the disciples to Jesus' call to become *fishers of men*. He writes, *"They immediately left their nets and followed Him,"* (Matthew 4:20). There is a strong emphasis on the "immediate" response of these men. The fact that James and John respond the same two verses later only heightens its importance. Matthew carefully relates to us other times when there was delay and hesitation. There was one disciple who wanted to go and bury his father before he followed Jesus. Jesus' reply was abrupt and forceful, *"Follow Me, and let the dead bury their own dead,"* (Matthew 8:21). There was no room for hesitation or postponement. The call was for an immediate response.

This is the archetype of the Scriptures. Archetype means "an original model or type after which other similar things are patterned." It becomes the prototype. The early response of these disciples established the pattern for all disciples. There must be no hesitation. If one diligently searches the Scriptures the "immediate response" is the consistent ingredient of every call from the heart of God. The revelation of God to man is never casual or optional. It is important and immediate! Hesitation undermines the sovereignty of God's will. It places man's will above God's will. It blaringly declares that we know better than God. God is so gracious; He gives us ample time to try the spirits. However, God requires response the moment we are sure of His call. This is not because it is best for Him; it is best for us. Let immediate response to Jesus be the pattern of my life. I am a Jesus pusher!!!

Jesus PUSHER | 251

I am a Jesus pusher!!! The disciples respond immediately to the call of Jesus (Matthew 4:20). This is the pattern of the Scriptures. In chapter three of the Book of Hebrews, there is a strong call to an immediate response. He uses the word "t*oday*" repeatedly. He quotes from the Book of Psalms stating what the Holy Spirit says. *"Today, if you will hear His voice, do not harden your hearts as in the rebellion,"* (Hebrews 3:7-8). He continues his emphasis by encouraging everyone to *exhort one another daily, while it is called "Today," lest any of you be hardened through the deceitfulness of sin* (Hebrews 3:13). He continues to quote the Book of Psalms, *"Today, if you will hear His voice, do not harden your hearts as in the rebellion"* (Hebrews 3:15). It must be noted that this same quotation is made again in the next chapter (Hebrews 4:7). The repetition of this quote gives us the strength of his emphasis. There must be an immediate response.

Paul writes with this same kind of urgency. He writes; *"We... plead with you,"* (2 Corinthians 6:1). Then he projects this urgency into a call for immediate response writing; *"Behold, now is the accepted time; behold, now is the day of salvation"* (2 Corinthians 6:2). It will never be easier for you to respond to Jesus. The circumstances will never be better or more conducive to your surrender to Him. Every day that passes without total response to Jesus only complicates relationships, circumstances, and your own inner heart. This is your moment! I commit to immediate response to Jesus. I am a Jesus pusher!!!

Jesus PUSHER | 252

I am a Jesus pusher!!! The disciples respond immediately to Jesus' call; why don't we? Disease responds immediately to the voice of Jesus. Jesus came down from the mountain after delivering the Sermon on the Mount. He put into living activity the theology He taught. A leper approached Him asking for healing. Jesus embraced him and spoke these words: *"I am willing; be cleansed." Immediately his leprosy was cleansed* (Matthew 8:3). His disease left immediately without debate or argument. Every illness must come under the control of Jesus without delay.

Two blind men cried out to Jesus. *So Jesus had compassion and touched their eyes. And immediately their eyes received sight, and they followed Him* (Matthew 20:34). Jesus approached another man lying by the pool. *Jesus said to him, "Rise, take up your bed and walk." And immediately the man was made well, took up his bed, and walked* (John 5:8- 9). Mark reports that Jesus took the hand of Peter's mother-in-law who was sick with a fever. *And immediately the fever left her. And she served them* (Mark 1:31). All of nature responds immediately to the call of Jesus. Is there any reason for us to do less? I am alert to His call; I will respond immediately. I am a Jesus pusher!!!

I am a Jesus pusher!!! When Jesus called two of His disciples, *"They immediately left their nets and followed Him"* (Matthew 4:20). It is the only proper response to Jesus. The Scriptures give us an excellent example of Jesus' response to us. After hours of frantically fighting to keep the boat from sinking in the night hours, Jesus appeared skipping from one storm wave to another. At first the disciples thought He was a ghost and were frightened. Jesus called out to them; He even encouraged Peter to walk on the water with Him. Peter made a feeble attempt. *But when he saw that the wind was boisterous, he was afraid and beginning to sink he cried out, saying, "Lord, save me!" And immediately Jesus stretched out His hand and caught him,* (Matthew 14:30). This reflected the love and concern of Jesus for Peter. It gives us a picture of the priorities in the heart of Jesus. You and I matter to Him.

Contained within the call of God upon our lives is the urgency of immediate response. The timing of your response is a reflection on the importance of the call. We respond to what is important to us. To set His call aside suggests our agenda is of greater importance and value than Him. The hour is pressing; the call is urgent; the response must be immediate. He has the supreme position in my heart. I will immediately respond to Him. I am a Jesus pusher!!!

———————

I am a Jesus pusher!!! The call of Jesus to the disciples required an immediate response (Matthew 4:20). The urgency is not found in the character of God; it is found in the nature of man's existence. In other words, Jesus does not necessitate the immediate response. He does not stand looking at His watch. He has not put a time limit on the call. It is not about Him; it is about you. This reality must be thoroughly understood. This may be contrary to your previous teaching or thoughts. I only urge you to carefully consider the truth.

Many have feared committing the "unpardonable sin." We missed the truth of the unpardonable sin because we misunderstand the concept. We view this sin as determined by God not by us. In other words, God set a time limit on our response. If the limit is not on time, it is certainly on the number of times we sin or reject. We think God is keeping a record. If we fail to respond to His call beyond His time limit, He simply withdraws the call. This leaves us without hope. The entire responsibility of my state is placed on God. I may realize what I have done and want to be forgiven; but God will not forgive me. Is He mad? Did I push Him beyond His limits? Has He lost patience with me and withdrawn His mercy and grace? Is there a different time schedule for every individual? Does God have more patience with some than with others? I want to convince you; this is not the case! The call of God needs an urgent response. The urgency is not because of God's requirements, but because of my personal time limitations. This is the moment to respond. I am a Jesus pusher!!!

I am a Jesus pusher!!! I marvel at the immediate response of the disciples to the call of Jesus. They established the pattern in the Scriptures for response. What if I hesitate in my response to Jesus? Have I committed the "unpardonable sin?" There is an unpardonable sin! The call of God does demand immediate response! However, the reason for the urgency of the response is not because of God. It is because of us! The condition and circumstances of our lives require immediate response. God is always willing to forgive. He has already forgiven everyone. The teaching of the Scriptures is that forgiveness is provided, and it is in place for every individual. Jesus paid for the sins of the entire world on the cross. There is no more payment necessary. In reality, God has already forgiven every man.

Therefore, the lack of forgiveness in our lives is not because God won't forgive. It is the condition of our personal hearts. This is why the call of God to repent must have an immediate response. Every moment I lack surrender to Him is a moment creating more obstacles to response. I must respond immediately! It is in my best interest! Jesus calls me to Himself. I will respond immediately. I am a Jesus pusher!!!

Jesus PUSHER | 256

I am a Jesus pusher!!!

The disciples respond immediately to Jesus' call (Matthew 4:20). Hesitation causes us to reflect on the loss of important opportunities. It is easy to be overwhelmed with guilt and despair over the loss of key moments in our lives. Our children, marriage, and career are affected. The Hebrew author speaks of such a situation. Esau was such a person. ***Esau, who for one morsel of food sold his birthright. For you know that afterward, when he wanted to inherit the blessing, he was rejected, for he found no place of repentance, though he sought it diligently with tears*** (Hebrews 12:16-17). This statement of the Hebrew author emphasizes that Esau missed his opportunity. It does not emphasize that God would not forgive him. It did not matter how much he repented or wanted the birthright; it was gone. Esau could not go back and regain his missed opportunity. No doubt all of us can think of many such situations in our lives.

If we have the courage to move beyond the guilt and despair of those missed opportunities, we feel like "second class" citizens in the Kingdom of God. It is not true. God in His sovereignty has an amazing way of redeeming the moments. His call on my life today demands an immediate response because this is His primary will for my life. Whatever might have been in the past is gone and God's best is being presented to me today. Therefore, the call of God for this moment demands an immediate response. It is not because of God; it is because of us. We live in a "time zone," which creates a past, a pressing present, and an unknown future. God does not live in this zone of time. The urgency of the response is found in the importance of this immediate moment in our lives. Do not miss the opportunity of "today!" Respond to Jesus now! I am a Jesus pusher!!!

———————

I am a Jesus pusher!!! Jesus called the disciples. Luke writes, *"They immediately left their nets and followed Him"* (Matthew 4:19). In regard to James and John Matthew wrote: *and immediately they left the boat and their father, and followed Him* (Matthew 4:22). Their response to the call of Jesus was not simply adding another activity to their schedule. They were involved in many activities but they could make time for one more. Their response to Jesus included the rejection of all other things. In order to embrace the call of Jesus with a positive response, they had to have a negative response to many other calls on their lives. Their *nets* and *boats* had been their focus. They repelled them to embrace Jesus. They could not do both.

This element is so important it colors their response. If it is removed, there is no response. The main subject and verb of each of the two groups is *"they left."* It is the translation of one Greek word (aphieme). This same Greek word is used sixteen different times for "forgiveness." It is used in reference to the departing of the devil in the "wilderness temptation" (Matthew 4:11). It describes the healing touch of Jesus forcing the fever of Peter's mother-in-law to leave (Matthew 8:15). There is a common element in the usage of the word. This Greek word (aphieme) does not refer to a simple change of location. It comes from two Greek words. The first is "apo" which is a motion term referring to changing locations. The second word is "hiemi" which means, "to send forth or away." It refers to a change of locations caused by a repelling. Responding to Jesus forces everything else to the circumference of my life. I am a Jesus pusher!!!

I am a Jesus pusher!!! The disciples left (aphiemi) their nets to follow Jesus (Matthew 4:20). The attitude of pushing aside something important to us seems to be a common characteristic in the lives of all those who embrace Jesus. The Rich Young Ruler found his life lacking. His question to Jesus revealed the lack, ***"Good Teacher, what good thing shall I do that I may have eternal life?"*** (Matthew 19:16). Undoubtedly, he considered this another activity to add to his already busy life. Jesus' final statement to the young man was a call to repel what was at the core of his focus. His riches were the heart of his value system. All other interests were strongly connected to his love of his riches, therefore, this is what he must repel.

Paul reported, ***"And I advanced in Judaism beyond many of my contemporaries in my own nation, being more exceedingly zealous for the traditions of my fathers,"*** (Galatians 1:14). His life was driven by the core value of his fathers' traditions. His career as a Pharisee, his persecution of Christians, and his zeal for Judaism were all driven by his zeal ***for the traditions of my fathers***. Jesus could never be an additional belief or interest to his life. He must push aside the traditions of his fathers' in order to embrace the call of Jesus. Jesus is worthy of my total focus. I am a Jesus pusher!!!

———————

I am a Jesus pusher!!! Peter and Andrew receive a call to follow Jesus. Up to this time they supported Jesus when they had time. Now the call of Jesus has come to them. They must repel their nets (Matthew 4:20) and their boat (Matthew 4:22). Their schedules, interests, and conversations will be driven by a different center. They will never go back to what they left. For James and John it was even more severe. *They left the boat and their father* (Matthew 4:22). It was a family business; they were carrying on the tradition of their family. This too must be set aside. At a later time Peter refers to what is being done as "*all.*" *Then Peter answered and said to Him, "See, we have left all and followed You"* (Matthew 19:27).

This theme of family is often highlighted in the Scriptures. As Jesus gave instruction to His disciples concerning ministry this issue appeared. He warned all disciples that persecution would come from within the realm of family relationships (Matthew 10:35-36). Jesus calls us all to love Him more than family relationship. He said, *"He who loves father or mother more than Me is not worthy of Me. And he who loves son or daughter more than Me is not worthy of Me"* (Matthew 10:37). Jesus is worthy of your total surrender of your total heart. I am a Jesus pusher!!!

Jesus PUSHER | 260

I am a Jesus pusher!!! For a moment I ask you to imagine going about your normal day. You have schedules to meet and obligations to fulfill. Jesus casually approaches you. You know Him and have experienced many of His crusades. His preaching powerfully moved you and brought you to a new hope. But there is something different about this particular experience. It is obvious that He specifically came to your place of work. He has come with a purpose. What does He see in you that attracts His attention?

His call is simple. *"Follow Me,"* (Matthew 4:19). *Follow* in the Greek language (deute opiso) is an expression of two words. The first word (deute) literally means, "come here." It is an imperative statement. The second word (opiso) means, "after." This identifies the place to which you are to come. Jesus says, "Your place is following after Me!" Is there any better place? This is to be your new location, dwelling place.

Matthew gives further clarity to this meaning as he describes the response of the four disciples (Matthew 4:20, 22). Matthew reports that they *followed Him*. The Greek word (akoloutheo) is a combination of "together" and "a way." The meaning is "to attend, to accompany, to go with, or follow a teacher." This Greek word occurs ninety times in the New Testament. Only eleven of these are found outside of the Gospels. In the Gospels, this word stands primarily as a term for discipleship to Jesus. Altogether seventy-three of the ninety occurrences of this verb refer to being a disciple of Jesus. This is my place; I am going after Jesus. I am a Jesus pusher!!!

I am a Jesus pusher!!! There is no reference in the Old Testament of "going after God" as a disciple. One can easily understand this lack. The Old Testament man had no vision of what God was like except for His qualities. They found it hard to conceive of following after Him. The idea is associated with idolatry. Many time the Israelites "went after other gods" (Judges 2:12; Deuteronomy 4:3; Jeremiah 11:10). But "going after" Jehovah could not be conceived in light of who He is.

Everything changed when Jesus came. This Greek verb (akoloutheo) seems to be reserved for being a disciple of Christ. There are a few exceptions when it is used in a general sense. This term referring to discipleship is confined to the four Gospels (except for Revelation 14:4). This is of major importance. In the Old Testament context the idea of being a disciple of Jehovah is not proposed. God is far removed from the people; His will is only known through His prophets. In other words, instruction and learning came by revelation from God through the prophets. In the realm of revelation there is no place for the master-teacher relationship. The authors of the epistles present the indwelling of God within the believer with an extremely different emphasis. However, in the Gospel accounts, Jesus, God in the flesh, is accessible to us. In Jesus, we know God! I am a Jesus pushing disciple of Jesus!

I am a Jesus pusher!!! A basic element in discipleship is obviously an EXTERNAL following. This was a strong element of the Jewish culture. There were many "disciples" who were designated as apprentices. In the Jewish setting, a disciple would select his teacher. The disciple received his value and esteem from the fame and importance of his teacher. In the New Testament, there were disciples of Moses (John 9:28), of the Pharisees (Matthew 22:16), of John the Baptist (Mark 2:18), and some indication of Paul (Acts 9:25). Certainly to be a disciple of Jesus was to externally attach oneself to Him. This physical attachment has strong precedence in the Old Testament. Joshua, the assistant of Moses, went where Moses went. Together Moses and Joshua ascended the mountain of the Lord (Exodus 24:13). Joshua was so diligent and faithful to Moses that he waited on the mountainside for him, staying forty days and forty nights until Moses returned with the tablets (Exodus 32:15-17).

I am a Jesus pusher, physically attached to Jesus. Think of **"Christ in you,"** (Colossians 1:27). Comprehend your entire physical existence coming under the control and presence of His person. Live in the reality of all the involvements of your physical life controlled by Him. What does this change? His presence and direction in your life can change old habits, eating patterns, wasting of energy, body drives, and interaction with others. What could be withheld from Jesus? I am a surrendered Jesus pusher!!!

I am a Jesus pusher!!! Another element in following Jesus is an EXCLUSIVE relationship. While Jesus walked the face of this earth, it was a common practice for people to attach themselves to a great teacher as a disciple. The purpose of this attachment was to learn a particular philosophy or theory. However, to be a disciple of Jesus was more than adhering to His teachings; He was the Messiah. The leaders of Israel did not have a problem accepting Jesus as another great teacher. It was His position as Messiah that threatened them. One could not embrace the teachings of Jesus without embracing Him as the Messiah. He was not one among many; He was the only One. Jesus said, *"I am the bread of life,"* (John 6:35 and 6:48). This statement comes from a discussion He had with the leaders of Israel. They quoted the Old Testament Scripture concerning their forefathers eating manna in the desert. Jesus reminded them that Moses did not give them the bread from heaven. It was His Father who promised that the true bread from heaven would give life to the world. Jesus claimed to be this bread.

A commitment to Jesus must be total abandonment to Him alone. This became evident when *from that time many of His disciples went back and walked with Him no more* (John 6:66). The statement *"went back"* has to do with "going away to the things left behind" or "no longer walking with him." These expressions mark the return of these disciples to the lives they lived before they followed Jesus. The twelve disciples expressed the true commitment necessary to be a disciple. *But Simon Peter answered Him, "Lord, to whom shall we go? You have the words of eternal life. Also we have come to believe and know that You are the Christ, the*

Son of the living God, (John 6:68-69). Count me in! I am an abandoned Jesus pusher!!!

I am a Jesus pusher!!! There were radical differences between being a disciple of Jesus and a disciple of another person of His day. One is Jesus CHOSE His disciples. Luke indicates there were a large number of disciples following Jesus. After praying all night He gathered them, ***and from them He chose twelve whom He also named apostles*** (Luke 6:13). This was unique among the Jews because it was normal for the students to choose their teachers. Also Jesus CALLED His disciples. ***Then He said to them, "Follow Me, and I will make you fishers of men"*** (Matthew 4:19). Both the "choosing" and the "calling" are strongly stated. A third difference is the COMMITMENT to leave everything. Discipleship to a rabbi was temporary. The students would assemble in a classroom and the teacher taught by question, repetition and memorization. It was expected that the disciple would render respectful service to his teacher during his apprenticeship. After this period of learning and listening, the student became the teacher. Jesus did not take His disciples to a classroom. He gave them "on the job training" in the field, on the sea, and in the villages. He engaged them in the marketplace of their lives. This way of teaching remains to this day. Since Jesus chose and called me, I will embrace the commitment. This life commitment is to be shaped and structured by His indwelling presence. But who wouldn't want to learn and be molded into His image? I am a committed Jesus pusher!!!

I am a Jesus pusher!!! The Greek word (akoloutheo) translated *followed* does not apply to the disciples after the Gospel accounts. It is extremely important to notice the use of the Greek word (matheteuo) translated ***disciple***. As a noun it appears two hundred and sixty-one times in the New Testament, however, it is only found in the Gospels and the Book of Acts. The verb form as used in the Great Commission (Matthew 28:19) only appears four times (Matthew 13:52; 27:57; 28:19; Acts 14:21). This amazed me! You would think the idea of discipleship as proposed by Jesus in the Great Commission would echo throughout the epistles. It is never mentioned in that form.

The idea of "following" or "discipleship" seems to disappear in the epistles. The Gospel approach of attachment to a physical Jesus with its external emphasis is swallowed up in the New Covenant approach of the indwelling of the Spirit of Christ. The shift from the external Jesus to the internal Jesus demands a shift in language as well. All of the old structure and language becomes old wineskins into which the new wine is poured. It cannot contain it! Jesus comes to indwell us! This takes us beyond just physically attending worship services in a physical building. We become the temple of the indwelling Jesus who transforms our lives. I am an indwelt Jesus pusher!!!

———————

Jesus PUSHER | 266

I am a Jesus pusher!!! Do not be drawn into "imitating" language. The Greek word (mimetes) translated **imitate** is in the noun form (1 Corinthians 11:1). This word group appears only eleven times in the New Testament. Eight of them are in Paul's writings. The verb occurs in the Book of Hebrews (13:7) and in the epistle of John (3 John 11). The noun form appears in the Book of Hebrews (Hebrews 6:12). The idea of imitation is not suggested as a style of Christian discipleship, but is connected to a certain activity or example which should be followed, imitated.

Let it be strongly stated that after the Gospels (the crucifixion, resurrection, and ascension of Jesus), there is no call to "follow" Jesus. He is no longer here to follow. Our relationship with Jesus drastically changed. For a moment, think of the radical difference between the God on Mount Sinai or in the Holy of Holies and the actual presence of Jesus, God in the flesh. The differences between these two manifestations form a sizable list. The kind of relationship each manifestation produced is radically different. Even more so is the difference between Jesus in the flesh and the indwelling Spirit of Jesus. The change in relationship from one manifestation to the other demands a total adjustment in language and experience. We no longer serve Him; He engages us in His service from within. We no longer do our best; He flows through us producing His best. We no longer live for Him; He is living through us! I am a privileged Jesus pusher!!!

I am a Jesus pusher!!! The Book of Acts begins with "filling" language. Luke describes the Pentecost event in four verses (Acts 2:1-4). His language is filled with Old Testament imagery such as **wind** and **fire**. However, his explanation of the coming of the Spirit of Jesus upon the believers revolves around the word **filled**. It is the standard translation in the event (Acts 2:2; 2:4). In the original language of the Scriptures, Luke uses two different Greek words, painting two different pictures of this "filling." He introduces the concept of "filling" with the Greek word "pleroo," (Acts 2:2). This describes Pentecost as an event in which the outside content (God) comes to be inside the container (the believer). The second Greek word (pletho) gives further insight into the "filling," describing it as a sponge. The picture is one of saturation, permeating, or infiltrating.

God does not indwell us as He lived in the Holy of Holies in the Old Testament. He does not dwell in some remote section of our lives in order to bark out orders or commands. He comes to saturate our lives as He saturated Jesus' life. He moves into every fiber of our being to totally source our lives. He merges with us for the sake of intimate partnership in living. The language of discipleship (following) does not describe the intimacy, sourcing, and oneness of this new filling! We can be filled, saturated, permeated, and sourced by Jesus. I am a filled Jesus pusher!!!

I am a Jesus pusher!!! The language of the Apostle Paul for relationship with Jesus is the preposition "in" (en). There are three small words used often in the English and Greek languages. "From" and "into" are motion terms, which indicate a change in location. However, "in" describes the location to which the motion brought us. It is the dwelling place, the abiding or remaining location. Paul developed the bumper sticker slogan of Christianity, *Christ in you* (Colossians 1:27). The phrases of "Christ in" and "in Christ" appear over two hundred times in Pauline literature. Jesus uses this same language in the Gospel of John as He describes what is about to take place in the fullness of the Spirit. He tells His disciples, *"At that day you will know that I am in My Father, and you in Me, and I in you,"* (John 14:20).

Being "in Christ" is not the loss of individuality, nor the absorption of the individual into the Divine person. We were created by God to be dependent upon Him. As an engine was built requiring oil, so we are created requiring Jesus. We find our full potential and fulfillment when we are "in Christ." Our full value is found here! The ideas of being "in Christ" and "Christ in you" are descriptions of the same basic union. It is the picture of "breathing." The air is in us and we are in the air. The desires of God are now dominating our mind and hearts. We are not "following" an instructor; we are not "imitating" an example. We are empowered by the very nature of Jesus. Everything is different when we are "in Christ" and Christ is "in us." I am a Jesus pusher!!!

———————

I am a Jesus pusher!!! The Biblical language of Jesus living in us must be brought into the language of our culture. God is not sitting on Mount Sinai, belching out His laws. He is not watching me closely to see if I "obey" His commands. Jesus comes to indwell me in the fullness of His Spirit. But His indwelling is not a simple relocation of the Old Testament God. He does not live within me to tell me what to do. Both views assume the approach of "performance" or "doing." He is intimate and one with my very inner being. I am not living in obedience to His orders; I RESPOND to His desires and nature. He does not give me a plan, and I am to accomplish it. He fills my life with His nature; moment-by-moment I respond to His desires, which fulfill His plan. He does not instruct me on what to do to be holy; He saturates my life with His holy nature. I respond to His urges rather than mine. His feelings are now mine; His emotions saturate mine. I live a life of response to Him. We are one!

I no longer view the disciples of Jesus in the Gospels with envy. Their opportunity of physically following Jesus does not begin to compare with the wonder of my responding to His indwelling presence. Thank you Jesus for being "in" me! This is far beyond "religion;" it is intimacy with Jesus. I am "an embracing Jesus" Jesus pusher!!!

I am a Jesus pusher!!! ***And Jesus went about all Galilee*** (Matthew 4:23). Jesus is not going about Galilee by Himself. This is clarified in the Greek word (perigu) translated ***went about***. It is actually a combination of two Greek words. The first is "peri" which means "about," and "gu" which means "to lead, carry, or go." This Greek word highlights not just the individual changing locations, but includes someone else as it happens. The emphasis of the word embraces the disciples who were called. They experienced the ministry of Jesus in Galilee as a member of the audience, but also participated with Him in its accomplishment.

As Jesus went around Galilee He was leading and He included these disciples. It is emphatic in the Greek text.

When Jesus originally called these men, He called them to be ***"fishers of men,"*** (Matthew 4:19). The focus of their lives was to change from a focus on self to others. Now they are experiencing practical ministry with Jesus fulfilling this focus. In three verses (Matthew 4:23-25), we are given a description of those included in this focus. He lists those possessed of ***all kinds of sickness and all kinds of disease*** (Matthew 4:23). He gives further details by including ***sick people who were afflicted with various disease and torments, and those who were demon-possessed, epileptics, and paralytics*** (Matthew 4:24). All the people we would normally shun, He embraced and changed. Jesus called this ministry! If I am filled with Him, what will He do through me? Would He not continue with this same focus? Because I am focused on Jesus, I am gripped with His focus. His heart becomes by heart! I am a Jesus pusher!!!

———————————

I am a Jesus pusher!!! Matthew gives a description of the people to whom Jesus ministers (Matthew 4:23-25). For instance, there are the INCURABLE. Nothing was too hard for this Spirit-sourced Man. There is no area, no condition, and no situation in which Jesus in not adequate. Matthew develops this in the chapters to come by carefully choosing illustrative examples.

When you couple this with His theme of the "Kingdom," it becomes evident God invaded the demonic control and authority. Not all sickness is a direct result of personal sin. Job suffered greatly, though he was blameless, upright, feared God, and turned away from evil (Job 1:1). On one occasion the disciples assumed that the man who was born blind was being punished either for his own sin or that of his parents. Jesus corrected them, *"Neither this man nor his parents sinned, but that the works of God should be revealed in him,"* (John 9:3). However, all sickness is indirectly the result of the curse of sin upon our world. Every miracle of healing is an invasion of the control and authority of the demonic Kingdom. It is a declaration that the Kingdom of God is present. There are none who are incurable; the forces of evil have no grip on anyone that cannot be released. There are no habits, no bondage, no sin, no guilt, and no situation the Spirit of Jesus cannot conquer. I am a delivered Jesus pusher!!!

I am a Jesus pusher!!! Jesus calls His disciples to the focus of His heart. His heart is focused on people. It is an INCLUSIVE focus! Matthew describes the multitudes to which Jesus ministered (Matthew 4:23-25). He lists three specific types. There are ***those who were demon-possessed*** (Matthew 4:24). It is clearly stated that many physical and mental afflictions are caused directly by demons. Jesus conquered the demonic authority and control. The issue was not the miracle but the people. Jesus is focused on people. Matthew goes on to list a second category, ***epileptics***. The Greek word (seleniazomai) translated ***epileptics*** literally means "moonstruck." In many cultures the mentally ill and those who have convulsions or seizures were thought to be under the influence of the moon. In our passage, demon possession and mental illness are separated. They are included in the ministry of Jesus; the issue is not the condition but the people! The third group was the ***paralytics***. This is a general term representing a wide range of crippling handicaps. The Jews of Jesus' day looked upon those who were handicapped with disdain. Along with the poor, they were barred from the temple. For Jesus the issue was not the condition of the person but the person.

These three terms characterize the three broad areas of man's great need, the spiritual, the mental, and the physical. Jesus invades the demonic territory; He conquers every situation and condition. ***And they brought to Him all sick people,... and He healed them*** (Matthew 4:24). The disciples are called to be "***fishers of men***." This is a call to all people; there are none excluded. I am an included Jesus pusher!!!

I am a Jesus pusher!!! Matthew writes, ***Then His fame went throughout all Syria; and they brought to Him all sick people*** (Matthew 4:24). The ministry of Jesus is INTERNATIONAL. In this passage, ***Syria*** refers to the region north of Galilee. The Greek word (akoee) translated ***fame*** means "to hear something." It is used for the idea of a rumor. The Gentiles all over Syria and to the north heard of what was going on in Galilee. The result was inevitable. Great multitudes of patients from all over Galilee and Syria came to Him

Christianity would never be contained within the boundaries of the Jews. It is exciting to read the Book of Acts. It is here we discover the explosion of Christianity to the whole world. Christianity could not be a sect of Judaism. Jesus came for the people of the world. If we have the mind of Christ, we cannot maintain racial barriers. The New Testament states, ***For He Himself is our peace, who has made both one, and has broken down the middle wall of separation, having abolished in His flesh the enmity, that is, the law of commandments contained in ordinances, so as to create in Himself one new man from the two, thus making peace*** (Ephesians 2:14-15). Jesus even embraced me! If all people are not included, I am not included. I am a thankful Jesus pusher!!!

I am a Jesus pusher!!! If people are the central issue with Jesus, how many would be enough? The number is INNUMERABLE! Matthew makes no attempt to count the miracles or the number of sick. Look at the words he uses: ***all kinds of sickness, all kinds of disease*** (Matthew 4:23), ***all Syria, all sick people, He healed them*** (Matthew 4:24), ***Great multitudes, from Galilee, and from Decapolis, Jerusalem, Judea, and beyond the Jordan*** (Matthew 4:25). Can you fathom the numbers of people involved?

There were two occasions which required feeding the crowd before they returned home. Jesus was concerned and said, ***"I have compassion on the multitude, because they have now continued with Me three days and have nothing to eat. And I do not want to send them away hungry, lest they faint on the way"*** (Matthew 15:32). The number of this crowd was four thousand men, besides women and children. In a previous setting Jesus fed five thousand men, besides women and children (Matthew 14:21). During Jesus' entrance into Jerusalem on Palm Sunday, the Pharisees reacted to the great crowd by saying, ***"You see that you are accomplishing nothing. Look, the world has gone after Him!"*** (John 12:19). We must not be content with just our little group. We cannot maintain our church facility and enjoy our fellowship. We are driven by the heart of Jesus to win our world. Do you have the mind of Christ? I am a driven Jesus pusher!!!

I am a Jesus pusher!!! If there is any doubt about this focus of ministry? Listen to His words in the Great Commission. ***"Go therefore and make disciples of all the nations, baptizing them in the name of the Father and of the Son and of the Holy Spirit"*** (Matthew 28:19). While this truth echoes within our minds, let it be stated that Jesus never focused on multitudes. He always focused on individuals. But individuals became innumerable. His concern and passion was for people. He must win all people, one at a time. It was not great numbers that mattered, but the individuals contained within those numbers. No one could be left out.

Age had captured Commissioner Samuel Logan Brengle, the leader of the Salvation Army. He was expected to address the great assembly of the Salvation Army. It would no doubt be his final words to them. But to their great disappointment, he became too weak attend. A telegram was sent in his place. With trembling hands the telegram was opened before this large expectant body. The last message they would hear from their beloved leader was read. His message to them was "Others! Others! Others!" This is the mind of Christ. If I would know His heart, it is a heart for others. You cannot embrace Jesus without embracing others. You cannot minister in Jesus without ministering to everyone. His heart changes my narrow, opinionated, and prejudiced thinking. I will be a platform for His life to touch others. I am a Jesus pusher!!!

I am a Jesus pusher!!! Matthew summarizes Jesus' ministry in three verses (Matthew 4:23-25). But there is one topic he does not mention. It is INCOME. Personal gain is never addressed. There seems to be no pay. Nothing is spoken of offerings or salary. In my translation of verse twenty-four the word *fame* is used, but not in the sense of power and prestige. The Greek word (akoee) translated *fame* means "to hear something." It is used for the idea of a rumor. We will find as His ministry progresses that *"Foxes have holes and birds of the air have nests, but the Son of Man has nowhere to lay His head,"* (Matthew 8:20).

If you study the four Gospel accounts carefully searching for a hidden agenda or an angle, you simply will not find one. There is no material gain involved; there is no power acquired. He never strives for a position of rule. The applause of the crowd quickly dismayed Him (John 2:24). The heart of His Father drove him. He wanted what the Father wanted. It must be understood! He did not have intimacy with His Father because He gave His life for others. NO! He gave His life for others because He was intimate with the Father. How will His disciples become *fishers of men*? He will not train them in techniques; He will not teach them skills of crowd psychology. He will reveal to them intimacy with His Father which gives a passion for men. Oh! I would be possessed by His heart! I am a burning Jesus pusher!!!

I am a Jesus pusher!!! The Kingdom of Heaven is a communication of "good news!" It is *the gospel of the kingdom* (Matthew 4:23). The Greek word (euaggelion) translated *gospel* literally means "good news." It comes from "eu" which is "good or well" and "aggello" which is "to proclaim or tell." The Greek word "aggellos" is an angel who bears the message of God. This is the root word of the *gospel* (euaggelion). In the Greek culture this term became a technical one for "news of victory!" A whole ritual surrounds the coming of the messenger who bears this news. All of this is combined in the announcement of the birth of Christ. The angel of the Lord bears the message to Joseph. It is the "good news" of victory. He said, *"And she will bring forth a Son, and you shall call His name Jesus, for He will save His people from their sins,"* (Matthew 1:21).

The focus of the *gospel* is "good news;" it is news of victory. It is not news of the awfulness of sin; it is not news of judgment. While both of these elements are true, it is not the focus of the *gospel*. The "good news" does not highlight hell with all of the consequences of sin. The wickedness and cunning of Satan is not the teaching of the *gospel*. The *gospel* is "good news!" Upon hearing it, the heart of man realizes there is hope. Life can be different. Sin can be forgiven; there is a way out! Why would we want to share anything else but the "good news?" I am a good new Jesus pusher!!!

I am a Jesus pusher!!! Matthew specifically attaches the *gospel* with *the kingdom*; it is the *gospel of the kingdom* (Matthew 4:23). It is the "good news" of the *kingdom*. The content of the *kingdom* is the content of the *gospel*. *Kingdom* in this context must be interpreted as the rule, which God establishes in the hearts of men when Jesus is received by faith. The focus of the Kingdom is not on size, amount, population, space, or finances. It is a focus on the King and more specifically on the ruling of the King. Where ever the King rules the Kingdom is present.

There is a reference to the Kingdom of God in its future state during which we will reign with Christ forever (Revelation 22:1-5). Even this is simply an expansion of the indwelling presence of Jesus reigning from the throne of our inner lives. If the content of the *gospel* is the *Kingdom* and the content of the *Kingdom* is Jesus, then the content of the *gospel* is Jesus. It is not simply the truth about Jesus; it is Jesus Himself! It is not the action or result of Jesus' coming; it is the actual reality of the person of Jesus. The *Kingdom* is found in the embrace of this person; intimacy with Jesus is the substance of the *Kingdom*. No one is in the *Kingdom* who does not have Jesus present within him or her. Jesus is the *Kingdom*. The content of the *Kingdom* is the actual person of Jesus reigning in the inner person of our lives. It is "good news." There has never been better news. Jesus forgives and cleanses us from all sin; He embraces us and fills us with His presence. The King indwells us. I am a good news Jesus pusher!!!

I am a Jesus pusher!!! "Kerygma" is a parallel Greek word to the word **gospel** (euaggelion). As a verb, it is the act of preaching or proclaiming. As a noun it is translated "preaching." Paul proclaims, **For since, in the wisdom of God, the world through wisdom did not know God, it pleased God through the foolishness of the message preached** (kerygma) **to save those who believe** (1 Corinthians 1:21). The "kerygma" is the content of the "euaggelion."

Preaching always deals with the content of the good news. It is a fixed content. Since preaching is the revelation of this content, there are elements of teaching present in preaching. No one can be said to be "preaching" if they are not exposing the content of the good news (**gospel**). The fixed content of the **gospel** contains seven truths. It is a revelation of prophecies fulfilled. Jesus is born of the seed of David in fulfillment of those prophecies. Jesus died on a cross for our sins. He was buried in a borrowed tomb; He resurrected from the dead through the power of the Father. He ascended to be King of the Kingdom while sitting at the right hand of the Father. He will return to restore all things! Notice all of these truths are about Jesus. The content of the **gospel** is to reveal the person of Jesus. There are only fifty-two Sunday mornings in our year. We cannot afford to use even one of them to highlight any issue other than Jesus. He is the content of the **gospel**. I am a Jesus pusher!!!

I am a Jesus pusher!!! We must clearly understand that the **gospel** (good news) is about the **Kingdom**. The **Kingdom** is about Jesus; therefore, He is the good news. If Jesus is the **Kingdom**, we must carefully consider what it means to be in Him (the **Kingdom**) and what it means for the **Kingdom** to be in us. The **Kingdom** naturally takes on the characteristics and mannerisms of the King. Who He is, what He desires, His passion must naturally become mine. The moment I embrace Him, His heart becomes my heart. What is His heart? It becomes very obvious as we saturate in our passage. The call of Jesus to the disciples is to "**Follow Me**" (Matthew 4:19). They are to attach themselves to Him. The automatic result of such a relationship will be **"and I will make you fishers of men,"** (Matthew 4:19). It is the by-product of engaging Him. The creative flow of His Spirit will shape and mold them into **fishers of men**. They can choose to embrace Him or not embrace Him; but they cannot choose the consequences of their choice. If they choose to embrace Him, they will become expressions of His heart's passion. It is others.

Our focus is always on Jesus. We are not task oriented. The **Kingdom** is not a career or job to accomplish. We do not meet quotas. We are people who are captured by Jesus. He spills His heart through us to win our world. Who will engage their world with the message of Jesus? It is the people who possess the heart of Jesus. Why would anyone embrace the need of someone else? It is because the heart of Jesus, the One they love, compels them. Why would someone go out of their way to win others to Jesus? The **Kingdom** is within them; what drives the King also drives them. I am a driven Jesus pusher!!!

I am a Jesus pusher!!! It is a summary (Matthew 4:23-25)! The focus is on three activities. They are ***preaching, teaching,*** and ***healing***. Matthew understood the importance of these healing miracles. God is doing something new through Jesus. Therefore, the healing miracles VALIDATE HIS PERSON (who He is). He is sourced by God to usher in the Kingdom of God. This must be seen against the absolute void of miracle workers in His day. There was no parallel among the rabbis. Schlatter states, "In Palestinian Judaism of the time there were no workers of miracles, nor were there any who were honored as such." Jesus did thousands of miracles. They created such a stir; Palestine and the surrounding region responded to His ministry. The Anointed One of God was among the people.

However, Jesus continually downplayed the spectacular aspect of these miracles. He constantly requested those receiving miracles not to tell anyone (Matthew 8:4; Mark 7:36; 8:26; 8:30). There were no theatrical activities to impress the crowds; there was no fixed pattern of action or words added to give drama to the healing. Jesus simply touched or gave a quiet word. He gave a simple command to an evil spirit. It was a private morning call to a "sleeping girl" (Matthew 9:25). A woman touched Him from behind (Matthew 9:21); He gave a word from a distance (Matthew 8:13). All was done naturally, informally, and simply. This bespeaks the very authority and character of His person. What could He speak into your life? I am a listening Jesus pusher!!!

I am a Jesus pusher!!! The healing miracles of Jesus mark a significant step beyond the ministry of John the Baptist. John consistently proclaimed Jesus as ***"One mightier than I"*** (Matthew 3:11). Priests and Levites from Jerusalem asked John the Baptist, ***"Who are you?"*** (John 1:19). They accused him of being Elijah, the Prophet, or the Christ. He denied all of these identifications and said, ***"I baptize with water, but there stands One among you whom you do not know. It is He who, coming after me, is preferred before me, whose sandal straps I am not worthy to loose"*** (John 1:26-27). While Jesus and John the Baptist preached the same message of repentance (Matthew 3:2; 4:17), the healing miracles placed Jesus far above the ministry of John. They identified Him as the One for whom John was the forerunner.

The healing miracles not only validated His Person as the Messiah, but they also pointed to the content and character of that Person. They were cures, blessings, and favors. The Spirit of God invades demonic territory in each miracle. It demonstrates the character of the Messiah as love, grace, and mercy. It is the call of a mother hen who gathers her chicks around her (Matthew 23:37). If ***God so loved the world that He gave His only begotten Son*** (John 3:16), would not the expression of that Son be one of great love? Did not God express His heart through the Messiah in compassion for the needs of His people? Oh, how He loves you. Embrace Him! I am a Jesus pusher!!!

I am a Jesus pusher!!! These miracles VALIDATE HIS PURPOSE (what is available) (Matthew 4:23-25). They announce the arrival of the Kingdom of God. Jesus allows us clarity in the statements to follow. We address no individual case of sickness in any specific person. However, the Scriptures do propose the view that sickness is the consequence of the universal corrupt nature of sin plaguing the earth. The fall of man (Genesis 3) resulted in total change of the human nature. Inwardly man was radically different which affected his perspective (Genesis 3:7). The curse of sin resulted in multiplication of sorrow (Genesis 3:16), and came upon the social life of mankind. The ground came under the curse of sin (Genesis 3:17). Death was experienced (Genesis 3:19). Paul speaks of this as *the sufferings of this present time* (Romans 8:18). He explains that there is an *earnest expectation of the creation* waiting for the redemptive hour (Romans 8:19). He pictures the entire creation groaning and laboring with birth pangs waiting for the relief of redemption (Romans 8:22). He explains that creation needs to be *delivered from the bondage of corruption into the glorious liberty of the children of God* (Romans 8:21).

The miracles of Jesus flow through a Spirit sourced man and are the first acts of the new Kingdom of God. Jesus delivered the paralytic by forgiving him of his sins. When the scribes questioned His right to do so, Jesus said, *"For which is easier, to say, 'Your sins are forgiven you,' or to say, 'Arise and walk'?"* (Matthew 9:5). Jesus reversed the effects of sin. I want to give my life to Him for this purpose. I am a receptive Jesus pusher!!!

———————

I am a Jesus pusher!!! There is theological controversy over the Messianic passage stated in the prophecy of Isaiah. *But He was wounded for our transgressions, He was bruised for our iniquities; the chastisement of our peace was upon Him, and by His stripes we are healed* (Isaiah 53:5). Forgiveness is found through His sufferings, the cross. However, the debate is over what else may be granted to us through His sufferings. Does "*by His stripes we are healed*" signify we can expect to be continually healed of every sickness as a provision of the cross? Whatever you may conclude about this issue, it is evident that the sacrificial death of Jesus does embrace the physical needs of my life. The cross of Jesus was not a bandage on the oppression of the demonic authority of the Kingdom of darkness. It was an invasion and overthrow of that authority.

The healing miracles of Jesus demonstrated the nature of God's kingdom as health-giving, down-to-earth, and relevant to the daily problems of the entire person. These miracles revealed the compassionate character of Jesus toward ordinary, undervalued individuals, degraded by Satan. The healing miracles left no doubt that a new power was at work in the world. A Spirit sourced Man was aggressively invading the devil's territory. I want to be such a Jesus filled person. I am a Jesus pusher!!!

I am a Jesus pusher!!! The healing miracles of Jesus must have numbered in the thousands (Matthew 4:23-25). These miracles VALIDATE HIS PLAN (who we are). Demonstrated in the healing miracles is the power of God fulfilling His plan to restore mankind from his fallen state. Revealed in this restoration is the revelation of the substance of who we are in God's mind and heart.

Jesus had numerous controversies with the Pharisees over healing on the Sabbath day. The Pharisees saw healing on the Sabbath as a medical procedure, which could wait for another day. On the Sabbath day Jesus healed a woman who had a spirit of infirmity for eighteen years. *But the ruler of the synagogue answered with indignation, because Jesus had healed on the Sabbath; and he said to the crowd, "There are six days on which men ought to work; therefore come and be healed on them, and not on the Sabbath day"* (Luke 13:14). Jesus saw healing as a manifestation of the Kingdom of God struggling against the Kingdom of darkness. Jesus *answered Him and said, "Hypocrite! Does not each one of you on the Sabbath loose his ox or donkey from the stall, and lead it away to water it? So ought not this woman, being a daughter of Abraham, whom Satan has bound – think of it – for eighteen years, be loosed from this bond on the Sabbath?"* (Luke 13:15, 16). Perhaps we misunderstand healing! It is not simply a physical correction but a complete spiritual change for life. I am a Jesus pusher!!!

I am a Jesus pusher!!! In the minds of some scholars there is a controversy between the structure of man as presented in the Old and New Testaments. I personally do not see the conflict. In the Old Testament, the structure of mankind is a dichotomy. The Hebrew concept held to man being twofold. Man is physical evidenced by his body. He is also spiritual evidenced by his inner spirit. The story of creation is a demonstration of that. ***And the Lord God formed man of the dust of the ground, and breathed into his nostrils the breath of life; and man became a living being*** (Genesis 2:7). Man's body was formed from the physical ingredient God had already created. Then God breathed into man's body the ***"breath of life."*** The Hebrew word translated ***breath*** (neshamah) can be translated "breath, wind, or spirit." Man received his ability of life from God. The Hebrew word translated ***"being"*** (nephesh) is used seven hundred and fifty-three times in the Old Testament. When this word is applied to a person, it doesn't refer to a specific part of a human being. The Scriptures view a person as a composite, whole, fully relating to God, and not divided in any way.

Jesus invaded the demonic hold Satan had on mankind by miracles (Matthew 4:23-25). He could not restore man physically without restoring him spiritually. When the spiritual life of man is whole it affects his physical life! Jesus ministers to the whole person. I invite Him into my whole person. I am a Jesus pusher!!!

———————

I am a Jesus pusher!!! Our view of the man's structure is important. A person is not a whole person without his body; a person is not a whole person without the inner life God breathed into him. Therefore, man is a dichotomy in structure consisting of his body and inner life. This is vividly demonstrated for us in the physical resurrection of Jesus as well as in the promise of our own personal resurrection. The body is not something to be discarded in the eternal state. It is not a temporary dwelling place for inner life as a tin can is a container for food. The body and inner life are paired together to form who we are. God created my personality and inner life; He did not casually place my inner life in just any "body." He tailor made my body to match my personality and inner life (Psalms 139). I am a matched set!

Medical doctors recognize the intimate connection between the physical body and the inner spirit. The physical sickness of the body can easily affect the attitude and response of the inner spirit. Likewise the state of the spirit can bring sickness to the body. One of the mysteries of redemption is the focus on redeeming the physical world. *For we know that the whole creation groans and labors with birth pangs together until now. Not only that, but we also who have the firstfruits of the Spirit, even we ourselves groan within ourselves, eagerly waiting for the adoption, the redemption of our body* (Romans 8:22-23). Man is not just a body or just a spirit (soul); He is the combination of the two. Both need redemption and both live eternally. I give both my spirit and body to Jesus. I am committed Jesus pusher!!!

I am a Jesus pusher!!! In speaking of the resurrection of the body, Paul said, *"It is sown a natural body, it is raised a spiritual body. There is a natural body, and there is a spiritual body"* (1 Corinthians 15:44). The body of man was designed for earthly existence and is mortal. Paul illustrates the death of this body as the seed, which a farmer sows. He says, *"Foolish one, what you sow is not made alive unless it dies"* (1 Corinthians 15:36). So the *natural body* must come to death so the *spiritual body* can live. When Paul speaks of a *spiritual body*, he does not exclude the physical. Both the *natural* and the *spiritual* are physical. The focus is on what sources or produces those bodies. The Greek word (pneumatikos) translated *spiritual* means what dominates or sources. The Spirit of God sources the *spiritual body*.

How does this dichotomy of the man's structure instruct us for today? Obviously God's concern is for the whole man. The movement of God in our lives calls for the whole man to respond. This is not just a spiritual response, but it is also a physical response. The fruits of the Spirit are not only to operate within the realm of my spirit but also in my physical body and its drives. I am bringing my mind, will, emotions, and body under the authority of Jesus. I am a surrendered Jesus pusher!!!

I am a Jesus pusher!!! In speaking of the resurrection of the body, Paul said, *"It is sown a natural body, it is raised a spiritual body. There is a natural body, and there is a spiritual body"* (1 Corinthians 15:44). The body of man was designed for earthly existence and is mortal. Paul illustrates the death of this body as the seed, which a farmer sows. He says, *"Foolish one, what you sow is not made alive unless it dies"* (1 Corinthians 15:36). So the *natural body* must come to death in order that the *spiritual body* might live. When Paul speaks of a *spiritual body*, he is not speaking of one that is not physical. Both the *natural* and the *spiritual* are physical. The focus is on what sources or produces the body. The Greek word (pneumatikos) translated *spiritual* means what dominates or sources. The Spirit of God sources the *spiritual body*.

How does this dichotomy of man's structure instruct us for life today? Jesus' obvious concern is for the whole man. The presence of Jesus in our lives calls for the whole man to respond. This is not just a spiritual response but also a physical response. The fruits of the Spirit of Jesus are not only to operate within the realm of my spirit but also in the realm of my physical body and drives. Both my body and spirit must come under the control of Jesus. I am a controlled Jesus pusher!!!

I am a Jesus pusher!!! Paul often discussed the relationship of the physical body with our spiritual life. He determined that all things were allowed for him; but ***all things are not helpful*** (1 Corinthians 6:12). The deciding factor is one of "control." He said, ***"I will not be brought under the power of any"*** (1 Corinthians 6:12). He uses the illustration of food. ***"Foods for the stomach and the stomach for foods"*** is his statement (1 Corinthians 6:13). The issue is Jesus' authority over both. Paul continues by illustrating sexual immorality. ***"Do you not know that your bodies are members of Christ? Shall I then take the members of Christ and make them members of a harlot? Certainly not!"*** (1 Corinthians 6:15). From this thought comes a resounding conclusion: ***"Or do you not know that your body is the temple of the Holy Spirit who is in you whom you have from God, and you are not your own?"*** (1 Corinthians 6:19).

God seems to allow the spirit to suffer in dark moments. An ancient saint spoke much of "the dark night of the soul." It is in times when Jesus seems to abandon us that He is the most present. He strengthens and grows the spiritual character of my life. James said, ***"Knowing that the testing of your faith produces patience. But let patience have its perfect work, that you may be perfect and complete, lacking nothing"*** (James 1:3, 4). If Jesus allows difficulties, pressures, and trials in our spirit's being will this not also be true in the physical? In fact, the avenue of trials may become the physical. I will trust Jesus with my spiritual and physical life. I am a trusting Jesus pusher!!!

Jesus
PUSHER | **291**

I am a Jesus pusher!!! Jesus never divides my spiritual from my physical! In other words, what happens in my physical activities is a direct response to my spiritual life; my spiritual life responds to my physical activities. We are a whole being designed to be controlled of Jesus.

Paul expressed this from his own experience, *"And lest I should be exalted above measure by the abundance of the revelations, a thorn in the flesh was given to me, a messenger of Satan to buffet me, lest I be exalted above measure"* (2 Corinthians 12:7). Evidently Paul had an infirmity in the flesh, which affected his spiritual condition. After desperately praying three times for its removal, he was reminded that the strength of Jesus is experienced in our weakness (2 Corinthians 12:9). Paul proclaimed that he would rather embrace and experience the infirmity and have the power of Christ, than to be without the infirmity and lack Jesus.

The call to intimacy with Jesus is to allow His Lordship to reign both in body and spirit, the whole man. If this means healing of physical infirmity, the Lord will be praised. If this means experiencing physical infirmity, the Lord will be praised. Either way Jesus is fulfilling the purpose and plan for my life. I am a committed Jesus pusher!!!

———————

I am a Jesus pusher!!! Matthew emphasizes a connection between the mountain and the Sermon on the Mount. He gives his overall assessment of the beginning of Jesus' ministry in Galilee and then flows into this sermon. The success of this ministry is profound; it affected foreign lands bordering Palestine. However, the multitudes did not motivate Jesus to preach The Sermon on the Mount; the disciples motivated him. *And seeing the multitudes, He went up on a mountain, and when He was seated His disciples came to Him. Then He opened His mouth and taught them* (Matthew 5:1-2). What did they hear? How did they respond? At the close of the sermon he reflects: *And so it was, when Jesus had ended these sayings, that the people were astonished* (ekplesso) *at His teaching, for He taught them as one having authority, and not as the scribes* (Matthew 7:28-29). This Greek word begins with "ek" for the of purpose intensity. "Plesso" means, "to strike out, force out by a blow." It means "knocking one out of his senses."

It was the great "Manifesto of the Kingdom of Heaven!" These Jews had only experienced the Old Covenant; Jesus presents the New Covenant. There are as many outlines of the Sermon on the Mount as there are scholars who study it. If their conclusion is Jesus, each one is legitimate. Only when He is at the center does the puzzle of the Sermon on the Mount become a complete picture. Jesus is not only the speaker of the sermon; He is the key unlocking the door to its entrance. You may ask, "How can I live this sermon out?" The answer is Jesus! The Sermon on the Mount is not impossible in Jesus. I am a Jesus pusher!!!

I am a Jesus pusher!!! As we approach the beginning of the Sermon on the Mount, please keep in mind the astonishment of the listening Jews; they were "knocked out of their senses." It was not because Jesus added new laws for them to keep or presented them with a new moral code of holiness. It was not a new standard of righteousness, but a new standpoint of righteousness. Outside of the Sermon on the Mount, every moral system is a road we must travel. It requires self-denial, discipline, struggle, and effort to arrive at the goal of morality. It is a goal finally achieved; it is the end result. Jesus' approach is the exact opposite. He does not end with the goal, but begins with it. He placed His disciples in the position other teachers presented as the end. What others labor to earn, Jesus gives! Others demand; Jesus bestows! The Sermon on the Mount is not a new law or moral system, but a new life.

Since this is true, the promises attached to many of the statements in the sermon are not rewards or results. They are the natural essence of the Kingdom. Look carefully at the "Beatitudes." You do not become **_poor in spirit_** and therefore enter the Kingdom. The **_poor in spirit_** dwell in a spiritual state; it is the spiritual state of the Kingdom. In other words, a description of the condition of the inner, present, spiritual reality of a member of the Kingdom is the eight Beatitudes. The inner awareness of the child of the Kingdom is one of absolute helplessness. Is this not the fundamental motivation which drives men to Jesus? King Jesus becomes our only source! I am a helpless Jesus pusher!!!

I am a Jesus pusher!!! Jesus begins the Sermon on the Mount by congratulating us on our arrival at the state of helplessness (***poor in spirit***). "Mourning" (the second Beatitude) is a natural state which results from being ***poor in spirit***. It begins with our heartbrokenness over self-sourcing. It becomes so dominate that the child of the Kingdom lives in the state of responding out of his helplessness. It compels him to Jesus, the King. The Kingdom is not a reward for those who ***mourn***; it is the dwelling place in the Kingdom.

One does not develop "meekness" (the third beatitude) as an attribute of life and receive the Kingdom as a reward for achievement. The Kingdom person is ***poor in spirit***, a constant recognition of helplessness. He understands and mourns over the disaster in his life produced by the "rich in spirit," the pride of life. He dwells in a state of aggressive anger against all such pride; this is called "meekness." Since he is ***poor in spirit*** he does not live with pride; he lives in the heart of Jesus; he thinks with the mind of the King. He conquers sin as he joins the dying of Jesus, the cross! He is gentle and mild. In other words, if you are ***poor in spirit*** (properly understood) you ***mourn***; if you ***mourn*** over the results of all self-centeredness, you are ***meek***. If you are ***meek***, you are in the Kingdom. If you are in the Kingdom, you are ***poor in spirit***, you ***mourn***, and you are ***meek***. The connecting link between each of these is Jesus. Since Jesus is the Kingdom, the only possibility we have of living in this state of being comes through Him. It is His grace and forgiveness which brings it to pass. I am a passionate Jesus pusher!!!

I am a Jesus pusher!!! Congratulations! You are ***poor in spirit***. That is the beginning of the Sermon on the Mount. It is an expression of total helplessness. This drives us to "mourning" (the second Beatitude). It is a recognition and admission of our condition of helplessness. In this response, Jesus, our total Resource, is able to fill us. The combination of our helplessness and His Person becomes the Kingdom of God. I am not the Kingdom; He is not the Kingdom; "we" are the Kingdom! Who He is becomes visible in us. Meekness (the third Beatitude) becomes our experience.

These three Beatitudes whelm up within the child of the Kingdom. A passionate, undying ***hunger and thirst for righteousness*** (the fourth Beatitude) becomes the appetite of those in the Kingdom. The Christian is not one who constantly tries to control his appetite for sin. The state of the Kingdom is not resisting, but embracing. We are not swimming upstream; He attracts us with the wonder of His love! We ***hunger and thirst*** for Him as a lover for his beloved. As the stomach longs for food, so my soul longs for Him. ***As the deer pants for the water brooks, so pants my soul for You, O God*** (Psalms 42:1). He fills my hunger for Him, which creates more hunger for Him. He is takes me to new levels of relationship. I am a filled Jesus pusher!!!

———————

I am a Jesus pusher!!! The first four Beatitudes focus on our direct response to Jesus; the last four Beatitudes focus on the flow of Jesus through us to our world. The first one is **_mercy_**. Expressed through the child of the Kingdom is a compassionate, benevolent, and merciful involvement of thought and action, the heart of Jesus. The mercy of Jesus is experienced in the Kingdom; therefore the child of the Kingdom is merciful. This enables Him to experience more **_mercy_**.

The child of the Kingdom who has this heart interacts with his world in a state of holiness. He is **_pure in heart_**. This purity is not contained in laws or duty, but in condition and inner sincerity. Is it his personal holiness? Can he claim ownership to it as if he produces it? All the previous Beatitudes declare, "No!" He dwells in the state of the Kingdom, Jesus. The nature of Jesus is now his nature. His helplessness, **_poor in spirit_**, drives him to "mourning" over the devastation and destruction of his own self-effort. "Meekness" and **_hunger and thirst_** compel him to focus on Jesus. **_Mercy_** and **_pure in heart_** are his living experience.

This child of the Kingdom lives in "peace." "Peace" radiates and permeates all his surroundings. It is not the absence of conflict, but the reigning of the King of Rightness. In fact, this dominates within the circumstances of "persecution." This child does not respond from outward pressure and conflict, but reacts from the inner heart of Jesus, the state of the Kingdom. Jesus embraces him. I am Jesus pusher!!!

I am a Jesus pusher!!! Immediately after the Beatitudes, Jesus begins an explanation of the formed Kingdom. The Old Covenant was introduced with God descending upon Mt. Sinai. The Israelites had a frightening experience "knocking them out of their senses." God gave them the Ten Commandments. Jesus, the King of the Kingdom, introduced the Kingdom of Heaven with the eight Beatitudes. The Ten Commandments were the Law written on tablets of stone; the eight Beatitudes are written on the fleshly tablets of the heart (Jeremiah 31:33). This is not the observance of the Law, but the realization of that Law by the Spirit!

The Ten Commandments in the Old Covenant were preceded by a Prologue (Exodus 19). The Eight Beatitudes are followed by an Epilogue (Matthew 5:13-48). This Epilogue begins with a clarification of the "state" of the child of the Kingdom (Matthew 5:13-16). If there is any confusion concerning the Kingdom of Heaven not being a reward for keeping the law, it is immediately made plain. Jesus adds a variety of images to help us. What is this "state" of being for the children of the Kingdom? It is *salt* (Matthew 5:13). The essence of *salt* is its flavor, but if it loses its flavor nothing comes from serving *salt*. It is *light* (Matthew 5:14-16). A light shines in darkness; it is not what it does, but what it is! Both of these images speak "state of being." They take place because of who we are in Him! In other words, we are helpless but Jesus makes the difference in our lives. I am a contented Jesus pusher!!!

———————

I am a Jesus pusher!!! *Salt* and *Light* are images of a state of being. The formation of the Kingdom is found in the Beatitudes. I am helpless; He is my resource. In this unity, the Kingdom is formed. I do not do the Kingdom or eventually become the Kingdom. We are the Kingdom, Jesus and me! The imagery of *salt* and *light* presents a state of being.

After this clarification, Jesus launches into the conclusion of the Epilogue. It is in this section that Matthew highlights the continuity of the Old and New Testaments. The Old Covenant is not destroyed but is fulfilled in Jesus (Matthew 5:17-20). This is the great message of the Sermon on the Mount. In the following verses, Jesus defines the "fulfillment" of the Law. He highlights the application of the Law as proposed by the scribes and Pharisees in contrast to the fulfillment of the Law in Him. Jesus says, *"You have heard that it was said to those of old,"* (Matthew 5:21, 27, 31, 33, 38, and 43). He then continues saying, *"But I say to you"* (Matthew 5:22, 28, 32, 34, 39, and 44). Every time Jesus takes the literal interpretation of the Law and internalizes it, He also intensifies it. The application of the Law moved from a duty to the flow of His nature in us; it is the Kingdom of Heaven, *salt* and *light*. In other words, the Law becomes who we are rather than what we do. It is not an obligation to keep or duty to maintain, but a nature that we have. We do not act because we have to; we act because we are! Even if we discipline ourselves to do the right thing, we will still not be Kingdom people. We experience Jesus in intimacy; our lives flow with His nature. I am a naturalized Jesus pusher!!!

I am a Jesus pusher!!! In the Sermon on the Mount, Jesus acclaimed a change in the Old Covenant. The Law proposed abstinence from the activity of murder. Judgment focused on those who did a murderous deed (Matthew 5:21). What about anger? How important is reconciliation with my brother who has something against me? Should I agree with my adversary? This is the law on a whole new level! It is internalized and intensified. The Kingdom of Heaven is a state of love. We dwell in His nature (Matthew 5:21-25).

The Old Covenant took pride in not committing adultery. Conquering the sexual drive of the body so as not to commit the act is the highest level of the old. But the child of the Kingdom has the mind of Christ. Men and women must see each other through the eyes of Christ. This applies to all of our body drives. The body must be a servant to the indwelling King (Matthew 5:27-30). This internalizes and intensifies the Old Covenant.

Marriage in the reality of the Kingdom is extremely different from the old approach. Those of old looked for an easy escape from marriage. Jesus said the reason for this viewpoint is *"hardness of your hearts,"* meaning "destitution of spiritual perception" (Matthew 19:8). It has to do with stubbornness and obstinacy. The old standard was self-centered and self-serving. Jesus, the King of the Kingdom, gives us a redemptive attitude toward our spouse (Matthew 5:32-33). This internalizes and intensifies the marriage vows. I am a Jesus pusher!!!

I am a Jesus pusher!!! The Sermon on the Mount presents a "new covenant." The "old" based honesty on "swearing." The command of the Old Testament was: *"And you shall not swear by My name falsely, nor shall you profane the name of your God: I am the Lord"* (Leviticus 19:12). The Jews interpreted this to mean that swearing falsely by any other name was allowed. God stated the law: *"If a man makes a vow to the Lord, or swears an oath to bind himself by some agreement, he shall not break his word; he shall do according to all that proceeds out of his mouth"* (Numbers 30:2). The old system interpreted this statement as permission to renege on oaths made to anyone but God. People would swear by "heaven," "earth," "Jerusalem," or their "head," which were all substitutes for God's name. When they were pressed to keep their word, they felt no obligation. After all, it was not an oath based on the name of God. The "old" created a system of manipulation, conniving, and twisting.

This thinking appalled Jesus. The Kingdom of God is a state of being: the King reigns in us. There is no need for swearing at all. There is no outward pressure for honesty; there is only the integrity of Jesus' heart dwelling in the believer. We are children of the Kingdom of Heaven (Matthew 5:34-37). This moves integrity from an outward pressure and internalizes and intensifies it as an expression of our lives. Jesus is intimate with us; we express His nature. I am a Jesus pusher!!!

I am a Jesus pusher!!! ***"An eye for an eye and a tooth for a tooth"*** (Matthew 5:38) is a quotation taken directly from the Old Testament (Exodus 21:24; Leviticus 24:20; Deuteronomy 19:21). It reflects one of the most ancient codes of law. It simply requires that the punishment exactly match the crime. We use this same principle in our day when we say, "Tit for tat." The expression of this law comes from a heart of revenge. There is a "get even" spirit in its essence. The good factor of this proposition is its limitation. You could "get even" with another individual, but only to the extent they injured you.

Jesus internalizes and intensifies the old standard. The state of the Kingdom of Heaven is the heart of Jesus. There is no revenge. It is a redemptive heart. Because I know the pain of the loss of an eye, I would not want to inflict that upon another. The cross is present in the beginning statements of Jesus' preaching (Matthew 5:38-42). It was not an event in the future for redemption; the cross style was the motive of His heart. The expression of God's heart is always redemptive. How should I respond to the misdeeds of another? I must always be redemptive. How do I handle arguments? I must always be redemptive. What is the will of God for my life? I must always be redemptive. This is the nature of Christ; we are partakers of the Divine nature (2 Peter 1:4). I never want to imitate Jesus; I want His nature to flow through me! I am a Jesus pusher!!!

I am a Jesus pusher!!! The righteous scribes and Pharisees said: *"You shall love your neighbor and hate your enemy"* (Matthew 5:43). They eliminated a key phrase in the Old Testament quotation. *"You shall love your neighbor as yourself:"* (Leviticus 19:18). And to this statement they added, *"and hate your enemy."* The Kingdom state of being makes no distinction between the people you like or dislike. At the heart of His explanation, Jesus gives us the display of His Father! *"He makes His sun rise on the evil and on the good, and sends rain on the just and on the unjust"* (Matthew 5:45). If we will be *sons*, this same nature indwells us. We are called to be *"perfect* (in love), *just as your Father in heaven is perfect* (in love)"* (Matthew 5:48). Jesus takes the outward actions of the scribes and Pharisees and internalizes and intensifies them for the child of the Kingdom. The Law of God becomes the nature of our lives and we have His very heart. None of this is possible unless the Spirit of Jesus indwells us. The old system to achieve and accomplish is replaced by experience and embrace.

What a privilege to be filled with Jesus. Christianity ceases to be activities I achieve and becomes who I am in Him! His nature becomes my nature. He changes me with His presence. I am filled with Him! Oh the wonder of living in Jesus as He lives in me. I am a Jesus pusher!!!

———————

I am a Jesus pusher!!! Matthew is a Jesus pusher!!! His writing has a basic theme that we cannot disregard. Every passage must be interpreted in light of this thrust. The Gospel of Matthew is a focus on the Jews. Matthew desperately wants to convince them that Jesus is the Kingly Messiah. This explains the opening genealogy of his book (Matthew 1:1-17). Jesus is in the lineage of King David; He fulfills God's promise to King David! Matthew presents the birth of Jesus as a declaration of His Kingship. Jesus is conceived of the Holy Spirit; He is born of a virgin (Matthew 1:20). The wise men seek the new King of the Jews (Matthew 2:2). The arrival of the new King creates incredible insecurity in Herod. He calls for the murder of all baby boys under the age of two in Bethlehem and the surrounding districts (Matthew 2:16).

John the Baptist heralds this new King (Matthew 3:1). The anointing of the Holy Spirit takes place as God, the Father, places His approval on His Son, the new King (Matthew 3:16-17). This new King battles Satan, and wins through the sourcing of the Spirit (Matthew 4:1-11). This King leads the Kingdom of Heaven as it conquers demonic territory (Matthew 4:23). The introductory language of the Sermon on the Mount emphasizes this reality. Jesus **was seated** on a mountain (Matthew 5:1). He sits like a king on his throne. ***His disciples came to Him*** (Matthew 5:1). They approach Him like subjects in a royal court. ***Then He opened His mouth and taught them*** (Matthew 5:2). He is the King delivering his inaugural address. It is the great "Manifesto of the Kingdom of Heaven." As a Jesus pusher, I am honoring this King!!!

I am a Jesus pusher!!! There are three chapters in the Sermon on the Mount. The first chapter (Matthew 5) sets the stage or establishes the foundation for this sermon. Jesus announces the PRESENT REALITY of the Kingdom. When the Kingdom of Heaven is announced as present, would not the laws of the Kingdom follow? But Jesus is not presenting a moral system. The reality of the Kingdom of Heaven is Himself. We are found in intimate relationship with Jesus, the King. Therefore, ours is the reality of the "state" of the Kingdom. We do not perform a moral code to be in the Kingdom; we are the Kingdom and the Beatitudes are our benefits (Matthew 5:1-10). The "state of being" is strongly contrasted with the Law of the old system (Matthew 5:21-48).

The middle section of the Sermon on the Mount is the pivotal section of the sermon. This chapter does not focus on the observance of basic religious *activities*: charitable deeds (Matthew 6:1-4), prayer (Matthew 6:5-15), or fasting (Matthew 6:16-18). This chapter focuses on the marvel of an intimate relationship with Jesus in the Kingdom that affects all activities of life, religious and non-religious. This chapter thunders to a close with ***"But seek first the kingdom of God and His righteousness and all these things shall be added unto you"*** (Matthew 6:33). What a summary! The Kingdom of God is an intimate relationship between Jesus and me. No wonder I am a Jesus pusher!!!

I am a Jesus pusher!!! The Sermon on the Mount is in no way a doctrinal dissertation. It is certainly not an organized, systematic belief system. Jesus does not prescribe an adjusted form of outward observance. He did not come to establish a university of higher education. He came to found a Kingdom! He does not propose a system, methodology, or structure of technique. He institutes an intimate fellowship. All disciples, both the original and those to follow, discovered doctrinal teaching which sprang out of fellowship with Jesus. This happened in the early disciples and it happens in those who are disciples now. He reveals Himself and they believe; when we believe, we learn the truth connected with Him; the truth springs out of Him. The seed of truth comes from the Sower who sowed the seed, ***the word of the Kingdom*** (Matthew 13:19), in our hearts. It comes from His Person!

In Matthew 5, Jesus presents a "state of being" not a moral system with rules to obey. Now, in Matthew 6, Jesus presents the practical application of living in this state. At the beginning (Matthew 5), he shifts our focus from a list of rules to the wonder of actually being in the Kingdom. Now how do we live beyond a mere observance of some outward commandments (Matthew 6)? We live in Him! Jesus is our total focus and motivation. No wonder I am a Jesus pusher!!!

I am a Jesus pusher!!! Jesus highlights three specific applications for life (Matthew 6). These three areas become the focus of every world religion. The three areas are "charitable deeds," "prayer," and "fasting." "Charitable deeds" is the consideration of materialism. "Prayer" points to our relationship with God. "Fasting" highlights the relationship of the physical to the spiritual. In each discussion Jesus begins with the negative approach and then moves to the positive explanation.

Jesus begins with **charitable deeds** (Matthew 6:1-4). His proposal is very clear from the start. The Greek word "dikaiosune," translated **charitable deeds,** in verse one is different from the Greek word "eleemosune," translated **charitable deeds,** in verses two, three, and four. "Dikaiosune" is the "state" commanded by God and standing the test of His judgment. It is most often translated "righteousness." "Eleemosune" comes from "eleemon," which is translated mercy. It is used thirteen times in the New Testament and is exclusively used for charitable deeds. Jesus begins speaking of **charitable deeds** with the word "righteousness." Every charitable deed must be seen in light of the nature of Jesus. What does the heart of God feel about this deed? Immediately Matthew makes us aware that the important thing is not the observance or the giving of money to help the poor. It is about the motive of the Kingdom, the nature of our King. If an individual follows the exact instructions of Jesus, and follows the proper mode of giving alms, he will not have the Kingdom. The heartbeat of the King must be experienced in every deed. I am one with Him in sharing with others. I am a Jesus pusher in the charitable deeds of my life!!!

I am a Jesus pusher!!! Intimate relationship with Him shared through daily living applies to the spiritual discipline of "prayer" (Matthew 6:5-15). Jesus moves from the negative to the positive in His teaching. In both the sections on **charitable deeds** and "prayer," the instructions focus on the motive of being **seen by men**. Jesus compares what man sees to what our Father sees. Our Father sees everything, even what we do in secret. This focuses not on the activity of prayer but on the motive behind prayer. The Lord's Prayer is given to us as an example or pattern for prayer (Matthew 6:9-13). This prayer section ends with a strong emphasis on the need for forgiveness (Matthew 6:14-15).

Once again Jesus brings us face to face with the reality of the basic message of His sermon. If we achieved the proper observance of the mode and method of prayer, what would be the point? If we avoid the externalism of the Pharisees and correctly follow the form of the Lord's Prayer, what will we gain? We must lay our inner man wholly before the penetrating light of our King. We must embrace the way that light changes and influences us. The call is not to bend to the form or moral code of performing deeds in certain ways. How would that be different from the Law that is fulfilled in Jesus? This is the Kingdom of Heaven. We are in relationship with Jesus, our King. His heart produces our observances. No wonder I am a Jesus pusher!!!

I am a Jesus pusher!!! Jesus again highlights secrecy in the third religious observance, "fasting" (Matthew 6:16-18). His insistence on secrecy is not the same as the kingdom of darkness. It is not about being underhanded or hidden. It is about pride. It is a focus on performing deeds for the sake of self-gain. He injects the idea of **reward**. Earning, meriting, and achieving are preset in this motive. Jesus begins with the negative, moves to the positive, and then returns to the negative. We must clearly see the correct motive in view of the two negatives. "Fasting" has to do with how the physical needs correspond to the spiritual reality. I can only properly understand this relationship as I am in the Kingdom of Heaven.

Jesus begins with **charitable deeds** (Matthew 6:19-24). In these brief verses He pounds the issue of your focus on treasure. He contrasts **treasures on earth** with **treasures in heaven**. Note the difference between **on** (epi) and **in** (en)! "Epi" primarily focuses on "rest" or "no motion." The focus of **treasures on earth** is **earth** rather than **heaven**. The **treasures on earth** are in constant motion or flux. They are eroding and always escaping. They are definitely limited to "upon" the earth. Treasures never take anyone beyond the physical aspect. The **treasures in heaven** never move, erode, or escape. A focus on Jesus builds and increases intimacy with Him. Jesus always takes us to greater levels. I am expanding as a Jesus pusher!!!

I am a Jesus pusher!!! In the Sermon on the Mount, the issue of **charitable deeds** is not about the deed itself but about the focus of your heart. *"For where your treasure is, there your heart will be also"* (Matthew 6:21). The outward performance of such deeds focuses on "how much," "how often," and "what do I get in return?" Jesus calls us to the heart of the Kingdom, His heart. This is not a law concerning materialism. Jesus pronounced the scribes and Pharisees as hypocrites in this area. He said, *"For you pay tithe of mint and anise and cummin, and have neglected the weightier matters of the law: justice and mercy and faith. These you ought to have done, without leaving the others undone"* (Matthew 23:23). They meticulously tithed everything down to the herbs on their back patios. Thus, they prided themselves in their achievement of the law. The call of the Kingdom is a focus of your heart on heaven, which liberates your heart for generosity. It frees you to flow love in the **charitable deeds**.

Jesus uses the imagery of **the lamp of the body is the eye** (Matthew 6:22) to state this focus. What your eye perceives determines if your body is full of light or darkness. It is impossible to focus in two directions at the same time. "No one can serve two masters;" (Matthew 6:24). *"You cannot serve God and mammon* (riches)*"* (Matthew 6:24). Jesus is the Kingdom; your relationship with Him is the focus that brings light to your life. All **charitable deeds** must flow from your relationship with Jesus. Again, the issue of **charitable deeds** is not about the deed itself but about your focus on Jesus! I am a Jesus pusher!!!

I am a Jesus pusher!!! Jesus expresses His heart in the spiritual discipline of prayer. It becomes difficult for us to distinguish between the clarifications on prayer and fasting in the remainder of the chapter (Matthew 6:22-24). In fact, the fundamental motive underlying the Kingdom person's involvement in **charitable deeds**, prayer, and fasting may all be one. Jesus distinctly contrasts two treasures; He even calls them **two masters** (Matthew 6:24). He says, "***You cannot serve God and mammon*** (riches)" (Matthew 6:24). You would initially apply this to the **charitable deeds**. If you focused on and were mastered by riches, this would definitely affect your giving of alms.

But let's apply this to prayer and fasting. If Jesus is your Master, the content of your prayers will be vastly different than if materialism is your master. If materialism is your focus, you will worry about the necessities of life. For instance, "***what you will eat or what you will drink***" becomes your highest priority (Matthew 6:25). You will focus your prayer life on these things. Worrying about your life will become the emotional state of your being. A Kingdom person's focus is on Jesus. He recognizes **life** is **more than food and the body more than clothing** (Matthew 6:25). Jesus said, "***For your heavenly Father knows that you need all these things***" (Matthew 6:32). **These things** are His concern for you! If He is concerned about these things for you, then you need not be worry. I am a Jesus pusher!!!

I am a Jesus pusher!!! Jesus said, *"For your heavenly Father knows that you need all these things"* (Matthew 6:32). *These things* are His concern for you! They are not your concern; they are His. We have an abundance of illustrations for this. Jesus said, *"Look at the birds of the air,"* (Matthew 6:26). Do they not depend on someone greater than themselves? They do not worry; in fact, they do not even prepare as in sowing or reaping. Jesus thunders the truth, *"Yet your heavenly Father feeds them"* (Matthew 6:26). He continues by proposing the question that we are of greater value to God than the birds! Look at the *lilies of the field* (Matthew 6:28). Consider the *grass of the field* (Matthew 6:30). In each case, God meets the necessities on their level of living. Will not your Father provide what you need on your level?

We are to be focused entirely on Jesus; He is concerned about all *these things*. We must allow the King of the Kingdom to be who He is in our lives. Then Jesus thunders into the conclusion of the whole matter. *"But seek first the kingdom of God and His righteousness, and all these things shall be added to you"* (Matthew 6:33). If our passion is Jesus, the King, the content of *charitable deeds*, prayer, and fasting will all change. They will not be religious observances gaining attention and fulfilling pride. Each of these areas will burst forth from Him; they will look like Him; they will be the result of His mind; He will drive us. He will be seen! It is a privilege to be a Jesus pusher!!!

———

I am a Jesus pusher!!! The first two parts of the Sermon on the Mount explain the final section (Matthew 7). Matthew 5 establishes the fundamental premise of the Kingdom of Heaven. All other systems are a road we must travel. They require self-denial, discipline, struggling, and effort to arrive at the goal or morality. Jesus does not present a new standard of righteousness to achieve, but a new standpoint of righteousness in His embrace. Others present ways to become the children of the Kingdom; Jesus simply states that you are a child of the Kingdom.

In the second section of the Sermon on the Mount (Matthew 6), Jesus highlights the intimate relationship within the Kingdom which affects all activities of life, religious and non-religious. How does the nature of Jesus in you affect "charitable deeds," "prayer," and "fasting? One person focuses on "materialism," another person focuses on "our relationship with God," the last person focuses on "the relationship of the physical to the spiritual." Every activity of life occurs within one of these three areas. There is one fundamental principle: ***But seek first the kingdom of God and His righteousness, and all these things shall be added to you*** (Matthew 6:33).

This final section flows with a concise focus on the inner heart of the individual. Jesus reveals the key pitfalls into which religious individuals tend to fall. The way to avoid such places is to be filled with the Kingdom. If Jesus is not living within you, you will eventually develop another moral system based on performance. However, you will miss the inner and secret rewards from the heart of God. They cannot be missed in Jesus. I am a Jesus pusher!!!

I am a Jesus pusher!!! In the final statement of the Sermon on the Mount Jesus begins with "The Statute of the Standard" (Matthew 7:1-6). This has to do with how you view your fellowman. All other moral systems focus on self-discipline, self-denial, and self-effort. Once mastered, you are able to compare yourself with others. This was the condition of the Jews of Jesus' day. The Law developed into six hundred and thirteen oral traditions. The Pharisees dedicated their lives to accomplishment and observance of these traditions. The nature of their moral system led them to judging others. Competition, superiority, and condemnation occurred in their relationships. They developed elitism. They stressed only the activities that did not tempt them. We do the same thing. For instance, those of us who are overweight may openly criticize those who smoke. Some rent movies to watch at home but actively criticize those who attend the theaters. Those who have been baptized in one mode criticize others who have are baptized in another mode. Those who prefer hymns criticize those who worship with choruses. Those who dress in one style criticize those who have another fashion. The list is too long to continue.

Do you realize the freedom Jesus proposes in the Sermon on the Mount? I am not measuring you or myself. We are both focused on Him! There is no competition between us. We are not performers; we are lovers of Jesus. Our goal is not to correct or judge your performance but to help you embrace Jesus. Nothing concerns us except the flow of the Kingdom among us. I am the Jesus pusher!!!

———————

Jesus PUSHER | 314

I am a Jesus pusher!! Jesus proposed the Kingdom of Heaven in not a moral system to achieve. In fact, if the Kingdom of God shapes our lives into the performance of a moral system, we are **hypocrites** (Matthew 7:5). Any form of judging others produces this state within us. We miss our personal correction from Jesus by giving personal correction to others. We allow large beams to be dangling from our eyes as we attempt to remove splinters from the eyes of others (Matthew 7:5). Jesus, the King of the Kingdom, is the only solution to such a state. I must focus on Him.

We also give the holy love relationship of the Kingdom to the dogs and swine of our existence (Matthew 7:6). The dogs to which this verse refers were not household pets. They were scavengers who ran in packs. They were filthy, dangerous, and untrained. Judgment, competition, and measuring others reduce the Kingdom to dog packs and herds of swine. It is ultimate destruction. It is the result of a moral system that demands achievement and performance. It produces competition as we compare ourselves to others. Feelings of self-worth and value whelm up in me. After all I do more than you do. The moment this happens in my life, I have joined the dog pack and herd of swine. There is only one deterrent to such a condition; I must fall in love with Jesus. It is in Him, I am enabled to see you as He sees you. It is the perspective of the Kingdom of Heaven. What a relief not to compete with you, but to love Jesus completely. I am a Jesus pusher!!!

———————

I am a Jesus pusher!! Jesus raises the issue of "source" (Matthew 7:7-8). If none of my energy is spent in criticizing, judging, condemning, or comparing myself to others, how will I spend my time? The opposite of judging is "seeking!" Seeking, openness, desiring, hungering, knocking, and asking become the core of my existence. Of course, in the Kingdom of Heaven my seeking is focused on Jesus! Jesus begins this section by stating the attitude of responding (Matthew 7:7-8). Then He illustrates this statement with a story of a father and son (Matthew 7:9-11). Therefore, the conclusion of this responsive attitude is Jesus' fulfillment of the **Law and the Prophets** (Matthew 7:12). Everything God wanted to accomplish in the Old Covenant will be fulfilled and accomplished in this embrace of Jesus, the Kingdom of Heaven.

While this way may be **narrow**, it is not difficult to find. Jesus ends this section with a contrast between the **narrow gate** and the **wide gate** (Matthew 7:13-14). The idea of **narrow** comes from the concept of being confined. It refers to obstacles surrounding and confining the area. If one is seeking, knocking, and asking through the focus of the moral performance system, it is impossible to locate. But in the Kingdom of Heaven, if you are seeking, knocking, and asking while focused on Jesus, there is a guaranteed finding. If you **"ask,** I guarantee **it will be given you,"** (Matthew 7:7). In other words, ingrained in the very "asking" is the receiving. If you will **"seek,"** I guarantee **you will find"** (Matthew 7:7). Ingrained in the "seeking" is the finding. You can read it, "If you will seek, you will be found." The same is true of "knocking." There is no way to miss the Kingdom. Jesus is the Kingdom; I am a Jesus pusher!!!

I am a Jesus pusher!!! Jesus moves the discussion in the Sermon on the Mount from a physically focused activity to a relationally focused activity (Matthew 7:9-11). He refers to a father and son relationship. Within this relationship is the constant care and concern of the father. He is not selfish; he does not withhold from his son. He does not play mean tricks on his offspring. If his son needs bread and asks for it, the father does not give him a stone (Matthew 7:9). The same is true if the son asks for a fish, the father does not give him a serpent (Matthew 7:10). The parallel is simple. If this is true in an earthly relationship, how much more is it true with our heavenly Father (Matthew 7:11)? If we *ask, seek,* or *knock,* He will give, find, and open.

Therefore, the fundamental principle of Kingdom living is not performing, doing, and accomplishing; it is asking, seeking, and knocking. If the *Law and the Prophets* pointed to and prepared us for the Kingdom of Heaven, this fulfills them (Matthew 7:12). Everything we need is in Jesus, and He desperately wants to be our supply. Therefore, live a life of asking, seeking, and knocking, focusing all on Jesus.

This automatically affects your relationship with your fellow-man. The good gifts you seek from your heavenly Father will be what you want for your fellowman. We find all of this in Jesus. I am a man with one focus; I am a Jesus pusher!!!

I am a Jesus pusher!!! In the Sermon on the Mount Jesus focuses on the internal (Matthew 7:15-23). If the moral system is a reward for the journey we makes, we must focus on performance and doing. We lose the internal substance. We have no time or energy to be concerned for that which does not matter. The heart substance of the individual is neglected and tragically decays. Jesus begins this section with a strong, revealing statement: ***"Beware of false prophets, who come to you in sheep's clothing, but inwardly they are ravenous wolves"*** (Matthew 7:15). False prophets will be those who travel the road, accomplish the disciplines, and receive the rewards for outward performance. They learned how to fit into ***sheep's clothing*** (Matthew 7:15). Their outward appearance is that of sheep, but ***inwardly they are ravenous wolves*** (Matthew 7:15).

This is a strong statement! They are not described as "misguided individuals." They are not "nice guys" who need further instruction. They are ***ravenous wolves*** that have an appetite for destroying sheep. Was Jesus not predicting the conflict He will experience with the leaders of Israel? These were men who achieved the highest positions of law keeping. They traveled the road and won the prize. Jesus described them as ***"whitewashed tombs"*** (Matthew 23:27-28). It is the tragic result of the moral system of achievement and performance. Only Jesus can save us from this! I am a Jesus pusher!!!

———

I am a Jesus pusher!!! Jesus uses illustrations from nature familiar to everyone. Grapes do not come from thorn bushes; figs do not come from thistles (Matthew 7:16). It is impossible for a good tree to bear bad fruit and for a bad tree to bear good fruit. They cannot be intermixed (Matthew 7:17-20). These illustrations focus our attention on the importance of what we are inwardly. This is the message of the Kingdom of Heaven. It is the inner state of being. Jesus is strong from the Sermon on the Mount to the end of His ministry as to the final result of such a condition. He clearly proposes that any tree that is not capable of producing good fruit is *cut down and thrown into the fire* (Matthew 7:19). Nothing less will be tolerated or allowed.

In case the illustrations or parables of this truth become confusing, Jesus boldly states the truth of the matter. Kingdom people are those through whom the nature of the Kingdom flows, accomplishing the will of the Father (Matthew 7:21). The Kingdom is not an outside performance; it is an inside flow. It is not an adherence to physical laws; it is a state of His presence generating His will. Jesus said, "This means there will be many who will say, *'Lord, Lord, have we not prophesied in Your name, cast out demons in Your name, and done many wonders in Your name?'*" (Matthew 7:22). They are the group who performed activities, accomplished duties, but did not know the intimacy of His presence. They practiced *lawlessness* (Matthew 7:23). They adhered to the law, promoted the law, and demanded the law. In the midst of the law, they were lawless! They did not have Jesus, the "substance" of the Kingdom! This is why I am a Jesus pusher!!!

I am a Jesus pusher!!! In the last four verses of the Sermon on the Mount, Jesus describes the Kingdom of Heaven in its relationship to the foundation of life. It is a parable. He pictures life with all of its difficulties; in fact, there is no life without storms. The options suggested by the story are not life with difficulties versus life without difficulties. It is failing versus not failing. Jesus clearly states the perimeters of the story. The story describes, *"whoever hears these sayings of Mine, and does them"* (Matthew 7:24) versus *"everyone who hears these sayings of Mine, and does not do them,"* (Matthew 7:26). When we view these statements as presented in the English translation, we are drawn again to the trap of accomplishment.

The Greek word "poieo," translated **does,** introducing this parable (Matthew 7:24) is used again in the middle of this parable (Matthew 7:26). This is the identical Greek word "poieo," translated **bears,** which Jesus used in the illustration of trees and fruit (Matthew 7:17-19). The clearest picture of this word "poieo," translated "doing," is found in a "tree bearing fruit." No one ever says, "This tree is doing fruit." Trees do not *do* fruit; trees bear fruit! It is a result of the inner nature of the tree. Trees are not following a list of rules or commandments; they respond to the urging of their inner state of being. Their fruit is not the result of a long road of activities for which they can be proud. It is the result of the inner condition of their being for which they are thankful. This describes the inner relationship of Jesus and the believer. Jesus is the source and life by which we live! This is the foundation of life that endures storms. I am a Jesus pusher!!!

I am a Jesus pusher!!! The Parable of the Wise and Foolish Man closes the Sermon on the Mount (Matthew 7:24-27). It is a focus on the foundation for life. The inner condition of the Kingdom, Jesus, is the stability of our lives. It is not a matter of storms or the lack thereof; it is about Jesus' presence. The focus is not on the outward structure of the building; it is on the inner foundation of His presence. We must be found in Him; rather, He must be found in us!

This is the Sermon on the Mount. ***The people were astonished*** (Matthew 7:28). It is a simple statement, radical both in Jesus' day and in ours. This Greek word "ekplesso" is found only here in the New Testament. It is used in the sense of "knocking one out of his senses." The King came to be within us; the Kingdom is established within us; we dwell in the state of the Kingdom. The results of this state are described in the Sermon on the Mount. We will see them demonstrated repeatedly in the life of Jesus. Patience in the midst of a busy schedule, betrayal by His friends, crucifixion resulting from injustice, and the continued list, are all storms of life. However, Jesus remained unshakable. It was the fullness of the Spirit living within Him. This is the one unshakable foundation for life. Jesus must indwell us; every other foundation is sand. No wonder I am a Jesus pusher!!!

I am a Jesus pusher!!! Approaching the Sermon on the Mount causes trembling. The content of the three chapters absolutely boggles my mind. At the close of the sermon, the people were **astonished** (Matthew 7:28). They were "ekplesso." They were "knocked out of their senses." If you acquire the courage to begin the journey, you shrink at the opening statements, which are united together as "The Beatitudes" (Matthew 5:1-10).

The approach you make stimulates the fright. If you come as a mountain climber you will be overcome with the danger and impossibility of the climb. Who can reach the heights of these standards? I can never dwell in such lofty altitudes. If you come as a racecar driver you will collide in wreckage at the first curve. If you come as a great and wise philosopher you will immediately dismiss the simplicity of the truth. If you cannot embrace the simple truth, how can you ever know the depths of wisdom? If you come as a builder who constructs a house of truth you will be paralyzed by the beauty of what has been provided. No addition, no remodeling, and no repairs are needed. How should we approach this sermon? We must come as a lover of Jesus. If we are head over heels in love with Jesus, we find that we belong in the high altitudes. Jesus drives us safely to all fulfillment of truth. He reveals Himself as the Truth, and you will know Him. You will dwell in Him and He in you. You will live this sermon. No wonder I am a Jesus pusher!!!

I am a Jesus pusher!!! Jesus gave eight Beatitudes. There is some argument about this number. Many have paralleled the Sermon on the Mount with the Ten Commandments, attempting to create ten Beatitudes. However, in verses three through ten, the verb of being (*are*) is not in the Greek text. A literal translation is *"Blessed! The poor in spirit,"* (Matthew 5:3). Again, this follows through until verse eleven, which contains the verb of being (*are*) (Matthew 5:11), giving us eight Beatitudes.

All eight Beatitudes have three parts. First is the "ascription of blessedness." All Beatitudes begin with **blessed** (makarios) as the first word. In the Greek language this becomes the highlighted thought of the sentence. You can accurately place an exclamation mark after each **blessed!** The second part is the "description of the person" to which this ascription applies. There is a definite article placed before each description in the Greek text. It the plural definite article *"the"* (hoi) before each noun used as an adjective. It is not just *"a poor in spirit,"* but is *"the poor in spirit."* It is *the mourning, the meek, the hungering and thirsting, the merciful, the pure in heart, the peacemakers, and the persecuted*.

The third part is a "subscription of this description." It is the reason for the condition or state exists in the ascription. Each state is experienced in relationship with Jesus. In other words, He is the state. We are blessed exclusively because of Him. I am a Jesus pusher!!!

I am a Jesus pusher!!! The essence of the Beatitudes is the word *"blessed."* It is the opening Greek word in all eight Beatitudes, and Jesus highlights it in each statement. In all eight Beatitudes the verb of being is missing. An exclamation mark could be placed at the end of the word: ***Blessed!*** Jesus exclaims the internal condition of the Kingdom of God. The Kingdom may be examined from several aspects. Jesus is the King of the Kingdom. His rule marks the character of the Kingdom. But what is the atmosphere surrounding everyone in the Kingdom? More specifically, what is the attitude of those experiencing the Beatitudes? They are ***blessed!***

Obviously this state of essence is not dependent on circumstances. If you are ***poor in spirit, mourn, meek, hunger and thirst for righteousness, merciful, pure in heart, peacemakers,*** or even ***persecuted for righteousness' sake***, you are still blessed! Whatever your circumstances, you are ***blessed*** in the embrace of Jesus! Circumstances do not add to or subtract from this state. They are the stage upon which the state of ***blessed*** takes place. This sounds so strange to us. The original crowds were "knocked out of their senses" at such statements. Circumstances constantly dictate to us how we feel, what we want, and how we react. How can anyone live without being sourced or controlled by the circumstances of the world? You have to be sourced and controlled by another world, the Kingdom of Heaven! Jesus is this Kingdom! I am a Jesus pusher!!!

I am a Jesus pusher!!! Circumstances, regardless of what they are, become the instrument through which the ***blessed*** state is experienced. If you are ***poor in spirit*** (helpless), this becomes the means by which you embrace ***blessed***. This attitude to some degree controls and determines what kind of circumstances you experience. The essence of this state of ***blessed*** can only happen in one who totally loses his life to Jesus in helplessness.

For instance, ***the poor in spirit*** (helpless) is never found or admitted among the proud and haughty. Those who ***mourn*** are only among those broken before Jesus. The self-sufficient never experience this state. You will never find those who are ***meek*** in the congregation of the self-righteous. The self-confident, those who are masters of their own destiny, never ***hunger and thirst after righteousness***. The legalistic, who are always right, are never ***merciful*** and do not realize they need ***mercy***. Those who are their own god never experience purity of heart and never ***see God***. They have no vision beyond themselves. Persecution comes only to those who are vulnerable and risk pouring out their lives to others. The self-centered exert their energy protecting themselves. They never experience the Kingdom; they are never ***blessed***.

Are you tired of being controlled by your circumstances? Jesus must control you! Are you exhausted by your state of circumstances? Jesus must be your new state; dwell in Him. I am a Jesus pusher!!!

I am a Jesus pusher!!! Many people have attempted to add to the Beatitudes in the Sermon on the Mount. Do we have the potential of copying or adding to Jesus' stated pattern in the Beatitudes? What other "attitudes" could we add to the "Beatitudes?" Is it an exhaustive list or just a suggestion? When looking at life are there vast areas of living not covered in the Beatitudes? Is additional insight and instructions required for the Kingdom of God?

For instance, can we add "love?" Isn't love the uniting and integrating of all eight Beatitudes? If "love" is listed as a separate beatitude, that destroys the necessity of all eight. If "love" were added to the Beatitudes, we would consider it separate from the other eight. But "love" is the combination of all of them in unity. If "holiness" were added to the Beatitudes, it would separate it from the flow of all eight Beatitudes. Holiness is the nature of God. Are not all of these Beatitudes an ingredient of such a nature? Jesus stated every possibility in the eight Beatitudes, and I believe them to be complete. Everyone in the Kingdom experiences the eight Beatitudes at the same time because they experience Jesus! They are **blessed**! I am a blessed Jesus pusher!!!

I am a Jesus pusher!!! Jesus congratulates us in the Beatitudes. He declares we are *"Blessed."* Blessed (makarios) is a difficult problem for translators of the New Testament Greek because it is displayed in a variety of ways. Several translations use the English word "happy." However, "happy" has as its primary meaning an emotional state. It comes from the old English "happenstance." It contains the root "hap," which means "chance." Human happiness is dependent on the chances and the changes of life. Life gives, but life also destroys. It contains the flavor of "fate" and has its roots in "luck." This is far from the meaning of *blessed*.

There is another Greek word translated *blessed*. It is "elougetos." We derive our English word "eulogy" from it. It means, "to speak good things" or "praise." Paul uses this word often in Ephesians. *Blessed be the God and Father of our Lord Jesus Christ, who has blessed us with every spiritual blessing in the heavenly places in Christ* (Ephesians 1:3). In this one passage Paul uses the word (elougetos) as an adjective, verb, and noun. This Greek word does not seem to be connected to our Greek word in Matthew. "Makarios" carries the idea "to be in a good position," that is, "to be in a favorable place to receive something good." It describes a joy that has its secret within itself. This joy is serene and untouchable; it is self-contained and independent from all the chances and changes of life. It describes the presence of God reaching in and through your life to accomplish His Divine will. It often carries with it suffering or hard circumstances; however, those circumstances are overshadowed by the wonder of His fulfilled plan and presence. This is the state in which the Christian dwells. We are blessed in the presence and will of Jesus. I am a Jesus pusher!!!

I am a Jesus pusher!!! Let me remind you, in the Beatitudes there is no verb connected with **blessed**. The word **"are"** is not present. Why is this? The Bible scholars state that Jesus did not speak the Beatitudes in Greek; he spoke them is Aramaic, which was what the Hebrew of Jesus' day spoke. Aramaic and Hebrew have a common kind of expression. It is an exclamation meaning, "O the blessedness of…" This expression is common in the Old Testament. The following is an example of a pronouncement, an exclamation!

> **Blessed** (O the blessedness of the man) **is the man**
> **Who walks not in the counsel of the ungodly,**
> **Nor stands in the path of sinners,**
> **Nor sits in the seat of the scornful;** (Psalms 1:1).

There is one particular use of this Greek word (makarios) by the Greek culture that gives us a clear description of this state. The Greeks always called the island of Cyprus, the "makaria." It was Cyprus, the blessed one. What did they mean by that? Cyprus was a lovely, fertile island. It had the perfect climate and was filled with flowers, trees, and fruit, lacking nothing. The minerals and natural resources contained within its coastline supplied all the materials for perfect contentment. Its inhabitants found everything they needed for sustenance and happiness within the boundaries of Cyprus. The island was **blessed** because its provisions were complete. This is the picture of Jesus for us! Our completeness, blessedness, is in Him. I am a Jesus pusher!!!

I am a Jesus pusher!!! Jesus presents a powerful and life changing conclusion. In the Beatitudes, He says, ***"Blessed are the poor in spirit, for theirs is the kingdom of heaven"*** ("O the blessedness of the poor in spirit!") (Matthew 5:3). Jesus applauds us! He shouts, "You have made it! You have arrived! Congratulations!" The Beatitudes are not pious hopes of what shall be; they are not prophecies of some future blessing. This is congratulations for what is now. The state of ***blessed*** is not postponed to some future world in heaven. This state of ***blessed*** exists here and now! It is not something Christians *will* enter; it is something we *have* entered!

You and I must take a moment to praise and adore Jesus! What a wonder to be a Christian! Oh, the bliss of being a Christian. There is great joy in Jesus' embrace. The depth of sheer delight is found in the intimacy of His presence. All we ever needed or longed for is now experienced in "knowing" Him. Indeed, the Trinity God placed all He wanted for us in Jesus. We are now in Him. The Kingdom of Heaven, the King, has arrived. We are now His! Defeat, dismay, or depression has no room here. We are ***blessed***! No wonder I am a Jesus pusher!!!

I am a Jesus pusher!!! Jesus called us ***"Blessed*** (makarios)!*"* An investigation of the use of "makarios" in the classical Greek reveals further insight. It was used as "makar." It is an adjective describing the gods as opposed to mortals; it is a Divine quality. One ancient scholar spoke of the gods as not born, but rather incorruptible, unchangeable, holy, and ***blessed*** (makarios). In Greek mythology the Greeks assumed that the gods were blessed in themselves. They were not affected by the outside world. The state of ***blessed*** originally meant a state that is neither produced nor affected by outside circumstances, but is intrinsic within the individual. This is the underlying principle and meaning in the use of the word in the Septuagint and in the New Testament. ***Blessed*** is a state not dependent on the chances and changes of life. ***Blessed*** is untouchable.

We must hasten back to the fundamental idea of the Sermon on the Mount. It is about Jesus. If our state of ***blessed*** cannot be altered by the world because the world does not source it, what is its source? Congratulations! You and I dwell in the new place, Jesus! He is our source. We do not accomplish the instructions of the Sermon on the Mount in order to get into the Kingdom; we are able to live the Sermon on the Mount because we are *in* the Kingdom. Circumstances vary, materialism decays and rusts, health declines, and the weather is forever changing. But Jesus is a safe and unchangeable place of ***blessed***. There is nothing more that you need. You have found your place. Jesus is your all in all. I am a Jesus pusher!!!

I am a Jesus pusher!!! The opening statements of the Sermon on the Mount are called "The Beatitudes." This title or word is not found in the Greek language. However, there is a structure and focus which places certain statements in both the Old and New Testaments in this form. Beatitudes are shaped by certain literary structure making them distinct from proverbs. A proverb is a simple and profound statement aimed at making an insight permanent. It strips the concept or truth down to its essence and presents it in a memorable phrase. A Beatitude is always a pronouncement of blessing. It is phrased in a literary formula beginning with "Blessed." Jesus begins the Sermon on the Mount with the Old Testament use of "Beatitudes."

The subject matter of the first Beatitude caused the response of the crowd to Jesus' message: ***The people were astonished at His teaching*** (Matthew 7:28). They were "ekplesso," "knocked out of their senses." Jesus pronounced a "blessing" on the poor. No one is congratulated for poverty. The rich are obviously "blessed" by God. No one envies the "poor." We long to be like the rich. In the kingdom of earth great value is placed on wealth. How strangely different the Kingdom of Heaven must be.

> *"Blessed are the poor in spirit,*
> *For theirs is the kingdom of heaven."*

The Kingdom of Heaven has a different value system than the Kingdom of earth! It is an eternal perspective! Jesus is at the heart of this value system. I value Him! I am a Jesus pusher!!!

———

I am a Jesus pusher!!! Jesus begins the Beatitudes by congratulating those who are poor! We must understand that the opening focus of this state of blessedness is our beginning point. Poor is the Greek word "ptochos." It comes from a verb meaning "to shrink, cower, or cringe." This was characteristic of the beggars in Jesus' day. The word refers to any person reduced to total destitution or helplessness. He trembles over being totally destitute of all life's necessities. He is reduced to crouching in a corner and begging. He holds out one hand for alms as he covers his face with the other hand. He is ashamed of being recognized. This term does not mean simply poor, but begging poor.

Contrasted with this word is "penichros." It is used for ordinary poverty such as the widow Jesus saw giving an offering in the Temple (Luke 21:2). She had very little (two small copper coins). She was poor but not a beggar. One who is "penichros" has some meager resources. But one who is "ptochos" is completely dependent on others for sustenance. He has absolutely no means of self-support. Jesus congratulates us on being in this condition in our spirit. The focus is not on materialism but on the spiritual. We respond to Jesus from this position. It allows Him to flow His resource in and through us. I am responding to Him in my weakness; He is my strength. I am a Jesus pusher!!!

I am a Jesus pusher!!! The first Beatitude of the Sermon on the Mount focuses on *the poor in spirit.* It is the strongest concept for poverty in the Scriptures. Jesus does not qualify its use, and offers no conditions regarding this poverty. He does not speak of activities accomplished or not accomplished. He does not distinguish between those who keep the law or are found guilty of breaking the standard. The poor are not those lacking in the observance of ceremonies or sacrifices. This state of helplessness is unqualified; it is not poverty that results from being handicapped. A person was not poor because he did not have proper parental upbringing, or because he did not have proper advantages as a teenager. The state of poverty is simply not qualified.

Since this reference to *the poor* is unqualified, and individual does not produce it. It is a condition in which he finds himself! His part is to recognize his state. If it is recognized and embraced in his spirit, everything changes. His entire perspective of life is altered. Being *poor in spirit* opens him to utter abandonment to Jesus, the Kingdom of Heaven. Spiritual helplessness is acceptance of all provisions found in Jesus. He becomes an unashamed beggar of Jesus who supplies the Kingdom. The great hindrance of this is self-resource. Why would anyone depend on Jesus when they can do it themselves? We live out of our own resource instead of His. Could this be the reason for our personal disasters? The recognize our personal need is to respond in openness to Jesus. Jesus is my total resource! I am a Jesus pusher!!!

I am Jesus pusher!!! ***"Blessed are the poor in Spirit"*** must be seen in the context of the Old Testament. An individual deprived of his inherited rights was considered poor. The inherited rights were focused on the land. The land was under God's legal possession; He gave it to the whole people. Therefore, there were no poor. In the law, God made comprehensive provisions for the poor. God protected the widow and orphan having no land. The right of gleaning was granted to them. The "corners" of the fields were not to be reaped, nor all the grapes of the vineyard to be gathered, and the olive trees not to be beaten a second time. The fatherless and the widow were allowed to gather what was left. It was a provision of the Lord (Leviticus 19:9-10; Deuteronomy 24:19-21).

When Israel was exiled, they were considered to be in this state of poverty. They had no land; they were destitute and helpless. Why were they in exile? They ceased to realize they were totally dependent upon Jehovah. In their arrogance and pride, they turned to other gods. This only proved their "poverty." The moment they ceased to recognize their helplessness, their circumstances proved it to them again. Israel had no chance of survival without their God. They were destitute and helpless.

This is the context of the first Beatitude. ***The poor*** are those totally destitute and helpless. They lack resource, inability in every area, and no hope. The only avenue of deliverance is God. Jesus came to be our source! I am a Jesus pusher!!!

I am a Jesus pusher!!! We must understand the proper location of *"Blessed are the poor in spirit."* It is in our spirit. Luke records this Beatitude as *"Blessed are you poor"* (Luke 6:20). In the original language the phrase *are you* is not present, nor does he include *in spirit*. You might think Jesus was referring to materialism. Matthew's account of this message clarifies any misunderstanding about the location of the poverty in the heart of the Kingdom of Heaven. The idea of economical poverty is not the focus of this statement. Jesus calls for a spiritual perspective of our attitude toward God. The helpless, destitute poverty is located in the spirit of the individual.

The *spirit* of man is the principle of life causing him to live. The spirit can live without the body, but the body cannot live without the *spirit* (Matthew 27:50). It is the breath breathed by God into man and will again return to God (Genesis 2:7). It is the spiritual entity in man. It is related to *the hidden person of the heart*, which is to be characterized by a *gentle and quiet spirit* (1 Peter 3:4). Therefore, the spirit would focus on the inner aspect of man, which determines the response of his living. His *spirit* causes his attitude, reactions, and perspective of life. This is the core of man's being. This is the location of man's poverty and helplessness.

This location is where Jesus wants to dwell. For the Spirit of Jesus to indwell man here would be fullness indeed. It affects the life, enables every avenue of existence, and strengthens every facet of his thinking. We are in desperate need of Jesus. I am a Jesus pusher!!!

———

I am a Jesus pusher!!! ***"Blessed are the poor in spirit"*** is our condition. The destitute-helplessness contained in being ***poor,*** is located in the ***spirit*** of man. Every attitude is determined by this driving awareness of helplessness. My first response to being possessed by such awareness is rejection. If you truly feel this way deep in your inner heart, you will live in constant fear. Such an individual will never accomplish anything. You will cower in the face of every obstacle. You will be labeled as having a psychological condition you need to overcome. But what if this helplessness is not a psychological state but is the truth? What if we are absolutely helpless in our spiritual condition? What if all of our physical successes in business, materialism, athletics, education, and many other fields of endeavor only serve to distract us from this simple bottom line of life? We are totally helpless. What if all our pride is only "make-up" applied to old scars? We cover up what is really there; we pretend we are strong, able, and conquering. In reality, we are weak, helpless, and failing.

Is this the message needed for our hour? It seems that in the midst of the despair and chaos of our lives, we need a message of encouragement. We can make it; we are able to accomplish the task; we will win the victory. The message of encouragement is found in Jesus. He is the answer! I am a Jesus pusher!!!

Jesus PUSHER | 336

I am a Jesus pusher!!! ***"Blessed are the poor in spirit"*** is distressing to one who thinks he is capable. However, grasping this reality allows me to clearly see Jesus. In this reality I become His. All dependency on myself is eliminated because of my helplessness. I depend on Him alone! Jesus tried to reveal this to the leaders of Israel. After a long discussion with them about this subject, His disciples came to Him. They seemed a bit disturbed about how abrupt Jesus was with these leaders. They asked Him, ***"Do You know that the Pharisees were offended when they heard this saying?"*** (Matthew 15:12). Jesus turned to His disciples and said again, ***"Let them alone. They are blind leaders of the blind. And if the blind leads the blind, both will fall into a ditch"*** (Matthew 15:14). Jesus saw the desperate need of the Pharisees. They were helpless! On another occasion He described them as ***"whitewashed tombs which indeed appear beautiful outwardly, but inside are full of dead men's bones and all uncleanness"*** (Matthew 23:27). If the best religious, law keeping people of that day are the helpless, what chance do I have?

Pride and self-sufficiency cause me to hide from the reality of my state of helplessness. But dare I risk missing Jesus? Do not the constant circumstances and pressures of situations beyond my ability and control tell me it is true? I am helpless! It is time for a total surrender to Jesus. I am a Jesus pusher!!!

I am a Jesus pusher!!! ***"Blessed are the poor in spirit"*** points me to Jesus. This is the truth of this Beatitude. I am totally helpless and destitute. I am full of dead men's bones; I am blind. This is the state in which I dwell. It is in this reality I can clearly see Jesus. But I am a "fixer." How can I go about fixing others when I am so broken ourselves? Ministry will shift from what I have learned, my skills, and my abilities to His flow. I will become an avenue for Him to demonstrate Himself to others. I must cease to be a performer to be admired and become the hands of Jesus to my world.

But I am "self-sourced." How can I possibly be self-sourced when I am so empty? When I operate out of myself, I live out of helplessness and despair. Why would I want to permeate the world around me with such a source? Jesus can source me! If I see the helplessness of my own self-sourcing, it will drive me to Him. How can I ever go back to such death and repulsive filth? My "poverty" becomes the clarity by which I see Him: He is all I need.

But it is just "who I am." How can I possibly remain who I am when I am filled with such poverty? Will I not run to embrace the One who can make me different? The helpless state of who I am becomes the springboard that launches me into who He is. I must live in Him. Congratulations! I am helpless, destitute, and poor. Jesus is my one need! I am a Jesus pusher!!!

I am a Jesus pusher!!! *"Blessed are the poor in spirit, for theirs is the kingdom of heaven"* (Matthew 5:3). The first and the last Beatitudes offer the promise of *the kingdom of heaven*. This promise is not a reward for "doing" something, but is the "result" of a state. In other words, everyone who responds to the state of poverty experiences *the kingdom of heaven*. The concept of the *kingdom* is a focus on Jesus, the King. The heart of the word, even in the English translation, tells us this truth. The focus is not on size, population, or palaces; it is on the ruling of the King. The Kingdom is where Jesus rules (or supplies).

This is what is so unique about the *kingdom of heaven*. In other kingdoms, the kings rule from without. Jesus rules from within. Other kings are satisfied as we supply them; Jesus wants to supply us. Other kings desire that we defend them; Jesus wants to be our defense. Other kings want us to serve them; Jesus wants to serve through us. In our absolute poverty, helplessness, we have nothing to offer Him. He can be our total supply and source His life through us. The only blockade to this relationship is our own self-sourcing.

The Kingdom of Heaven is not a location; it is a relationship with Jesus. He is not the Kingdom by Himself; I cannot be the Kingdom on my own. When He fills me, we become the Kingdom. The Kingdom is not a "me" or "Him;" it is an "us!" My helplessness is filled with the resource of His great person; we become the Kingdom of Heaven. I am a Jesus pusher!!!

I am a Jesus pusher!!! ***"Blessed are the poor in spirit, for theirs is the kingdom of heaven"*** (Matthew 5:3). As He sources us, we begin to recognize others are as ***poor*** as we are. If they could experience the resource we have! ***The kingdom of heaven*** becomes a community of poverty stricken individuals who totally depend on Jesus. This community is easily recognized because each person in the community looks like Jesus. This is not a likeness in physical activities or ceremonies, but in attitude and heart. Everyone is being sourced by the nature of God.

This community is easily recognized because it lacks of competition. No one is jealous of the other because everyone is poverty stricken. Since Jesus is our only source, competition means that Jesus is competing against Himself. How ridiculous! We become the "body of Christ." He is our head. If there is division among us it comes from self-sourcing. We have ceased to be ***poor***.

This community is easily recognized because there are no stars. No one "lords" it over another. How can we? Jesus sources us all. In our poverty we have no claim to any position or authority. We are called by His sourcing to serve. ***"As the Son of Man did not come to be served, but to serve,"*** so we are an expression of this same nature (Matthew 20:28). We are ***poor*** and helpless, being empowered by our King. Our only desire is Jesus! I am a Jesus pusher!!!

I am a Jesus pusher!!! ***"Blessed are the poor in spirit, for theirs is the kingdom of heaven,"*** (Matthew 5:3). Lets review! ***"Blessed"*** must be understood as "congratulations" or "you are fortunate." The Speaker of the word sees you in an ideal position. The opening word of the Sermon on the Mount congratulates us on having arrived! We are not on a journey to the Kingdom of Heaven; we have arrived in the Kingdom of Heaven. This is not a road filled with attempts, discipline, struggles, and trying until we reach our final destination. We begin our journey in the Kingdom. Jesus is the Way; He is the Goal. When we are in Him, we are on the Way; therefore, we have already arrived.

"The poor" is the state of being for those within the Kingdom of Heaven. The Greek word (ptochos) translated ***poor*** is specific. The word refers to any person reduced to total destitution or helplessness. Jesus pinpoints the exact location of the destitution. It is ***in spirit***. The ***spirit*** of man is the principle of life causing him to live. It is the spiritual entity in man and focuses on the inner aspect that determines the response of man's living. Man's ***spirit*** causes his attitude, reactions, and perspective of life. This is the location of man's helplessness. Man did not become helpless; he has always been helpless. This was God's design for the existence of man at creation. At the core of man's life, he is to depend entirely on God. God and man will be partners in the production of man's life. As God sources man in his ***spirit***, man will be the demonstration of the Spirit of God. Man's helplessness is not a negative; it is a positive. I am created to be filled with Jesus. I am a Jesus pusher!!!

I am a Jesus pusher!!! ***"Blessed are the poor in spirit, for theirs is the kingdom of heaven,"*** (Matthew 5:3). This location of poverty is where we discover the disaster of sin. Instead of allowing God to source him in his helplessness, man depends on himself. This is the demonic nature of self-centered carnality. Man enters into the kingdom of darkness as he lives out of himself. What a tragedy! The issue is rather simple. I am either linked with the Spirit of Jesus or linked with the demonic nature. Jesus either sources me or I am sourced by the devil. This is the deciding factor between the Christian and the non-Christian.

The demonic sourcing allows me to deny my helplessness. I live out of my ego, rights, and abilities. I strengthen my abilities in physical areas giving me the appearance of success. All the time, at the heart of my ***spirit***, I am helpless. This helplessness appears in my broken relationships, affects my attitude, and demonstrates itself in my mannerisms. I attempt to compensate and overcome this state of helplessness through self. I can always find someone who is not doing as well as I am in an attempt to cover my helplessness. I excel in physical and academic areas, giving me a sense of worth. I contribute to my self-worth by grabbing for position and power over others. All the while, at the heart of my life, I am helpless. "Helpless" is not something to get over, but to embrace. We live in the state of helplessness embracing Jesus as our source. This is the Kingdom of Heaven! Jesus is my source! I am a Jesus pusher!!!

I am a Jesus pusher!!! ***"Blessed are the poor in spirit, for theirs is the kingdom of heaven,"*** (Matthew 5:3). The location of ***the poor in spirit*** in the list of Beatitudes is important. It is significant that the first and the last Beatitudes contain the phrase, ***"For theirs is the kingdom of heaven"*** (Matthew 5:3; 10). All the other beatitudes include, ***"comforted," "inherit," "filled," "mercy," "see God,"*** and ***"sons of God."*** These are all aspects of living in the Kingdom. They are aspects of intimacy with Jesus! The foundational state of this relationship is my helplessness. As my helplessness embraces Jesus, I experience the Kingdom in my life.

The opposite of this embrace is "pride." The heart of sin is "I." No one filled with "self-sourcing" is a part of the Kingdom. The door to the Kingdom is low, and no one who stands tall will ever go through it. Jesus cannot make me worthy until I recognize my unworthiness. He cannot fill me until I realize I am empty. His life cannot be mine until I admit I am dead. This is the basic state of my relationship with Jesus. ***"Blessed are the poor in spirit."***

In our modern day theology, we find little emphasis on death to self-centeredness. Our Christian books are filled with self-helps. We focus on happiness, how to have a good marriage, and steps to recovery. Deny self and take up your cross does not seem to be popular. We focus on success not death to pride. Yet this is the message of Jesus. It is the first step to the Kingdom; in fact, it is the only step! ***"Poor in spirit"*** precedes everything else. I am responding to Jesus. I am a Jesus pusher!!!

———————

I am a Jesus pusher!!! "How do we become ***poor in spirit***" (Matthew 5:3)? This question spills forth from pride and self-sourcing. If we can "do" this, we are not helpless. Monasticism, asceticism, physical self-denial, mutilation are all foolish and futile attempts. They only increase pride rather than subdue it. Anything that gives us a reason to boast in what we have done or not done pushes us further from ***poor in spirit***. Self-sourcing is a trap. Any attempt of self to deliver itself from self-sourcing only produces more self-sourcing. Martin Luther had a daily list of things to do and not do. Every day he failed in some aspects of the list. Finally the day came when he realized he measured up and had accomplished everything on his lists. That is when his elation turned to horror, for he knew he had committed the worst of all sins, "pride."

Therefore, there is no list of steps to take, methods to master, or techniques to learn. We are helpless, ***poor in spirit***. Jesus must move on our lives. But this is the Sermon on the Mount. Jesus says that He is here. The Kingdom of Heaven is at hand; will you respond? In seeing my poverty, I can now embrace Jesus as my Source. Response is not a "doing" activity; yet, it involves the act of my will to participate. Jesus came to them; they did not come to Him. Jesus delivered the message; they did not discover it. Jesus taught them; they did not teach Him. His coming brings revelation of our helplessness. The answer is found only in Jesus. I am a Jesus pusher!!!

I am a Jesus pusher!!! One might think God's plan is to do something to eliminate our helpless state. In other words, He will move us from *"the poor in spirit"* condition into the Kingdom of God (Matthew 5:3). But that is a misunderstanding of His plan. Jesus is not going to change our helplessness. This state of *poor in spirit* was the intent of God from the beginning. The Trinity, in the creation moment, intended us to be dependent upon God. The disaster of sin is the declaration of independence by mankind. Man denied his helplessness and sourced himself. The shift is to admit our helplessness and embrace it.

There are some vivid pictures of this condition that may help our understanding. No one can deny the strong crucifixion language of Pauline theology. *I have been crucified with Christ; it is no longer I who live, but Christ lives in me; and the life which I now live in the flesh I live by faith in the Son of God, who loved me and gave Himself for me* (Galatians 2:20). This language strikes a blow at our independency, separation, and self-sourcing. We do not die and then resurrect from the dead. We embrace the reality of death (helplessness) and remain there. Then the life of Christ can live through us. *It is no longer I who live, but Christ lives in me.* I must stay crucified. The difference in my life is *I live by faith in the Son of God.* A Biblical definition of *faith* is "invoking the activity of the second party." Up to this time I have invoked the activity of the first party, myself. I live in this helpless state of continually, constantly invoking His activity in my behalf. Jesus is my source! I am a Jesus Pusher!!!

I am a Jesus pusher!!! ***"Blessed are the poor in spirit, for theirs is the kingdom of heaven,"*** (Matthew 5:3). Jesus congratulates us for existing in the state of ***poor in spirit.*** It is not a temporary state; it must continually be embraced in order that His resource might fill us! In the embrace of our helplessness and His person, we become the Kingdom of Heaven. One of the beautiful pictures of this posture is found in the Pauline theology of "in Christ" and "Christ in." This concept is dominant in Paul's writings; it is a central theme.

The bumper sticker slogan of Christianity is ***Christ in you*** (Colossians 1:27). In the midst of my helpless state, Jesus comes. He does not rescue me from my helplessness. He does not give me resource apart from Himself. He does not place resource in an account where I can draw on it when needed. He places me in Himself and Himself in me. It is in this embrace I experience adequate life in my helplessness. It is the old picture of the hand inside the glove. The glove is helpless without the hand; the glove is helpless with the hand. It is not about the glove; it is about the hand. The hand empowers the glove in the midst of its helplessness. The Trinity created me to be helpless and dependent on Jesus. This is my permanent posture; this is where I live!

Why would I attempt to be something that I am not? Why would I credit to myself that which I cannot do? Jesus is my only hope! I am a Jesus pusher!!!

I am a Jesus pusher!!! The first Beatitude ends on a positive note. *"For theirs is the kingdom of heaven."* Jesus repeats this statement using the same grammar in the last Beatitude (Matthew 5:10). At first glance, you might think the Kingdom of Heaven is a reward or the result of being *poor in spirit*. The way to achieve or enter into the Kingdom is to become helpless. The Greek word "hoti," translated *for*, does not refer to results. It portrays the idea of "for this reason. Jesus says the helpless, *the poor in spirit*, are *blessed* `because of their involvement in the Kingdom of Heaven. The Kingdom of Heaven is not theirs because they are helpless. The helpless are fortunate because of their involvement in the Kingdom of Heaven.

The subject of this statement is *the kingdom of heaven*. The main verb is the Greek word "esti," translated *is*. It is the third person, singular, present indicative of "eimi," which is "I am." There is coupled with the Greek word "autos," translated *theirs*. Jesus is not saying that the Kingdom of Heaven belongs to *the poor in spirit*. This word, "autos," has a stronger emphasis on the pronoun than normal. It is often used as a reflective pronoun such as herself, himself, or themselves. The antecedent of this pronoun is used in *the poor in spirit*. This pronoun is a genitive, which shows relationship between nouns. The idea is that *the poor in spirit* (theirs) is (equals) *the kingdom of heaven*.

The Kingdom of Heaven is not merely the presence of God. The Kingdom of Heaven consists of God and man in this embrace. When helpless man experiences the filling of the Spirit of Jesus, the Kingdom of Heaven is reality. The Kingdom is the unity or oneness of the embrace between Jesus and you. This is why He created you! I am a Jesus pusher!!!

I am a Jesus pusher!!! ***"Blessed are those who mourn, for they shall be comforted,"*** (Matthew 5:4). How can anyone possibly highlight and promote "poverty" and "mourning" as desirable? Can there be a major problem with the perception of our world? From the wicked individual to the most religious, riches, joy, and laughter are desired qualities. Is there something wrong with the nature of all individuals that causes us to place value on things of lesser value? Have the most valuable things of the heart been demeaned in light of physical and emotional comfort of the flesh?

Why do the world religious systems promote a reward structure that focuses on comfort, ease and pleasure? Jesus proposed a different approach. Congratulations! You are absolutely helpless, destitute, and ***poor in spirit***. It is within the confines of this helplessness you experience all that is available in the Kingdom of Heaven. Congratulations! You are mourning. As you are overcome with the spirit of mourning, you will embrace the comfort of life. You are comforted within the boundaries of mourning. Congratulations! You are crucified. It is while you are being crucified that you live. The moment you escape the cross, death overcomes you. Life is found in dying; the Kingdom of Heaven is embraced in helplessness; comfort of the soul comes in mourning. None of these are rewards, or even by-products. They are engrained within the state of being ***poor in spirit***, the state of ***those who mourn.*** Jesus is the only explanation for such thoughts. It is in the state of helplessness and mourning, we are able to totally embrace Him. I am a Jesus pusher!!!

I am a Jesus pusher!!! ***"Blessed are those who mourn, for they shall be comforted,"*** (Matthew 5:4). The subject of the sentence is the Greek word "ho," translated ***those***. It is an article such as "the," "this one," or "that one." The Greek word "penthountes," translated ***who mourn***, is a present participle, indicating continuous action. This participle is a verb acting as an adjective, which gives content to the subject, ***those***. The subject becomes "the mourning ones." Its usage in the Old Testament Septuagint is focused on mourning and lamenting at death. It is grief that is too deep for concealment. It is often joined with the Greek word "klaio," translated "weep," "to weep audibly."

If you look exclusively at this second Beatitude without its context, there is no basis to judge the source of the mourning. Is Jesus referring to difficult circumstances of life? Is He highlighting eternal life that shall overshadow all grief connected to death? Perhaps His concern is persecution as related in the last Beatitude.

The context of our passage gives a ready answer. Evidently mourning is that feeling which is birthed from the sense of our spiritual poverty. The second Beatitude is but the complement of the first! It is in the context of realizing our poverty that we are enabled to ***mourn***. Mourning takes on the quality and depth of helplessness. The strength of poverty becomes the expression of mourning. Mourning is the proper response to our helplessness that opens our lives to Jesus. He becomes the source of our lives. I am a Jesus pusher!!!

I am a Jesus pusher!!! ***"Blessed are the poor in spirit,"*** (Matthew 5:3). ***"Poor"*** is a translation of the Greek word "ptochos." It comes from a verb meaning "to shrink, cower, or cringe." It presents a picture of total destitution of all life's necessities. This condition is located ***in spirit***. This is not a result of sin or anything we have done. God created us this way! Jesus is our source! A glove is not criticized because it is helpless; it is made that way. It finds strength and life when indwelt by the hand. ***"Blessed are those who mourn"*** (Matthew 5:4). When we recognize our helplessness, our mourning becomes a proper response. In lamenting our destitution we respond to the source. How open will we be to Jesus? The extent of our mourning is determined by the depth of our realized helplessness.

Once we embrace our total helplessness, mourning is spontaneous. We do not decide to ***mourn***; we do not produce mourning. It is not something to do or to seek. It can be forgotten; no one needs to concentrate on it. The issue is not "do we ***mourn***?" The issue is ***poor in spirit***. Do we embrace our helplessness? Our state is proven by our failures. The circumstances of our daily lives repeatedly prove our condition. Surely we are ***poor in spirit***; therefore, we ***mourn***. Mourning is launched by our helplessness. If we refuse to embrace our helplessness, we cannot ***mourn***. Don't miss His resource for your life; don't miss Jesus. I am a Jesus pusher!!!

———————————

I am a Jesus pusher!!! ***"Blessed are the poor in spirit, for theirs is the kingdom of heaven"*** (Matthew 5:3). The location of poverty is ***in the spirit***. This is the principle of life causing man to live. It is the spiritual entity in man and focuses on the inner aspect that determines the response of man's living. Man's spirit carries his attitude, reactions, and perspective of life. When man's spirit embraces his helplessness, the first Beatitude becomes reality. He is to be congratulated.

"Blessed are those who mourn, for they shall be comforted" (Matthew 5:4). The first Beatitude gives birth to the second Beatitude. As man's ***spirit*** embraces his helplessness, he begins to ***mourn***. Helplessness is the mind and will expressing itself through mourning, which is the emotional aspect. We follow the pattern of Isaiah, the prophet: poverty ***in spirit*** admits its helplessness and says, ***"I am undone!"*** This causes a great mourning that breaks forth in the form of a lamentation, ***"Woe is me, for I am undone!"*** (Isaiah 6:5).

In the Sermon on the Mount, Jesus does not propose a set of rules or activities to be acknowledged intellectually and adhered to physically. He does not present emotional feelings we are to experience at certain times. He presents a combination of the mind and will, embracing the reality of a state of helplessness that will break forth with emotional expression and feeling of mourning. Thus the whole being of man, including mind, will, and emotion responds to his state of being ***poor in spirit***. None of this can be left out. This enables us to embrace Jesus! I am a Jesus pusher!!!

I am a Jesus pusher!!! ***"Blessed are those who mourn, for they shall be comforted"*** (Matthew 5:4). Everything that applies to ***poor in spirit*** (the first Beatitude) also applies to mourning (the second Beatitude). We cannot choose the areas of life where we will embrace poverty. We cannot decide to be helpless is one area while we let our pride and self-sourcing rule in other areas. Based on Jesus' Sermon on the Mount, this is not possible. He says poverty is ***in spirit*** and is the heart of every area of living. We are helpless at the core of our existence, thus, our living is permeated with helplessness.

If our understanding is complete, we see our helplessness as a journey. At any given moment we are completely helpless. As our awareness of our helplessness expands, so does our embrace and response to this helplessness, and our mourning parallels this expansion. In this sense, we are always total and complete. Jesus exposes who we are as He reveals who He is. The more I embrace Him and His revelation, the more I realize my need and I ***"mourn."*** Jesus is the answer to realizing my need as well as satisfying my need. I am a Jesus pusher!!!

I am a Jesus pusher!!! Before Adam fell in the Garden of Eden, he was the ideal picture of man. His sin caused all of that to change. Now Jesus is the picture of the ideal man, and He verifies and reveals God's intent and dream. When man is aware of his poverty *in spirit*, he fully embraces God's sourcing. There is no arrogance, pride , or self-sourcing. Man is complete in the fullness of the Spirit and fulfills God's design. Adam and Eve were created to live this way and did so until the fall. Jesus, the Second Adam, lived this way!

However, this has not been true for us. Sin entered the picture. Sin is not a deed or activity; sin is the denial of our helplessness. Let's return to the illustration of the glove. The glove is totally helpless. Its condition is not one of partial poverty; it is absolute. Man's creation by God parallels this example. Man within himself is totally helpless; therefore he is totally dependent on God. God is the hand who now fills him and man finds purpose in this filling. Imagine the glove deciding to source itself. In rebellion to the hand, the glove acts independently. What arrogance! This is the heart of sin. Sin is not a deed or activity; sin is the denial of helplessness and a rejection of Jesus' sourcing. In reality, we have all rejected Jesus as our source. We have all sinned! On this level, we must all *mourn*. The stupidity of our arrogant independence from Jesus demands a continual state of mourning. Such a state should repel us from all self-sourcing and drive us to dependence on Jesus. We are constantly repulsed by any appearance of pride and self-acclamation. We *mourn* what we have been and are driven to never choose such a state again. It presses us to Jesus. I am a Jesus pusher!!!

I am a Jesus pusher!!! There is another level of mourning (Matthew 5:4); we become deeply aware of the condition of others. In recognizing our helplessness and mourning over every moment we source ourselves, we become aware of the self-sourcing of our world. David cried out, *"Rivers of water run down from my eyes, because men do not keep Your law"* (Psalms 119:136). Men grab tightly to successes in business, athletics, education, and a thousand other areas to compensate for the fact they are helpless. We have power struggles in our organizations because we attempt to overcome our state of poverty. We live for applause and self-gratification; it enables us to deny that we are *poor in spirit*. Once we see this in our life, we then see it in others. We *mourn* our denial of poverty and we weep continuously for the plight of those around us.

Paul expressed the mourning within himself and creation. There is an *earnest expectation of the creation eagerly waits for the revealing of the sons of God* (Romans 8:19). He went on to explain that *the whole creation groans and labors with birth pangs together until now. Not only that, but we also who have the firstfruits of the Spirit, even we ourselves groan within ourselves, eagerly waiting for the adoption, the redemption of our body* (Romans 8:22-23). This mourning is the driving force of evangelism. If you are not aggressively winning others to Jesus, you are not mourning; if you are not mourning, you have not adequately embraced your helplessness. Jesus is the solution. I am a Jesus pusher!!!

———

I am a Jesus pusher!!! ***"Blessed are those who mourn, for they shall be comforted,"*** (Matthew 5:4).In order to be honest with our text, we must highlight the continual state of mourning. The Greek word "penthountes," translated ***mourn,*** is a participle in the nominative case. This means it is a verb functioning as an adjective. It gives content to the subject of the sentence. The subject becomes "the mourning ones." This participle is in the present tense. In Greek grammar this highlights continual action. In other words, there is to be a constancy of mourning based on the constancy of the poverty. God creates us in a state of poverty; therefore we live in a state of mourning.

The mourning is a product of embracing our helplessness. In establishing the connection between these two elements, the consistency is also established. If we were created in a state of consistent helplessness, would not our mourning also be consistent? Since God intended us to be helpless in order that He might source us, the recognition of this poverty is the core of our submission. Mourning is the fiber of our response that allows Jesus to live through us! The secret to all the wonder found in Christianity is discovered in this combination. What Jesus longs to produce in and through our lives is only experienced through this interaction of poverty and mourning. Everyone is ***poor in spirit*** but may not recognize it. Those who embrace it will ***mourn***. However, this does not guarantee comfort. Our passage must be seen in light of the One who speaks these words! Jesus is our solution! I am a Jesus pusher!!!

I am a Jesus pusher!!! ***"Blessed are those who mourn, for they shall be comforted,"*** (Matthew 5:4). There is a wonderful story about the gravel-walk and the beautiful flower.

"How fragrant you are this morning," said the gravel-walk.

"Yes," said the beautiful flower, "I have been trodden upon and bruised, and it has brought forth my sweetness."

"But," said the gravel-walk, "I am trodden upon every day, and I only grow harder."

What makes the difference?

Mourning is not a reference to the difficulties of life, although they will undoubtedly be present. "Trodden upon and bruised" is not the result of sickness or natural disasters. Mourning produces the fragrance of Jesus and is only found in fully embracing the helplessness of the spirit. In my state of brokenness, I mourn over every feeble attempt of self-sourcing. This state of mourning flows with a constant submission to the presence of Jesus; I am ***comforted*** in Him! One might ***mourn*** over their personal condition and never be ***comforted.*** The mourning is only a response that allows Jesus to be the Comforter in our lives. I am a Jesus pusher!!!

I am a Jesus pusher!!! *"Blessed are those who mourn, for they shall be comforted"* (Matthew 5:4). The Greek word "parakaleo," translated *shall be comforted*, is the verb form of the noun for one name of the Holy Spirit (Paraclete). Jesus told the disciples, *"And I will pray the Father, and He will give you another Helper* (Parakletos)*, that He may abide with you forever"* (John 14:16). This title is given to the Holy Spirit four times in this discourse of Jesus (John 14:16, 26; 15:26; and 16:7). It is used one other time in John's writings. *My little children, these things I write to you, so that you may not sin. And if anyone sins, we have an Advocate* (Parakletos) *with the Father, Jesus Christ the righteous* (1 John 2:1). In these verses John refers to Jesus as "The Comforter."

The basic verb "parakaleo" means "to summon, to call to one's side, to call for help, to appeal, to request, to encourage, to comfort, or to cheer up." The ministry of the Spirit of Jesus can easily be described as "The Comforter." He brings conviction to our state of helplessness. Without His direct ministry to our inner spirit we will never realize our poverty *in spirit* and we will never *mourn*. Even the ability to cry out in mourning over our helpless state only happens in the power of the Holy Spirit. We are helpless; we are poverty stricken. Thus, the Spirit of Jesus reveals our helplessness and enables us to mourn over our condition. Then He becomes the answer to our need. Our mourning delights our soul as we find life in the midst of death. Our complete helplessness becomes the substance of our strength, for He embraces us! The Spirit of Jesus has come! I am a Jesus pusher!!!

I am a Jesus pusher!!! ***"Blessed are those who mourn, for they shall be comforted"*** (Matthew 5:4). In the Gospel of John, Jesus refers to the Holy Spirit as "The Comforter" (Parakletos) four times. In the Epistle of First John, John refers to Jesus as "The Comforter" one time. Jesus clarifies this by saying, ***"And I will pray the Father, and He will give you another Helper*** (Parakletos)" (John 14:16). The Greek word "allos," translated ***another***, becomes important. It means "another but of the same kind." It is in contrast to the Greek word "heteros" meaning "another qualitatively, other, different one." The indwelling of the Spirit is of equal quality to Jesus. Jesus designates the Holy Spirit as equal with Himself.

Everything Jesus was in the flesh with the disciples, the Spirit of Jesus will be in the believer and more. The revelation and involvement of His presence in us is taken to a greater level. Can you imagine aiding, coming alongside a limp and helpless glove? You carefully lift each finger trying to improve its abilities. You can speak with the most detailed instructions, but nothing happens; the glove is helpless. The answer is not found in outside comfort; it must come from within the glove. When the hand is implanted within the glove everything changes. It is not instruction; it is empowerment. It is not prompting; it is provision. He is our comfort. The fullness of His presence in the believer is the relationship with the Kingdom. The ***poor in spirit*** are to be congratulated for they are in the Kingdom of Heaven. It would be better to say, "Congratulations, the Kingdom of Heaven is in you." Mourning is the state of receptivity that recognizes the state of helplessness and embraces His presence. The Comforter has come! I am a Jesus pusher!!!

———

I am a Jesus pusher!!! ***"Blessed are those who mourn, for they shall be comforted"*** (Matthew 5:4). It is necessary to note that the Greek verb "parakaleo," translated ***shall be comforted***, is in the passive voice. This proposes the fact that the subject is not responsible for the action of the verb. Those who embrace their helpless state and ***mourn shall be comforted***. "Comfort" will come because they are acted on. It comes from outside ourselves; after all we are helpless.

There is reality to embrace. Comfort is not intrinsic in the mourning. Surely all understand this. You must not focus on the mourning. You must not say, "I must ***mourn*** in order to receive comfort." You cannot earn comfort; it will never be merited. Do not imagine God patiently waits for you to perform poverty, do the right activities, or reach the proper level in order to reward you with comfort. Comfort is not a reward, payment, or merit. If you could achieve mourning, you would still lack comfort. Comfort is not in mourning; comfort is in Jesus. Mourning is the posture of our lives when acknowledging our helplessness. This position allows Jesus to come to our lives in His full comforting Spirit. The solution is not mourning; the solution is the Spirit of Jesus. No wonder I am a Jesus pusher!!!

I am a Jesus pusher!!! ***"Blessed are those who mourn, for they shall be comforted,"*** (Matthew 5:4). Comfort never finds its source in what we do. It comes from beyond us. We must not live within the realm of our capacity; we must live beyond our limits. In embracing our helplessness, we naturally live in mourning. The interaction of these two elements is only possible because Jesus reveals it to us. The moment we respond He becomes our comfort. Jesus is everything your mind can conceive in comfort! Jesus is not an idea; He is a Person outside of, and independent from us. Some try to convince us that positive thinking brings a storehouse of comfort, but that is a rejection of our state of helplessness. There is only One who can "be" comfort in us and that is Jesus. He must act on us.

The statement, "I do my part; God does His part," brings no comfort to the helpless. Our state of helplessness embraces the inability to do our part. When have we ever done our part? We mourn over our failure to meet the slightest degree of righteousness. The best we can accomplish on our brightest day is filthy rags in His sight. We are ignorant of our helplessness unless He reveals it. So from the start to the finish, it is Jesus. I must respond moment by moment to Him: He is my Comforter. I am a Jesus pusher!!!

———————

I am a Jesus pusher!!! ***"Blessed are those who mourn, for they shall be comforted"*** (Matthew 5:4). If comfort is really a Person, it is relational. Those who embrace their helplessness are in the Kingdom of Heaven. Those who mourn experience comfort. If the Kingdom of Heaven is Jesus, the comfort is Jesus. In the embrace of the Spirit of Jesus I find resource for living. The Greek word "parakaleo," translated ***shall be comforted***, points to the Spirit of Jesus. Jesus uses the noun form of this word as a title for His Spirit, the Comforter. The passive voice of this word points to the Spirit of Jesus acting on us to bring comfort. We can take no credit for the comfort. It comes only through His embrace.

The mood of this verb (parakaleo) is the indicative, which is a simple statement of fact. It is not "maybe" as in the subjunctive. It is not a "command" as in the imperative. It is a simple statement of reality. Here is the truth of the matter. Jesus does not present arguments; He does not debate. As King of the Kingdom of Heaven, He boldly proclaims the fact of the state! We must make a decision concerning His offer. We can live in the pitiful actions of self-sourcing out of helplessness or we can be filled with Jesus, our Source. In this relationship, the Kingdom of Heaven is formed; we experience comfort. Pride seems to be the great deterrent to this fulfillment. Logically it makes little sense to live out of weakness when such strength is available. When we view the advantages and disadvantages, there is only one conclusion. I am responding to the coming of Jesus; I am a Jesus pusher!!!

I am a Jesus pusher!!! ***"Blessed are those who mourn, for they shall be comforted"*** (Matthew 5:4). The verb tense is significant. It is the future tense and is translated ***shall be***. However, further research reveals in a more technical sense, it is the aoristic future (A.T. Robertson, Grammar of the Greek New Testament, page 872). This tense combines the aorist tense with the future tense. The aorist tense is the non-tense. It is punctiliar and focuses on the action of the verb rather than the time of its occurrence. This idea is now included in the view of the future.

The verb "parakaleo" with the combination of future and aorist tenses has a distinct purpose. It does not indicate the time of action but the effectiveness of action that Jesus has in our lives as we mourn. It is a past accomplished fact experienced in the future. Jesus underlines comfort as a certainty. It is already accomplished. In other words, we do not recognize our poverty and ***mourn*** which causes Jesus to rush in to comfort us. The comfort of His person is already ours; it has been there all this time. As we respond to our helplessness and mourn we find comfort. Jesus comfort is consistent and is not dependent on troubled times. There will be the constant, uninterrupted, and effective indwelling of the Spirit of Jesus within us. I am a Jesus pusher!!!

———————

I am a Jesus pusher!!! ***"Blessed are the meek,"*** (Matthew 5:5). The disciples constantly misunderstood. They expected a military Messiah who would restore the nation of Israel back to the pomp and glory of the days of Solomon (Acts 1:6). Due to the great oppression of Rome, the Jews longed for deliverance from domination. It was expected that Jesus would use His miracle power for military victory. A meek Messiah leading weak people was not their idea of a Messianic Kingdom. Peter rebuked Jesus when He expressed His meekness in terms of bleeding, suffering, and dying. Military victory and miracle power are understood; the power of meekness is incomprehensible.

The Old Testament prophecies clearly proclaimed the meekness of the Messiah. Isaiah the prophet pictured Him as ***despised and rejected by men, a Man of sorrows and acquainted with grief*** (Isaiah 53:3). In describing His role, Isaiah said, ***"Surely He has borne our griefs and carried our sorrows; yet we esteemed Him stricken, smitten by God, and afflicted. But He was wounded for our transgressions, He was bruised for our iniquities; the chastisement of our peace was upon Him, and by His stripes we are healed"*** (Isaiah 53:4, 5).

Jesus said, "Congratulations belong to the ***meek***." That is just as startling as "Congratulations to ***the poor in spirit***" or "Congratulations to ***those who mourn***." It is the reverse of everything we have thought or projected in our culture. It is so foreign to our basic philosophy of life we cannot reconcile it. Jesus sourcing my life will produce this great quality. His presence will be the only way I can share in "meekness." I am a Jesus pusher!!!

I am a Jesus pusher!!! ***"Blessed are the meek"*** (Matthew 5:5). We must understand this condition of meekness in the sequence of the Beatitudes. Jesus begins with ***the poor in spirit***. It is a state of being in which the individual is helpless. The location of this helplessness is in the ***spirit***. It is poverty at the inner core of our spiritual lives, the principle of life. We are to live in and through the Spirit of Jesus. Once this is recognized and embraced, it produces mourning. Mourning is the spirit's expression of embarrassment over its condition. How can I deny the heart of who I am? I am driven to embrace my poverty. This is the attitude of my inner spirit before God. This attitude becomes the posture of acceptance as the fullness of Jesus adequately embraces me. This embrace of helplessness is mourning.

This immediately changes my nature. In this infusion of His Divine presence, the first quality expressed is "meekness." "Meekness" is the expression of His Divine nature as He supplies and resources my life. "Meekness" is not achieved or earned. It is not developed or a product of discipline. It is not practiced and mastered. It is not copied from others. It is not to be the focus of our desires. It is not a goal to reach. It is a natural aspect as we exist in the Kingdom of God. It is a by-product of Jesus. After all I am helpless, so how can I produce meekness? Jesus is the source! I am a Jesus pusher!!!

———————

I am a Jesus pusher!!! ***"Blessed are the meek,"*** (Matthew 5:5). Jesus is the sole source of "meekness." Each step in the sequence of the Beatitudes forces me back to His sourcing. He is the source of my "helplessness." He is the great creator who designed me; His intent from the beginning was for me to be ***poor in spirit***. But, I have lived among a people who have always acclaimed self-sourcing as admirable. How can anyone discover the falsehood of pride? Jesus is the source! The darkness of self-sourcing is blinding; no one ever discovers truth without Divine revelation.

Once we embrace the truth of helplessness, "mourning" springs forth. It is the attitude of acknowledging my poverty. I am embarrassed over all self-sourcing, which increases my mourning. I live in the attitude of acceptance and response to the Source for which I was made. I do not produce this response because that would be more self-sourcing. Even my mourning is caused by His presence. My heart is drawn to Him. I did not come to Him in order to acquire "meekness." It was the furthest thing from my mind. Jesus captured my heart. I did not come to Him for benefits but for Himself. He is not an escape route; He is my Lover. As I lounge in His arms and dwell in His presence, meekness is present in my life. Meekness can only result from His indwelt presence. He is the source. I am content in Him! No wonder I am a Jesus pusher!!!

Jesus PUSHER | 365

I am a Jesus pusher!!! ***"Blessed are the meek,"*** (Matthew 5:5). In the Book of Galatians, Paul highlights our freedom in Christ. False teachers attempted to present "Jesus plus" Christianity. They wanted to add laws to Jesus. They taught that Jesus died to save us, but there were additional items needed to make salvation complete. Paul would not accept this premise. We are "in Christ" and that is sufficient. As Paul comes to chapter five of his presentation, he parallels living in the flesh with living in the Spirit of Jesus. As the nature of the flesh sources an individual in their helplessness, all of the characteristics of self-sourcing appear. Self is denying its poverty. Flowing from this life dependent on itself is hatred, envy, selfish ambitions, dissensions, and the like.

Both self-sourced and Spirit-sourced individuals are equally helpless. The picture of the Spirit-sourced individual is altogether different. The nature of Jesus fills him. He lives in the strength of the Spirit not in the weakness of the flesh. He embraces the sourcing of Jesus. The nature of the Spirit of Jesus is now manifested through his life. ***The fruit of the Spirit is love, joy, peace, longsuffering, kindness, goodness, faithfulness, gentleness*** (meekness)***, self-control*** (Galatians 5:22, 23). This is impossible without the sourcing of the Spirit. Jesus calls this the ***"kingdom of heaven."*** He fills our helplessness with Himself. I am a Jesus pusher!!!

Additional Resources

Stephen Manley has numerous resources to "push" you closer to Jesus Christ. Learn more about his books, sermons, DVDs, courses, and more at:

CrossStyle.org

Stephen has also started a college which teaches the Word of God in a practical hands-on ministry setting. Learn more about the Cross Style School of Practical Ministry by visiting:

School.CrossStyle.org

About the Author

written by Nathan Johnson and Jeremiah Bolich

Stephen Manley is a Jesus Pusher. It sounds a bit odd perhaps; some people "push" drugs or alcohol, sex or entertainment, and I guess in our own ways we all have something we "push." But I have met few individuals with such an intense focus on one thing. For Stephen Manley, his one thing, his only passion, his single desire is Jesus. In his own words:

I am a Jesus pusher!!!! I am an undaunted, courageous, stout-hearted, bold, adventuresome, brave, fearless, gallant, heroic, lionhearted, unafraid, unflinching, valiant Jesus pusher. I cannot help myself. He is startling and He has overwhelmed me. I do not speak of ideas about Jesus or historical information concerning Him. I speak about Him. I am a Jesus pusher!!!! I am a mastered, possessed, addicted and obsessed Jesus pusher. There seems to be no way to quit. But who would want to?

And Stephen does everything he can to "push" Jesus on everyone. No, Stephen is not aggressive, mean, or harsh, but he is intense, focused, and dedicated. Perhaps that's because of the foundation God laid in his life at a young age.

The Foundation

Stephen Manley, born July 18, 1942, grew up in the home of an Indiana Methodist pastor, which provided the basis for his early spiritual growth. Stephen received his call to ministry at the age of seven and began filling his father's pulpit at the age of eleven. But as a young man entering high school, he was conflicted and torn with the reality of his spiritual life.

There must be something more.

During the lunch hour one afternoon, Stephen stole away from the high school and walked across the street to his dad's church, hiding himself in a classroom to think and pray. There was no emotional surge, no lights in the sky, no booming voices, but Stephen left the church radically altered in heart and mind; Christianity is about intimacy with Jesus! Stephen concluded if the essence of Christianity is oneness with Jesus – the outside God getting to be inside, living and sourcing one's life – then it is critical to keep one's focus upon Jesus throughout the day, not merely a few minutes each morning in devotions and prayer.

As a way to develop such a habit of focus, Stephen decided every time the school bell rang he would pray: "Thank you Jesus for living inside of my life." This became so much fun he decided every problem he had, he would bring to Jesus and allow Him to be a part of the solution. Soon, he involved Jesus in every good thing; desiring His involvement and activity moment-by-moment throughout the day.

During these formative high school years, Stephen devoured every book he could get his hands on about the depths of intimacy with Christ. It was then he discovered he did not invent the concept of "practicing God's presence," but found great encouragement by those who had written about such a life long before his own. This concept became a growing aspect in young Stephen's life. He was constantly growing in intimacy and oneness with Jesus in an attitude of surrender and dependency.

None of his reading compared to his desire for the Word of God, which became the bedrock and platform for Stephen's life. Stephen found that as he dove into the written Word (Bible) he was diving into the Living Word (Jesus). The Bible was not a dreary book to study in order to prepare sermons, it was an exciting avenue through which he could experience the living Person of Jesus, develop deep intimacy with Him, and be continuously pressed and transformed by Truth (Jesus). As he is so fond of saying, "We do not handle the Word of God; it handles us." Even now, some fifty years later, the Word continues to become more precious and important in his life.

At age seventeen, now attending Taylor University and pastoring a local Methodist church, Stephen met, and two years later, married Delphine Oliver. For the next five years, Stephen and Delphine ministered in the pastorate of both the Methodist and United Missionary Church Denominations.

While in the pastorate, the Manleys adopted their first child, Stephen Christopher Manley, in March 1967. The following year, July 1968, they adopted their second child, Evangeline Faith Manley (Vangie). The expansion of the Manley family came at a critical time in Stephen and Delphine's call to ministry. After pastoring for seven years, Stephen, now twenty-four, made the leap into full-time itinerant evangelism, which became his call for the next forty-one years.

For his first four years in evangelism, Stephen travelled alone. In 1971 he moved his ministry under the umbrella of the Church of the Nazarene; and in 1972, Stephen brought his wife and children onto the road, where they ministering together for the next ten years.

Again in 1982, Stephen found himself traveling alone as the two children, now in their high school years, stayed at home with Delphine. As young Steve and Vangie attended high school, Delphine established and administered the office for Stephen Manley Evangelistic Association (SMEA), based out of their home in Upland, Indiana. It was only after Steve joined the army and Vangie graduated high school that Delphine joined Stephen back on the road.

The international arm of SMEA began in February 1985,

continuing for the next fifteen years. Stephen and Delphine dedicated nearly three months of every year to international evangelism, traveling throughout Africa, Central and South America, and Europe. In 1989 they spent six months within nine different countries in Africa. These trips often consisted of pastoral training during the day and evangelistic meetings in the evenings.

In addition, the Manley's began an evangelist intern program, taking young men and women on the road with them during the summer months. The emphasis of the intern program was on practical ministry as well as Biblical training and transformation. The interns would minister to the children and teens at the summer camps and church meetings Stephen preached, while attending a daily one-hour training with Stephen that included sessions on: theology, evangelism, saturation Bible study, practical ministry, and sermon preparation. For the next twenty years over 65 interns experienced life on the road with Stephen and Delphine Manley – seeing holiness, a servant-hearted lifestyle, and evangelism lived out in day-to-day living. Since the program's inception in 1987, Stephen had a desire to begin a one-year school of practical ministry that would invest, train, and mentor a new generation of people called to ministry. His desire was to give individuals an opportunity to learn how to study the Word, experience growth and transformation, and provide practical ministry training within a needy community. However, the desire for the school would have to percolate for a few years.

In 1986, Nazarene Bible College invited the Manleys to teach at the school, even with their busy preaching schedule. During winter semesters, Stephen and Delphine would live in their RV in Colorado Springs so Stephen could teach Monday night through Wednesday morning and then catch a flight to preach at a revival meeting Wednesday night through Sunday. Delphine was also an adjunct professor teaching under Verla Lambert in the Women's Study Series during several of those NBC years between 1986 and 1992.

The Lord soon pointed Stephen and Delphine toward Tennessee. In December of 1998, they responded to the Lord's leading and moved SMEA's ministry headquarters from Upland, Indiana to Lebanon, Tennessee; not realizing at the time that this would become the location of the practical ministry school Stephen had long felt a divine stirring over.

The Future

After 41 years in itinerant evangelism, the Manleys felt a clear call from God to come off the road for the purpose of starting the Cross Style School of Practical Ministry. The basis for this school required a church body to partner in the lives of the students and in the ministry training. In September 2009, twenty-two years after the dream began, Cross Style Church of the Nazarene was established in Lebanon, Tennessee with Stephen as the lead pastor.

Over the last several years, Cross Style Church has aggressively ministered within the community. Whereas some churches are inward focused, Stephen has wanted from the beginning for the pastoral staff, the congregation, and ministry students to be outward focused. The church now runs an emergency-housing program for the homeless and needy, provides food boxes and serves a daily free hot buffet dinner to the community. Cross Style is invested in nursing homes, the community little league, the local Kiwanis Club, and has recently started a transformation program for those with addictions and people coming out of prison or jail. The ministry opportunities have been expanding and opening up in ways that can only be ascribed to Jesus.

In 2013, Stephen and the Cross Style team officially launched the *Cross Style School of Practical Ministry*. The outflow and ministry potential as well as the practical investment in the lives of these students cannot be overstated. It is the passion of everyone in Cross Style, especially Stephen, to have the opportunity to invest in and train up the next generation of leaders, pastors, evangelists, missionaries, and ministers.

As such, the Cross Style School of Practical Ministry is focused on three types of individuals: high school graduates who want to spend a summer, semester, or year grounding themselves in the Word to have a Biblical filter before entering college; individuals called to ministry and want practical ministry training; and laymen who want to take their depth and intimacy with Jesus and their Biblical understanding to another level. Summer internships, much like the original evangelist intern program Stephen began, are still available for those who desire to spend a summer immersing themselves in the Word of God and learning servant-hearted ministry through practical hands-on experience.

Stephen, now in his 70s, has joked that he has been doing things backwards. Often pastors retire into evangelism but he has been slowly moving out of evangelism to become a full time pastor. Stephen still travels in evangelism, averaging one meeting a month and several camps throughout the summer, but his focus has become the church, school, and community within Lebanon, Tennessee. If you were to ask him when he might consider retiring for good, he would respond with a smirk and tell you it will never happen. And after a lifetime of full time ministry, you might think burnout might become an issue, but long ago Stephen found the solution for burnout: getting into the Word of God. As he says, you never hear a pastor or leader express how exhausted he/she is, and follow that with "let me tell you of the riches I've been discovering in the Word, how Jesus has been transforming my life, and the intimacy I've been experiencing with Him." Burnout is impossible when one's life is built upon the foundation of the Word and intimacy with Jesus.

For Stephen, his life is wrapped up in a total saturation of Jesus and the Word of God. Time in the Word is more than an activity or duty to schedule in his day. It is the delight of his heart and the focus throughout his day because it draws him deeper into intimacy with Jesus Christ. He wants his "moment-by-moments" saturated with the Person of Jesus and the Word. He longs for Jesus to ever increase and expand in and through His life.

Stephen's life, testimony, and preaching has been used throughout the last six decades to touch, influence, and transform the lives of countless people around the world. But in honest humility, Stephen downplays himself in order to lift up and "push" Jesus. His life is not his own; it is the stage upon which Christ acts, the glove Jesus wears, the voice through which Jesus proclaims Himself to the world, the hands Jesus uses to touch, minister, and love a hurting and needy world. Stephen is a Jesus pusher. He has no other focus than Christ.

"Jesus is present in every situation of my life. There is no conversation in which I do not feel His presence. He participates in all my recreation. He is everywhere I go. Who would want to be without Him? He is the protection for my life. He is the fragrance I constantly smell. He is the flow of my spiritual blood giving me life. He is my constant nutrition making me healthy. I cannot survive without Him. I am a Jesus pusher!!!!

I want to push Him on you. I want you to join me in this obsession. You do not have to work at it; it is not a discipline. It is as natural as breathing. Please let Him pull you to His heart."

–Stephen Manley

Made in the USA
Charleston, SC
04 January 2015